Who Believes Is Not Alone

Other Books of Interest from St. Augustine's Press

Who Believes Is Not Alone

My Life Beside Benedict XVI

GEORG GÄNSWEIN

WITH SAVERIO GAETA

Translated by Daniel B. Gallagher

ST. AUGUSTINE'S PRESS
South Bend, Indiana

Published by arrangement with The Italian Literary Agency
Original title *Nient'altro che la Verità: La mia vita al fianco di Benedetto XVI*

Manufactured in the United States of America.

2 3 4 5 6 28 27 26 25 24

Library of Congress Control Number: 2023941757

Jacketed Clothbound ISBN: 978-1-58731-073-7
Ebook ISBN: 978-1-58731-076-8

∞ The paper used in this publication meets the minimum requirements of the American National Standard for Information Sciences – Permanence of Paper for Printed Materials, ANSI Z39.48-1984.

St. Augustine's Press
www.staugustine.net

Cover art is an original watercolor and ink by Anastassia Cassady entitled, *Eigenleben*.

Table of Contents

Prologue

When Cardinal Joseph Ratzinger asked me to be his personal secretary in February of 2003 and introduced me to my new role at the Congregation for the Doctrine of the Faith, he also announced that both of our appointments were "provisional." The staff at the congregation acted surprised at this rather unusual description of our respective roles, so he went on to explain that he intended to step down from the congregation as soon as possible since he had already shouldered the burden for over two decades. This is precisely why he described the arrangement as "provisional." As it turned out, he remained prefect for only a little while longer, and I didn't stay much longer, either.

From another perspective, this "provisional" arrangement did endure; indeed, up until the time of his death. I assumed duties as his personal secretary on 1 March 2003 and performed that role for the rest of his time at the Holy Office until Pope John Paul II's death in April of 2005. I continued in this role for all eight years of his pontificate up until the time of his resignation in 2013, and throughout the remaining years of his life as "pope emeritus."

These were grace-filled moments that allowed me to get to know the true face of a man who has revealed himself to be one of the most important historical figures of the twentieth century, a figure often belittled in the popular media and by detractors who have labelled him *Panzerkardinal,* or "God's Rottweiler," a title that was meant to criticize convictions that were in fact nothing more than signs of his profound fidelity to the Church's Tradition and Magisterium, and his commitment to defend the Catholic faith. The weighty responsibility of serving as his personal secretary, together with my role as Prefect of the Pontifical Household during the papacy of Pope Francis, gave me the opportunity to take part in every important ecclesial event over the last two decades.

Each year had its joys and disappointments, its moments of excitement and exhaustion. There were certainly problems, of course, such as the clerical sexual abuse crisis and difficulties with Vatican finances. But there were also beautiful, precious moments that revealed a true faith, especially among the young, which bolstered a legitimate hope that the Church has a bright future.

These pages present a personal testimony of the grandeur of a humble man, a superb scholar, a cardinal and a pope who helped shape the history of the world today and who will be remembered as a beacon of theological acumen, doctrinal clarity, and prophetic wisdom. But they also present a first-hand account that attempts to shed light on misunderstood aspects of his pontificate and describe—from the inside—the truth of the world known as "the Vatican."

Georg Gänswein
Titular Archbishop of Urbisaglia

1
The Unconventional "Predestined"

Perpetually provisional

Having spent many years around the Vatican hierarchy, I can say one thing with certainty: every member of the College of Cardinals, in the silence of his heart, harbors a keen awareness that one day Christ might ask him to become His Vicar on earth.

I also realize that no one—unless he suffers from some deep psychological abnormality—really has any ambition to occupy the Chair of Peter, since he is well aware of the concrete, everyday demands of the office, and especially the spiritual responsibility. Consequently, every cardinal tries to expunge the thought of becoming pope from his head, and acts as if it were the unlikeliest of scenarios.

That is precisely the thought that flashes into my mind whenever I think back to 14 February 2003, the day Cardinal Joseph Ratzinger, then-Prefect of the Congregation for the Doctrine of the Faith, made an announcement that personally affected me—in fact, it radically changed the course of my life at the time, and even more radically in the years to come.

It happened during a coffee break from the *congresso particolare,* a sort of executive staff meeting that takes place every Friday morning during which staff members at the congregation update their superiors on the important items of concern.

Two days earlier, it was announced that Monsignor Josef Clemens, who had been Cardinal Ratzinger's personal secretary for two decades, had been appointed Undersecretary for the Congregation for Institutes of Consecrated Life and Societies of Apostolic Life (he was subsequently named Secretary of the Pontifical Council for the Laity on November 25th and elevated to the episcopacy).

We were all standing around, chatting in small groups, when Cardinal Ratzinger asked for silence. He cleared his voice and, on behalf of the entire congregation, congratulated Monsignor Clemens on his promotion and cordially thanked him for the work he had done both for the Congregation of the Doctrine of the Faith and for himself personally.

Then, with a warm smile, he motioned for me to come over and said, "You all know *Don Giorgio* (that's how I was always known at the congregation): I've called him to my side so that you may see more clearly *due provvisori* [i.e., two 'provisional' appointees]." This caused a buzz in the room since the German accent made it sound as if he had said *due professori* [two professors].

Noticing the confusion, Cardinal Ratzinger said more clearly: "No, I indeed meant to say *provvisori* since he is becoming my personal secretary, but only for a short period of time. You all know that I have been prefect here for twenty-one years, and I have asked John Paul II to allow me to retire according to the norms since I marked my seventy-fifth birthday two months ago. Now I only have to wait for Pope Wojtyła's acceptance of my request."

More mumbling circled the room, indicating that everyone thought he was innocently naïve. Even if the cardinal were entirely convinced that what he said were true, everyone doubted that such a letter—even if it had been written and sent—would even make it to the desk of His Holiness.

Afterward, when the cardinal had an opportunity to speak to me alone about how slow Pope John Paul II's response was, I tried to lighten things up by suggesting that he should allude to it in the course of one of his usual Friday afternoon meetings with the Holy Father, perhaps giving a coy hint that something was wrong with the courier service between the apostolic palace and the Holy Office [i.e., the *palazzo* housing the Congregation for the Doctrine of the Faith]. But he only managed to flash one of his wry grins and said nothing. I understood immediately that he didn't want to talk about it anymore, so I made no further comment.

In fact, this was just one of the countless times Ratzinger distanced himself from the "ecclesiastical world," as we often joked, and operated on a more ethereal level than his fellow cardinals, refusing to admit out loud that many fellow cardinals considered him the most *papabile* as a conclave seemed inevitably on the horizon. Or perhaps it was simply his way of dispelling the fear that such Vatican whispers might actually come true. In any case, the prospect of him becoming pope was completely foreign to his desires and way of thinking.

Truth be told, the cardinal thought he had done a decent job of arranging things such that the doors were flung wide open for his successor. In addition to the transfer of Clemens and the recruitment of some new officials at the congregation (especially Monsignor Charles Scicluna as Promoter of Justice), the secretary of the congregation and Ratzinger's main collaborator since 1995, Tarcisio Bertone, was nominated Archbishop of Genoa.

The official commencement of Bertone's new assignment on 2 February 2003 allowed Cardinal Ratzinger to make this frank remark in a February 16th interview with Esther Betz, a German journalist based in Rome whom Ratzinger had known since the Second Vatican Council: "It's no surprise that rumors are becoming more intense as I approach the end of my term at the congregation. Thanks be to God that we've found some new, qualified personnel. In any event, I will be happy to know that more peaceful times await me."

In his memoirs, Monsignor Bruno Fink, Ratzinger's secretary while he was Archbishop of Munich and during his years at the congregation until Christmas of 1983, remembers that as soon as they arrived in Rome in February of 1982, the cardinal had told him that he planned to serve as prefect for no more than two five-year terms so that he could return to the house he had built in Pentling, on the outskirts of Regensburg, and there he would have enough time to finish writing the theological works he had in mind.

On 25 November 1991, exactly ten years after his nomination, Ratzinger tried to ask John Paul II to allow him to retire, explaining that the death of his sister Maria on the previous 2nd of November had deprived him of precious domestic help, and that the cerebral hemorrhage he had suffered the previous September had caused serious vision problems in his left eye and constant physical exhaustion. But the Holy Father decided to reconfirm him anyway for another five-year term.

So, between the time his first mandate expired at the end of 1996 and his seventieth birthday at the beginning of 1997, the cardinal pulled some strings to have it suggested to John Paul II that Ratzinger himself might make a good archivist and librarian for the Holy Roman Church. A new nomination for that position was indeed expected given that Cardinal Luigi Poggi had already turned eighty.

The Salesian priest, Raffaele Farina, appointed Prefect of the Vatican Library on 25 March 1997 (and later elevated to the College of Cardinals by Benedict XVI in 2007), had a conversation with Ratzinger a few weeks later, during which the latter asked a few questions about the responsibilities of the cardinal librarian. Although he showed indifference, the thought of a happy retirement surrounded by books and precious historical documents was certainly appealing to Ratzinger. But once again John Paul II apparently didn't even consider the idea.

With a hint of nostalgia, Benedict XVI alluded to this during a visit to the Vatican Library on 25 June 2007, when he said to Cardinal Jean-Louis Tauran: "I must admit that, on my seventieth birthday, I would have been delighted if our dear John Paul II would have permitted that I dedicate my time to studying these fascinating documents and treasures entrusted to your care, invaluable for our understanding of human history and of Christianity. But it seems the Lord in His divine Providence had other plans for me."

Faithful to Providence

From his youngest years, John XXIII took a saying of Saint Francis de Sales and made it his own: "Desire nothing, refuse nothing." These words easily describe Cardinal Ratzinger as well, as evident from a letter written to his friend Esther Betz on 9 August 1997: "I never plan for anything (I never really have). I rather allow myself to be carried along by divine Providence, which has never been harsh with me, even though it has taken me places I never would have imagined."

In fact, from the time of the Second Vatican Council, Ratzinger had unknowingly caught the eye of Pope Paul VI, who closely followed his academic career. Ratzinger was publishing articles of ever-increasing import, and he personally thought that this would be his natural path forward. To keep the young theologian in touch with Rome, Pope Paul VI made him one of the thirty initial members of the newly founded International

Theological Commission, together with the likes of Hans Urs von Balthasar, Carlo Colombo, Yves Congar, Henri de Lubac, Jorge Medina Estevez, and Karl Rahner. The group met twice a year at the seat of the Congregation for the Doctrine of the Faith.

Pope Montini considered Ratzinger not only a fine theologian, but also a dedicated shepherd, leading the pontiff to invite Ratzinger to preach the spiritual retreat at the Vatican in 1975: "I was not confident enough with Italian and French to dare do such a thing, so I had to tell him 'no,'" the cardinal later revealed. The preacher thus ended up being Anastasio Ballestrero, the Archbishop of Bari at the time, and later appointed Cardinal Archbishop of Turin. The following year, a cardinal from Kraków by the name of Karol Wojtyła preached the retreat. Ratzinger, however, was granted a second chance in 1983 when Pope John Paul II invited him to preach. This time, Cardinal Ratzinger warmly accepted the invitation.

After Cardinal Julius Döpfner died of a sudden heart attack on 24 July 1976, Paul VI had little trouble in evaluating the set of three possible candidates to succeed him as Archbishop of Munich and Freising. He announced his personal choice of forty-nine-year-old Joseph Ratzinger on 25 March 1977. The young appointee had barely received his episcopal consecration on May 28th before receiving news that the Holy Father also intended to elevate him to the cardinalate the following June.

He conveyed a clear sense of his new responsibilities during the consecration ceremony at the cathedral in Munich on 28 May 1977: "A bishop acts not in his own name, but as a fiduciary of Jesus Christ and the Church. He is not a manager or a boss, but a steward on behalf of someone else. Hence, he cannot change his opinion or act according to personal preferences, first defending this and then that in whatever way seems convenient to him. He is not here to spread his personal ideas, but is rather a messenger called to deliver a message greater than himself. He will be judged precisely on this fidelity: fidelity is his very duty."

The consistory that took place in Rome on the following June 27th was relatively small. In addition to Joseph Ratzinger, the other new cardinals were the Theologian of the Papal Household, Mario Luigi Ciappi, the President of the Pontifical Commission *Iustitia et Pax,* Bernardin

Gantin, and the Archbishop of Florence, Giovanni Benelli. The Apostolic Administrator of Prague, František Tomášek, was also present, having been nominated *in pectore* the previous year. It was indeed a rather atypical consistory for Paul VI, since the number of new *porporati* fluctuated between twenty-one in 1976 and thirty-four in 1969, with twenty-seven created both in 1965 and in 1967, and thirty in 1973.

The motive was undoubtedly the Holy Father's wish to elevate the ex-Substitute of the Secretariat of State, Giovanni Benelli, who had just been nominated Archbishop of Florence on June 3rd. Indeed, the pope was probably feeling pressure from some members of the Roman Curia who considered Benelli's leadership style too authoritarian, although Montini probably utilized this aspect of Benelli's personality to make changes in several key curial positions. Ratzinger—perhaps *per* Benelli's suggestion—was included in the list of new cardinals at this time, seeing as the Diocese of Munich had traditionally been a cardinalature see since the beginning of the 1900s, and there was a push to create cardinals outside the usual sphere of the Roman Curia.

Reflecting back on that day, Ratzinger recalled the deep affection he felt from pilgrims who had made the journey from Munich to Rome for the occasion: "I had a great advantage over the other four new Cardinals when receiving the biretta from Paul VI. None of them came from a big family. Benelli had worked in the Curia for long time and he wasn't very well known in Florence, so not many *Toscani* were present at the ceremony. The iron curtain prevented most of Tomášek's flock from travelling to Rome. Ciappi was a theologian who had always worked on his little 'island.' Gantin was from Benin and it was not easy for anyone to make the journey from Africa to Rome. But so many people had come to celebrate with me! The hall was virtually full of people from Munich and Bavaria, so the applause was much more noticeable when I received the red hat. Paul VI seemed to take this as a confirmation that he had made the right choice."

In his speech, the pope explained that what was mostly required of the new cardinals was the "absolute fidelity which they are called to live out in this post-conciliar period full of great promise but also division. They must be constantly available, unwavering in service, and totally dedicated to Christ, his Church, and to the Pope, unbending, unhesitating, uncompromising." With regard to Ratzinger, he said that his "outstanding theological teaching at prestigious German universities and numerous and expert publications have shown that theological research—following the path of *fides quaerens intellectum* [faith seeking understanding]—cannot and must not ever be disconnected from a profound, free, creative adherence to the Magisterium which is the authentic interpreter and communicator of the Word of God."

The commemorative card Father Ratzinger had printed for his first Mass twenty-six years earlier featured a verse from the Second Letter of Saint Paul to the Corinthians, *audiutores gaudii vestri* ("collaborators of your joy" 2 Cor 1:24). He developed this idea further in his episcopal motto taken from verse 8 of the Third Letter of Saint John, *cooperatores veritatis* ("collaborators of the truth"). In his autobiography, he explained that this development was meant to "represent a continuity between my prior priestly service and my new episcopal duties. Even though there are differences between them, I essentially felt called to do the same thing: to follow the truth and to place myself at its service. And given that the theme of 'truth' has all but disappeared in today's world because it seems far above man's capacity to understand—though at the same time, everything collapses if there is no truth—this episcopal motto seemed to me well suited for modern times, especially in the positive sense of 'truth.'"

When the time came for me to choose an episcopal motto before my consecration in January of 2013, I didn't have to think about it for very long. I had already been blessed to take part in Benedict XVI's own dedicated service to the truth and to talk with him about what that meant to him, and it had been precisely my duty to assist him in his daily service of "collaboration" in the truth. So I selected chapter 18, verse 37, in John's Gospel—*testimonium perhibere veritati* ("to give witness to the truth")—and I was obviously quite happy that the pope supported my choice and expressed his fond approval.

On my coat of arms, I depicted the dragon slain by Saint George, a fourth-century martyr who, according to the *Legenda Aurea,* killed the terrific beast in the name of Christ and thereby converted everyone who had been threatened by it. In the history of Christian art, this image became emblematic of the earthly struggle between good and evil. I even joked with Pope Benedict at times, telling him that Saint Corbinian—the eighth-century bishop of Freising honored on his coat of arms—only tamed a bear, but my patron saint killed a dragon!

Cardinal Ratzinger actually chose three images for his archepiscopal coat of arms. The Moor's head, traditionally a symbol of the bishops of Freising, was represented twice. Ratzinger once explained that "the origin of the symbol is unknown, but for me it is a beautiful expression of the universality of the Church, which knows no distinction of race or class since 'we are all one' in Christ." A scallop shell also appears: a sign we are all pilgrims in this world. The symbol also recalls a story told by Saint Augustine. He was walking along the shore trying to wrap his head around the mystery of the Trinity when he came across a boy using a shell to pour sea water into a small hole on the beach. The boy allegedly replied, "I am emptying the sea into this hole." In this image, Augustine understood that no man was able to penetrate the depths of God's mystery.

The third image refers to Saint Corbinian, founder and patron of the archdiocese entrusted to Cardinal Ratzinger. On 9 September 2006, returning from an apostolic visit to Munich, Benedict XVI recalled the significance of this image: "As a child, I was fascinated with the legend of Saint Corbinian, whose pack horse was killed by a bear while they were travelling through the Alps. Corbinian severely rebuked the animal and then, as punishment, placed all his baggage on the bear's back and commanded him to carry it to Rome."

Cardinal Ratzinger explained in 1977: "I recalled an interpretation Saint Augustine gave to verses 22–23 of Psalm 72 when he was in a situation very similar to mine prior to his ordination to the priesthood and episcopate. He applied the words 'I was like a brute beast in your presence' (the word for 'beast' is *iumentum* in Latin) to an agricultural animal used in North Africa to plow fields, and he compared himself to that animal, describing himself as God's 'beast of burden' insofar as he was weighed down by his responsibilities, the so-called *sarcina episcopalis* (episcopal baggage). The Bishop of Hippo's story and the bear of Saint Corbinian were a constant source of inspiration for me to persevere in my service and perform it with joy and faith, both thirty years ago and now as I renew my 'yes' to God daily." Then, with a bit of irony, Pope Ratzinger added,

"Saint Corbinian, after successfully arriving in Rome, let his bear go free. In my case, the 'Master' had something different in mind."

The "just prophet"

In August of 1977, Cardinal Ratzinger spent a couple of vacation weeks in the diocesan seminary of Bressanone. Cardinal Albino Luciani, Patriarch of Venice, was President of the Episcopal Conference of Trivento (which also includes Alto Adige) at that time. The patriarch heard that his brother cardinal was staying there, so he decided to pay him a visit. He was a great admirer of Ratzinger's theological writings, especially of his commentary on the Apostolic Constitution *Lumen Gentium.* They conversed in Italian, which Ratzinger had learned during the Council, even though he spoke it a bit awkwardly, having used the 33 RPM vinyl-record method. He would later improve his skills in Rome by speaking Italian every day.

That was the first time the two had met. Ratzinger recalled how deeply he admired Luciani's "great simplicity, but also his vast culture. He was telling me how well he knew the area, having come there as a child with his mother on pilgrimage to the shrine of Pietralba, an Italian-speaking Servite monastery a thousand meters above sea level and a popular destination for many Venetian faithful."

During a public homily on 16 August 1977, Luciani referred to this meeting with Ratzinger: "A few days ago, I had the pleasure of spending time with Cardinal Ratzinger, the new Archbishop of Munich, in a Catholic Germany that, he says, suffers in part from an anti-Roman, anti-papal complex, but in which he had the courage to proclaim that 'the Lord is to be sought where Peter is.' Ratzinger appears to me a just prophet in saying this. Not everyone who writes and speaks has the same courage today. By going along with the crowd or out of fear of not being 'modern,' some of them accept only an edited or truncated version of the Creed pronounced by Paul VI in 1968 at the close of the Year of Faith. They criticize papal documents and speak continually of ecclesial communion, but they never speak of the pope as a necessary point of reference for anyone desirous of remaining in true communion with the Church. Others go beyond 'prophecy' and act like smugglers, taking advantage of their position and peddling their own opinions as if they were Church doctrine, sometimes even changing doctrine into ideologies diametrically opposed and rejected by the Church's Magisterium."

The next personal meeting between the two had to wait until the conclave in the summer of 1978, after the death of Pope Montini on August 6th. From what I can tell, Ratzinger's high esteem for Luciani led him to join the movement supporting the Patriarch of Venice to be the next pope, which indeed did occur on August 26th after only four votes. At the ceremony marking the beginning of John Paul I's papal ministry on September 3rd, the two exchanged words about the cardinal's upcoming trip to Ecuador, since, in a letter dated September 1st, John Paul I—in one of his first acts as pope—appointed the Archbishop of Munich and Freising as the Pontifical Legate to the Marian Congress in Guayaquil. The appointment was appropriate since the German and Ecuadorian dioceses had been "twins" for some time, and it was indeed the local archbishop, Bernardino Echevarría Ruiz, who had suggested that Ratzinger represent the pope at the congress.

In words that seemed to exceed the normal formula for this kind of letter, Pope Luciani wrote, "We desire to take part in this solemn celebration in some way so as to make its importance abundantly clear. Therefore, we write this letter to announce that we have chosen you as we create and proclaim you our 'extraordinary legate,' and we entrust you with the mission of presiding over these celebrations in our name and with our authority. You have distinguished yourself through your deep understanding of sacred doctrine and, as we know well, you burn with love for the Mother of Christ Our Savior and Our Mother. We have no doubt, therefore, that you will perform your duties in this matter with intelligence, wisdom, and success."

To express his own affection even more, John Paul I sent a message to the participants of the congress on September 24th, inviting them to make the motto of the congress, "'Ecuador for Mary and Christ,' the entire program of their lives and apostolic action: may Mary, Mother of Christ, Mother of the Church, and the sweetest Mother of all of us, always be your model, your guide, and your way towards our Brother and Savior of all, Jesus."

Ratzinger read the message publicly and, in the name of all the faithful present at the congress, thanked the pontiff for his genuine paternal care. It was for this reason that the unexpected death of John Paul I came as a great blow to Ratzinger. The news reached him in a rather bizarre way. Benedict XVI explained: "I was sleeping at the residence of the Archbishop of Quito. I had not closed the door because I felt as if I were resting in the bosom of Abraham in that house. But in the middle of the night, a beam of light suddenly entered my room, and I could barely make out the figure standing in front of me, dressed in a Carmelite habit. Blinded by the light and startled by this 'messenger of death,' I couldn't tell if I was dreaming or awake. Later, I learned that the mysterious figure who had come to tell me the pope had died was the Auxiliary Bishop of Quito, Alberto Luna Tobar."

On 6 October 1978, at a memorial Mass in Munich for Pope John Paul I, the cardinal archbishop foreshadowed words Pope Francis would utter years later at John Paul I's beatification ceremony on 4 September 2022: "The only greatness in the Church is to be saints. And it is his saints that show us the way like a pillar of fire. From now on, he too will belong to this pillar of fire. And what he gave us in the space of a mere thirty-three days shines as a light that will never be taken away from us."

In his biography of Wojtyła, George Weigel writes that Ratzinger once said to him: "We were convinced that the election [of Luciani] was made in correspondence with God's will, not simply in a human way … and if one month after being elected in accordance with God's will he died, God had something to say to us."[1] Remembering the days of the conclave, Ratzinger later remarked: "The election of Luciani was not a mistake. Those thirty-three days had a purpose in the history of the Church. His sudden death opened the door to the unexpected possibility of a non-Italian pope. Cardinal electors were mentioning this possibility at the previous conclave, but it was not a very likely scenario since Albino Luciani was such an appealing figure. After that, however, there was a need for something utterly new."

1 George Weigel, *Witness to Hope* (Cliff Street Books, 1999), p. 252.

The prevailing "double name"

Cardinal Ratzinger departed for Ecuador on 19 September 1978, and he stayed there until the end of the month. It was precisely at this time that a Polish delegation of bishops headed by Primate Stefan Wyszyński and Cardinal Karol Wojtyła arrived in Germany to meet with their brother German bishops. This was the result of a long journey that had begun thirteen years earlier, on 18 November 1965, with a letter signed by the Polish bishops who participated in the Second Vatican Council: "From the benches of the Council that approaches conclusion, we extend our hands, granting pardon and asking pardon." On the following December 5th, the German bishops gave their response: "We, too, ask to forget, and we beg forgiveness."

Ratzinger and Wojtyła did not meet on that occasion; neither did they meet during the Council, and even though they had collaborated in the formulation of some of conciliar documents they never crossed paths. As Prefect of the Congregation for the Doctrine of the Faith, Ratzinger would later emphasize, "Naturally we had heard of his work as a philosopher and pastor, and I had wanted to meet him for some time. For his part, he had read my *Introduction to Christianity* and had cited it during the spiritual retreat he preached for Pope Paul VI and the Roman Curia during Lent in 1976. So, both of us were hoping for an opportunity to meet in person sooner or later." That encounter finally took place in October of 1977 during the Synod of Bishops dedicated to the theme of catechesis, at which both were present.

According to journalistic reconstructions of the conclave that took place from 14–16 October in 1978, the Archbishop of Genoa, Giuseppe Siri, and the Archbishop of Florence, Giovanni Benelli, were locked in a tie in the initial rounds of voting, essentially cancelling each other out. On the eighth ballot, the Archbishop of Kraków's name emerged. This was no surprise to Ratzinger, however, as he himself admits: "I supported him. Cardinal König had spoken highly of him. And even though I didn't know him very well, the personal interaction I did have with him persuaded me that he was indeed the right man."

Upon his election, Pope John Paul II immediately began to gather a team around himself in the Roman Curia. He definitely wanted

Ratzinger on that team. So, less than a year after his election, the pope invited him to become Prefect of the Congregation for Catholic Education to replace Cardinal Gabriel-Marie Garrone who was about to retire. But the Archbishop of Munich managed to present a counter-argument to Pope John Paul II, responding: "I have only been in the archdiocese for two years, and I think it is impossible to leave the see of Saint Corbinian so quickly. My episcopal consecration symbolized a certain fidelity toward my native diocese. So, the pope decided to nominate Cardinal Baum of Washington instead, assuring me that he would be tapping my shoulder for a different job sooner or later."

In the fall of 1980, there were two additional opportunities for John Paul II to get to know Cardinal Ratzinger better. The first was in the Vatican, when, from September 26th to October 25th, Ratzinger was the general *relatore* at the Fifth Assembly of the Synod of Bishops dedicated to the theme "The Christian Family." The second was in anticipation of John Paul II's first pontifical voyage to Germany from 15–19 November, for which the cardinal had prepared various drafts of the pope's speeches and homilies. Ratzinger once told me a story that dates back to that time. Noticing John Paul was a little exhausted, he offered him a room in the archepiscopal residence to take a rest. But a smiling Wojtyła replied, "There will be lots of time for rest in heaven!" It was precisely then that the pope gave free reign to the idea of appointing Ratzinger to be the new Prefect for the Congregation for the Doctrine of the Faith.

On 6 January 1981, Cardinal Ratzinger arrived at the Vatican for the episcopal consecration of Monsignor Ennio Appignanesi, pastor of Santa Maria Consolatrice at Casal Bertone, which was Ratzinger's titular church according to the old custom of making cardinals "members" of the Roman clergy. John Paul II met with him privately and brought up the subject of the appointment once again, but the Archbishop of Munich had prepared a way out, saying that he would accept the nomination only if he were allowed to continue publishing theological works in his own name in addition to the official documents of the dicastery.

After consulting with collaborators about Ratzinger's request, John Paul II discovered that Cardinal Garrone had published several books while serving as Prefect of the Congregation for Catholic Education. This gave Ratzinger no escape! On one occasion, the cardinal told me that his nomination to Munich had already contradicted every one of his expectations for the future, let alone an appointment to a Roman congregation.... But then he realized that he could not resist repeated requests from John Paul II, and it was also clear what role would best allow him to pursue his personal studies while simultaneously serving the universal Church.

Forty years ago, placing conditions on the acceptance of an assignment presented by a pope would have seemed like hubris and pride, both of which were entirely foreign to Ratzinger's character. The reality is that, from that time on, he considered his activities of writing and publishing precisely as a service to the Church with a pastoral end. The cardinal never produced theological work out of vainglory; rather, he was fully aware that his writing was an authentic service to the Church. He would have viewed any truncation of his personal participation in theological debates as an amputation no less harmful to others as to himself.

I had the opportunity to understand his reasons for persevering in theological writing while he was working on the three-volume *Jesus of Nazareth* series as pope. Benedict XVI was criticized for spending more time on writing than on governing the Church which, some argued, was his primary duty. Taking Saint Bonaventure and Pope Benedict XIV as guides, he made it clear to me that writing is also a form of governance since it gives spiritual food to the faithful in addition to the magisterial activity he was obligated to perform as pope.

I hope I am not too bold in offering the following anecdote to underscore this point. On 7 June 2013, I was seated next to Pope Francis during a meeting in the Vatican with students from Jesuit schools. A little girl asked him why he chose to live at Casa Santa Marta rather than in the apostolic palace. Pope Francis answered, "I did it for psychiatric reasons, because it is my personality." I immediately thought similar reasoning could be applied to Ratzinger, both as cardinal and as pope, in his choice to continue writing. On several occasions, Benedict XVI said to me with conviction, "Writing is not a burden for me, but rather a means of freedom that does me good. It doesn't take energy away from me, it gives energy. It comes down to two different forms of energy, and both must be wielded." I would say that, essentially, if he had not had the outlet of producing theological material, the "pressure cooker" of his intellect would have lacked an escape valve and would have led to an explosion.

Watch dog or promoter?

Ratzinger's appointment to the Congregation for the Doctrine of the Faith became official on 25 November 1981. His farewell ceremony in Munich took place on 28 February 1982. He once told me that his flock bade him farewell with "one eye joyfully smiling at his promotion, and the other sadly tearing up at his departure." The Bavarian Prime Minister, Franz Josef Strauss, reflected the conflicted heart of his people, saying, "We would prefer that you not go to Rome, Your Eminence." The cardinal replied, "I will always remain Bavarian even when I am in the Vatican."

While working at the congregation, I had the opportunity to hear several staff veterans reminisce about Ratzinger's first years as prefect. Some harbored hopeful expectations, and others were seriously apprehensive about how he might act. Everyone was curious to see what changes he had in mind, he who had already been given the nickname *la Suprema* inasmuch as he had been the inspiration for a speech given by Cardinal Joseph Frings on 8 November 1963, in which he disparaged "processes and procedures not in line with the times and indeed harmful to the Church and scandalous to many people." These words had elicited thunderous applause from the participants at the Second Vatican Council.

Since the congregation was stuck at a crossroads, John Paul II probably chose someone who was both a theologian and a pastor rather than the usual diplomat and canonist. The same motivation likely lay behind Paul VI's decision to change the name from "The Sacred Congregation of the Holy Office" to "The Sacred Congregation for the Doctrine of the Faith," while maintaining the pope as president but designating a cardinal secretary to direct daily activities.

Paul VI made further changes to the congregation on 15 August 1967, establishing a cardinal prefect as head of the congregation and entrusting him with the task of "safeguarding doctrine with regard to faith and morals throughout the entire Catholic world." The overall mission of the congregation, however, was still framed in negative terms: "It is to examine new teaching and opinions that are being spread in any way, to promote the study of this material, and to organize meetings of experts; it is to condemn those teachings that are contrary to the principles of faith after having received the input of local bishops in the area, if they indeed would like to participate in the process. They are to examine books that are brought to their attention, and, if necessary, to condemn them, but not before having granted the author a hearing and an opportunity to defend himself. It is also the responsibility of the Congregation to judge errors regarding the faith according to the norms of the ordinary process."

Ratzinger's task of updating norms in accord with John Paul II's request began primarily with the new Code of Canon Law promulgated in 1983, where his influence on canons connected with ecclesiology, the Magisterium, episcopal conferences, and the relationship between bishops and the Roman Curia is unmistakable. This ultimately led to a reorientation of the congregation in positive terms as is evident in the Apostolic Constitution *Pastor Bonus* promulgated on 28 June 1988. The proper duty of the congregation was now to "promote and safeguard the doctrine on faith and morals in the whole Catholic world."[2]

To carry out this task, "The Congregation fosters studies so that the understanding of the faith may grow and a response in the light of the faith may be given to new questions arising from the progress of the sciences or human culture. It helps the bishops, individually or in groups, in carrying out their office as authentic teachers and doctors of the faith, an office that carries with it the duty of promoting and guarding the integrity of that faith. To safeguard the truth of faith and the integrity of morals, the Congregation takes care lest faith or morals suffer harm through errors that have been spread in any way whatsoever. Wherefore: it has the duty of requiring that books and other writings touching faith or morals, being published by the Christian faithful, be subjected to prior examination by the competent authority; it examines carefully writings and opinions that seem to be contrary or dangerous to true faith, and, if it is established that they are opposed to the teaching

2 Apostolic Constitution *Pastor Bonus,* art. 48.

of the Church, reproves them in due time, having given authors full opportunity to explain their minds, and having forewarned the Ordinary concerned; it brings suitable remedies to bear, if this be opportune; finally, it takes good care lest errors or dangerous doctrines, which may have been spread among the Christian people, do not go without apt rebuttal."

On 22 April 2007, during a pastoral visit to the Diocese of Pavia (where the remains of Saint Augustine are preserved), Benedict XVI seemed to make an autobiographical connection to the Bishop of Hippo and the saint's life after his episcopal ordination. Citing a passage from Augustine's *Sermons*, Benedict said, "His beautiful dream of a contemplative life had vanished, and his life was radically changed. Here is how the saint described his daily life: 'correcting the undisciplined, comforting the weak, supporting the faltering, and confounding enemies … exhorting the negligent, keeping the quarrelsome in check, helping the needy, freeing the oppressed, approving the good, tolerating the bad, and loving everyone."

That is precisely what I experienced working by the cardinal's side day by day as he demonstrated anything but the characteristics of a *Panzerkardinal* or "God's rottweiler," nicknames shamelessly spun by critics and pundits who had not the slightest clue of what Ratzinger was really like. His collaborators encountered in him a new style of governance because the implementation of the norms and procedures (the so-called *Regolamento*) of any Roman congregation depends entirely on who is in charge and the working climate he is able to create.

Ratzinger was always convinced that the only way to truly create an atmosphere of mutual respect and trust demands people getting to know one another well. He therefore gave the highest priority to human interactions and lots of space for meeting with people personally. This is most evident in the way he worked with the International Theological Commission, local episcopal conferences, and superior generals of religious orders and institutes, especially in his attempts to clear up misconceptions about the congregation that had accumulated through the years.

Among Cardinal Ratzinger's initiatives was a meeting of the congregation every Friday morning. All of us were required to prepare an outline of discussion questions and submit them by Thursday afternoon so that the prefect could study them at home and thoroughly prepare to discuss them the next morning. The regular practice was to begin with the youngest officials such that no one would fear to contradict the positions of his superiors.

The last word went to the prefect, but he always respected the opinions of others and listened to them carefully. If he found someone's solution to a problem convincing, he would happily accept it. Otherwise, after synthesizing what he understood the official to have said, he would say, "You have evaluated this case from a viewpoint that in itself is correct, but perhaps it's incomplete. Maybe there's another perspective that might lead to a different conclusion, which would go something like this…." In other words, he would never humiliate anyone—rather, he would indicate a solution that would seem reasonable once everyone took a moment to reflect on it.

On Mondays, there was a consultative meeting with experts led by the secretary of the congregation, and on Wednesdays a meeting with cardinals and bishops (the so-called *feria quarta*), presided over by the cardinal prefect. The atmosphere was relaxed and informal to the extent that bantering and joking were not unusual. In fact, one characteristic of Ratzinger that few had the opportunity to experience was his easy sense of humor. For example, on 4 January 1989, he was delighted to receive an award in Munich named after the comedian Karl Valentin. During the acceptance speech, he drew attention to the Pauline verse, "We are fools on Christ's account" (1 Cor 4:10), saying that "in the courts of the most powerful leaders in the ancient world, the jester was often the only one allowed the luxury of telling the truth. And since it is my very business to tell the truth, I am exceedingly happy to have been—or at least accepted to be—in the category of those who enjoy this privilege. Whoever does not feel he is a bit of a clown when he tells the truth will too easily become an autocrat."

I also remember a humorous exchange between Ratzinger and the Archbishop of Milan, Cardinal Carlo Maria Martini. The thinking of the two was quite different in many ways, but they did share mutual esteem for one another. After Martini boasted that he had never written a book, Ratzinger reparteed that he had read at least fifteen books in German bearing Martini's name as author. Martini replied, "But I never have to sit down for hours at a desk like you do. I speak, they record my voice, and then someone transcribes it, and that's that." Ratzinger gave a playful wink and suggested that the rather fragmented quality of Martini's work would give someone the impression that such indeed was his *modus operandi!*

2
The Philosopher and the Theologian

Two souls in harmony

"I thank God for the presence and help of Cardinal Ratzinger who has been a loyal friend." These words were etched in stone by Saint John Paul II in his 2004 memoir, *Rise, Let Us Be on Our Way,* about a man he collaborated with closely after appointing him Prefect of the Congregation for the Doctrine of the Faith. Joaquín Navarro-Valls, John Paul's spokesperson and close confidant, has this to say about the memorable passage: "The words Pope John Paul II wrote a year before his death are unprecedented in that they mark the first time he had ever explicitly and effusively praised a living collaborator and expressed such deep gratitude and genuine friendship. This alone makes it clear that they had an extremely close relationship."

Benedict XVI did not forgo any opportunity to in turn express his own esteem for Wojtyła. I can personally attest that among Ratzinger's highest priorities upon his election was to fulfill the program left uncompleted by his saintly predecessor, beginning with his pastoral visit to Bari for the conclusion of the National Eucharistic Congress on 29 May 2005, and the apostolic voyage to Cologne for World Youth Day taking place from August 18th to the 21st in 2005.

At the beginning of his pontificate, Benedict XVI requested that I tie up several loose ends regarding John Paul II's private appointments. I fondly recall the testimony of the journalist Filippo Anastasi, who at that time was the coordinator of religious programming for *Giornale Radio Rai:* "Shortly before he died, I had expressed to Wojtyła my desire to introduce my collaborators to him. The pope agreed to grant us a private audience, but later that day, he was admitted to Gemelli Hospital. We all know how it ended. A couple of months after the election of

Benedict XVI, I got a phone call from his personal secretary: 'Benedict would like to honor the appointments his predecessor was unable to fulfil, so he is inviting you to the apostolic palace for a private audience.' So, we all went."

Subsequently, Pope Benedict decided that his first foreign journey would be to Poland from 25–28 May of 2006. In his address to members of the Roman Curia on December 22nd of that year, the pope explained, "The journey to (John Paul's) homeland was an intimate duty of gratitude for all that he gave to me personally and above all to the Church and to the world during the quarter century of his service. His greatest gift to all of us was his steadfast faith and the radicalism of his dedication."

Few know that the house in which Karl Wojtyła was born—now a museum in Wadowice—hosts several items contributed by Benedict XVI himself: three rings John Paul II had given him as gifts while he was prefect, three letters from John Paul, and a photograph of the two taken at Pope Wojtyła's tenth anniversary celebrations on 30 October 1988. Benedict personally visited the museum in Wadowice during his trip to Poland on 27 May 2006, leaving a bas-relief of Our Lady and writing a special message in the guest book.

The two undoubtedly had different personalities and different leadership styles. Karol Wojtyła was a philosopher by training, whereas Joseph Ratzinger was a theologian (the cardinal once told me that John Paul II confessed to him that he always felt more well-versed in philosophy than theology). Wojtyła gravitated more toward philosophical investigation and intellectual research, whereas Ratzinger preferred theological clarity and hermeneutical rigor. Yet it was evident to all that these strengths were wonderfully complementary.

Professor Alfred Läpple, Ratzinger's formation director at the seminary in Freising, summarized Ratzinger's and Wojtyła's thought in an interesting way: "The philosophical-theological foundation of both Wojtyła and Ratzinger was personalism, but initially received and developed through different channels. In Poland, personalism was spurred by a hope for freedom as an alternative to the political-cultural domination of Soviet Marxism. Dialogical personalism was ultimately the bridge that connected the thought of the Polish pope to the German prefect:

man not as a 'something' but as an 'I,' who, in dialogue, lives as a 'you' in the encounter with the Divine Person."

On various occasions, I had the opportunity to observe how, whenever they were not completely in agreement on a specific idea or initiative, there was nonetheless an on-going sense of mutual openness and trust and the willingness to give the other the benefit of the doubt, something that always gave the cardinal motivation to do anything in his power to support whatever were John Paul II's designs. In some ways, Ratzinger considered those years at the congregation a sort of apprenticeship: "My spiritual and theological journey would have been unimaginable without him," he said on 4 July 2015 while receiving an *honoris causa* doctorate at Castel Gandolfo from the Pontifical University of John Paul II and the Academy of Music in Kraków.

In my opinion, Ratzinger's deep admiration for John Paul II was also the reason for the sympathy he felt for cries of *santo subito* that rang out at Pope John Paul II's funeral, as the faithful begged for a dispensation from the five-year waiting period before opening the process of canonization. Benedict XVI was so moved by this popular enthusiasm that he asked Cardinal José Saraiva Martins, Prefect of the Congregation for the Causes of Saints, to prepare a decree to be read on 13 May 2005 in the Basilica of Saint John Lateran at the conclusion of the Holy Father's audience with the clergy of Rome, paving the way for a rapid beatification on 1 May 2011 and a canonization on 27 April 2014.

Shortly after his election, Pope Ratzinger publicly testified to the holiness of Wojtyła: "Throughout my time collaborating with him, there were ever clearer signs that John Paul was a saint. He had an intense relationship with God. He was completely immersed in communion with the Lord, who was the source of John Paul II's radiant joy even while he was burdened with heavy responsibilities. Then there was the courage with which John Paul carried out his duties in an extremely challenging period of world history. He never sought recognition, and he was never anxious about how his decisions would be accepted. His faith and deep-seated convictions were the inspiration for his every action, and he was constantly ready to accept hardship. The courage to speak the truth is, in my estimation, one of the foremost criterion for holiness. The only explanation for his tireless pastoral activity was his intimate relationship with God. Whenever I think of him, I am filled with gratitude. I never tried to—nor would I have been able to—imitate him, but I have tried to carry on his legacy and program as much as possible. So, I am sure that I benefit from his goodness and enjoy the protection of his blessing even today."

The intimate relationship Ratzinger had with Wojtyła is further evident in words he shared on the commemoration of the twentieth anniversary of John Paul II's pontificate: "It is safe to say that one got more of an idea of who John Paul II was by concelebrating Mass with him and being drawn into the silence of his prayer than by analyzing his books or speeches. One touched the core of his nature more by participating in his prayer than by listening to his words, however powerful they may have been. It is on this basis that we can understand why he, although a formidable intellectual, possessed a unique and important voice in today's cultural dialogues. He always carried himself with a simplicity that allowed him to communicate effectively with every single person."

A weekly appointment

Of extreme importance for the strengthening of the relationship between Ratzinger and Wojtyła was the so-called *udienza di tabella,* a weekly meeting at 6:00 p.m. every Friday to discuss not only documents in preparation at the Congregation for the Doctrine of the Faith, but also the general state of the Church and the world. Ratzinger once told me that, at times, the scope of the conversation grew so wide as to include cultural topics since Pope Wojtyła was quite fond of German literature and wanted to hear Ratzinger's opinions on certain contemporary authors whose work caught his eye.

In addition to these official audiences, the pope often invited Cardinal Ratzinger to attend more informal gatherings on Wednesday mornings when various church leaders would share ideas relating to John Paul's weekly catechesis, current events, discussion topics proposed by bishops in town for their quinquennial *ad limina* visit, and new issues that had arisen in theological circles. The cardinal noted how these meetings often carried over into the lunch hour, during which attendees would tell jokes over a meal while thoroughly enjoying one another's company.

These interactions also led Ratzinger to recognize problems that had arisen from the reform of the Roman Curia as desired by Pope Paul VI. The Secretariat of State—first under the leadership of Agostino Casaroli until 1991 and then under Angelo Sodano—was the primary means of coordinating the activities of the various dicasteries, and the secretariat often found itself in the position of having to choose what to prioritize: the reinforcement of doctrine or the flexibility of diplomacy. Even though the Prefect of the Congregation for the Doctrine of the Faith tried to remain on good terms with everyone by smoothing out wrinkles whenever possible, from time to time an internal situation would require closer attention and he would need to support solutions proposed by John Paul II that were at odds with those proposed by the Secretary of State.

Allow me one memorable example. In the second half of the 1990s, there had been a constant, heavy stream of correspondence between the Secretariat of State, the Congregation for the Doctrine of the Faith, and the German Bishops' Conference on the issue concerning whether counselors and social workers associated with the Catholic Church in Germany could continue, in good conscience, to issue certificates testifying that a woman seeking an abortion had first spoken with someone about her decision. The nature of this certification process was ambiguous given that—even if it was originally intended to open a dialogue and allow a woman to reflect before choosing an abortion (and, thanks to earmarked state subsidies, it allowed Catholic counselors and social workers to continue offering services that would give them an opportunity to impress upon women the importance of choosing life)—it had, in fact, been transformed into an authorization to proceed with a non-punishable abortion during the first twelve weeks of pregnancy.

There was a difference of opinion between Sodano and Ratzinger about how to deal with this situation. The former was more attentive to the political ramifications and the importance of maintaining good relations with the president of the German Bishops' Conference, whereas Ratzinger was sharply focused on the ethical-moral dimension of the issue as well as the doctrinal and pastoral consequences that might ensue from making a poor decision. The behind-the-scenes debate went on for some time until finally, on 11 January 1998, Pope Wojtyła sent a letter to the German bishops clearly stating that "ecclesiastical counseling centers or those connected with the Church would no longer issue the certificate." But at the same time—and I cannot recall any other examples of this kind—Ratzinger made it perfectly clear how heated the disagreement between the two sides had been: "… [M]any people, including those who are involved in and support the Church, have firmly warned against a decision that would leave women in conflictual situations without the assistance of the faith community. With equal firmness believers of every rank and station have also pointed out that the certificate involves the Church in the killing of innocent children and makes her absolute opposition to abortion less credible. I have taken both opinions very seriously and I respect the impassioned search by both sides for the right path the Church should take in this important matter."

Prior to this, there was another moment of tension between Ratzinger and John Paul II, this time regarding the interreligious meeting for peace that was to be held in Assisi on 27 October 1986. Cardinal Ratzinger thought it inopportune for him to participate in the gathering. He thought that the unqualified gathering of such a vast range of cultic expressions represented by the sixty-two religious leaders assembled in the city of Saint Francis would cause serious confusion, and he feared his mere presence at the event would suggest that the pope saw no problem with it. Indeed, the program did include some ceremonies in local churches that were simply inappropriate, such as the placement of a statue of Buddha near the tabernacle and a peace pipe upon the altar. Moreover, during the midday prayer service in the main square outside of the lower basilica, the ordering of the prayers—even though there was a pause for silence between them—had an air of syncretism and the ring of relativism.

My conversations with Cardinal Ratzinger led me to believe that he had made his concerns clear to Pope Wojtyła about the Assisi event, but the latter was wholly convinced that the gathering presented an opportunity, so he asked the cardinal to help prepare for the event in whatever way he could. The cardinal was fully aware of his responsibility to caution the pope about the possible consequences, and he did not withdraw when John Paul II made it clear that he wished the event to go forward. In any case, according to Ratzinger, the pope realized that the cardinal's reservations were not going away, and so he asked him to be involved in preparations for a reprisal of the event on 24 January 2002. Even though as late as the day before the event Ratzinger's name was not included among the participants, he ultimately decided to contribute after the Holy Father's gentle coaxing.

Pope Wojtyła's collaborators testify that he never made an important decision without first consulting Cardinal Ratzinger, and I saw with my own eyes the many letters forwarded by John Paul II to the Congregation for the Doctrine of the Faith with a note such as, "Ask Cardinal Ratzinger" or "Please, forward to the cardinal prefect." In such cases, my fellow officials and I would read the letter with utmost attention in order to get the gist of it, formulate a response, and consign it to the cardinal so that he could approve a final response to share with the Holy Father at their weekly meeting.

After I was made the prefect's personal secretary, I often received phone calls from the Holy Father's personal secretaries, Monsignors Stanisław Dziwisz ("Don Stanislao") and Mieczysław Mokrzycki ("Don Mietek") relaying the Holy Father's request that Ratzinger come to the apostolic palace for a meeting with the pope and some other cardinals, or with the pope alone. Lunch meetings, however, were more rare, since it was increasingly more difficult for Pope John II to swallow his food. One was scheduled, however, after I had been appointed the cardinal's personal secretary, since Ratzinger wanted to introduce me formally to John Paul II and his closest collaborators in the papal apartments. I was rather intimidated, but both Pope John Paul II and his secretaries were extremely cordial to me, and shortly thereafter I was completely at ease working with them.

The challenges faced by the prefect

Soon after arriving at the congregation, Ratzinger had to confront one of the thorniest issues of his entire tenure. Canon 2335 in the Code of Canon Law promulgated by Benedict XV in 1917 stipulated that "whoever joins the Masonic sect or any other similar association which plots against the Church or legitimate civil authorities incurs *ipso facto* an excommunication reserved to the Holy See alone." In the new Code approved by John Paul II on 25 January 1983, canon 1374 basically expresses the same law but in a much-diluted formulation: "A person who joins an association which plots against the Church is to be punished with a just penalty; however, a person who promotes or directs an association of this kind is to be punished with an interdict." This change opened up a polemic on various fronts both within and outside of the Catholic Church, prompting Cardinal Ratzinger to draft an explicit declaration signed by Pope Wojtyła and published on November 26th (i.e., the day before the new Code entered into force).

The text clearly explained that the lack of an explicit mention of Masonry is "due to an editorial criterion which was followed also in the case of other associations likewise unmentioned inasmuch as they are contained in wider categories," and that therefore "the Church's negative judgment in regard to Masonic association remains unchanged since their principles have always been considered irreconcilable with the doctrine of the Church and therefore membership in them remains forbidden. The faithful who enroll in Masonic associations are in a state of grave sin and may not receive Holy Communion." Moreover, since it had come to light that some bishops were in favor of modifying the Church's stance against Masonry, Ratzinger added a peremptory clause to the declaration: "It is not within the competence of local ecclesiastical authorities to give a judgment on the nature of Masonic associations which would imply a derogation from what has been decided above."

This declaration was followed by a document published in the following year containing "reflections" on the "irreconcilability between Christian faith and Freemasonry," which highlighted Masonry's "philosophical ideas and moral conceptions opposed to Catholic doctrine," even though a "dialogue" had been "undertaken by some Catholic personages with representatives of some Masonic lodges which declared that they were not hostile, but were even favorable, to the Church." The reflection continues: "Prescinding therefore from consideration of the practical attitude of the various lodges, whether of hostility towards the Church or not, with its declaration of 26 November 1983 the Sacred Congregation for the Doctrine of the Faith intended to take a position on the most profound and, for that matter, the most essential part of the problem: that is, on the level of the irreconcilability of the principles, which means on the level of the faith, and its moral requirements."

Masonic leadership was disappointed (to say the least) with the election of Joseph Ratzinger to the papacy in 2005. This was evident in a congratulatory message sent by the Grand Master of the *Grande Oriente d'Italia* to Pope Francis in 2013: "Perhaps nothing will ever be the same in the Church. It is our hope that the Pontificate of Francis will signal a return to the 'Word-Church' from the institutional Church, (in the hope that) a Church of the people will discover the ability to dialogue with all men of good will and with Masonry." It was clear to me that this was not only a "welcome" to Pope Francis—someone whom I am quite certain they knew virtually nothing about—but also a "good-bye" to Pope Ratzinger!

A further challenge confronting the Congregation for the Doctrine of the Faith under the leadership of Cardinal Ratzinger was the so-called "theology of liberation" that had been spreading throughout Latin America in the 1970s, and which had been interpreted in Europe and North America as a just stance in favor of the poor. The problem, Ratzinger explained, was that this theology took only a partial perspective on salvation history and Christian doctrine: "Forms of immediate assistance to the poor and reforms that improve their condition are condemned as reformism that reinforces to the prevailing system. Therefore, a great upheaval is needed that can give rise to a new world. The Christian faith is instrumentalized as the means to this revolutionary movement, consequently transforming it into a kind of political force and weakening true love for the poor."

The cardinal frequently consulted John Paul II on this issue. Having had direct experience of the Marxist ideology underlying liberation theology, the pope gave clear direction and affirmed that the Church must act for freedom and liberation not in a political way, but by awakening men and women through faith and making them aware of authentic liberation. Ratzinger recalls John Paul II's guidance: "The pope directed us to address both aspects: on the one hand, to unmask a false conception of liberation, and on the other, to manifest the authentic vocation of the Church to liberate man." It is from these premises that the two instructions on liberation theology take shape: *Libertatis Nuntius* in 1984 and *Libertatis Conscientia* in 1986.

Even when the congregation's critique of liberation theology required it to take provisions against a specific theologian, the prefect always sought to make the intervention in a spirit of love and justice. "My collaborators and I always strove not to lose sight of the dignity of the person upon whom we had placed sanctions, and to do it in such a way that the individual himself could recognize why we had decided to take such action. We did not want to simply punish him with an excommunication, but to place ourselves at the service of the community as a whole, and therefore to place ourselves at his service as well. Yet above all, we felt the need to defend the faith of simple believers."

I believe that Ratzinger was motivated to publish the congregation's 1990 instruction on the ecclesial vocation of the theologian precisely because of his experiences in correcting and dialoguing with liberation theologians: "The obligation to be critical, however, should not be identified with a critical spirit born of sheer feeling or prejudice. The theologian must discern in himself the origin of and motivation for his critical attitude and allow his gaze to be purified by faith.... Never forgetting that he is also a member of the People of God, the theologian must foster respect for them and be committed to offering them a teaching that in no way does harm to the doctrine of the faith."

Among the many themes central to Ratzinger during his years as prefect of the congregation was the relationship between the political sphere and the grave responsibility Catholics have to base their political decisions on the faith they profess. On 26 November 1981, the day after he was formally appointed prefect of the congregation, Ratzinger delivered a homily as Archbishop of Munich to the Catholic representatives in German Parliament during a time of diplomatic crises that severely challenged their Catholic identity: "The state does not constitute the totality of man's existence and does not embody all of man's hopes. Man and his hopes transcend the reality of the state and go beyond political action.... The primary service that faith performs for politics is therefore man's liberation from the irrationality of political myths, which indeed are a real threat to our times.... Political morality consists precisely in resisting the seduction of grandiose words that distort the humanity of man and his full capability. The moralism of chimerical political aspirations is immoral because it intends to realize things that no one but God can bring about. Rather, morality demands that we accept our human limitations and strive to achieve what we can within those limits of our finite nature. It is not the absence of compromise, but compromise itself that is truly moral in the domain of political activity."

This acknowledgment of the limitations of political outcomes motivated Cardinal Ratzinger to issue a doctrinal note as prefect of the congregation on 24 November 2002 on some questions regarding the participation of Catholics in political life. This important document, requested by John Paul II as a response to questions he had received from bishops across the globe, has not lost any of its relevance. The doctrinal note begins with the assertion that "the history of the twentieth century demonstrates that those citizens were right who recognized the falsehood of relativism, and with it, the notion that there is no moral law rooted in the nature of the human person, which must govern our understanding of man, the common good and the state." The document states that "if Christians must recognize the legitimacy of differing points of view about the organization of worldly affairs, they are also called to reject, as injurious to democratic life, a conception of pluralism that reflects moral relativism. Democracy must be based on the true and solid foundation of non-negotiable ethical principles, which are the underpinning of life in society."

The doctrinal note unequivocally asserts that "by its interventions in this area, the Church's Magisterium does not wish to exercise political power or eliminate the freedom of opinion of Catholics regarding contingent questions. Instead, it intends—as is its proper function—to instruct and illuminate the consciences of the faithful, particularly those involved in political life, so that their actions may always serve the integral promotion of the human person and the common good. The social doctrine of the Church is not an intrusion into the government of individual countries. It is a question of the lay Catholic's duty to be morally coherent, found within one's conscience, which is one and indivisible. There cannot be two parallel lives in their existence: on the one hand, the so-called 'spiritual life,' with its values and demands; and on the other, the so-called 'secular' life, that is, life in a family, at work, in social responsibilities, in the responsibilities of public life and in culture." All of this was in line with the teaching of the Second Vatican Council, which exhorted the faithful to "fulfill their duties faithfully in the spirit of the Gospel."

Ratzinger the orchestral conductor

The fourteen encyclical letters of John Paul II were, for Ratzinger, tiles in a mosaic, inseparable from one another when viewed within the overall project of Saint John Paul's pontificate. The cardinal considered the first, *Redemptor Hominis* (1979), to be the foundation of the others, although Ratzinger himself did not collaborate in the composition of that encyclical since he was still serving as Archbishop of Munich.

Redemptor Hominis anticipated themes that would arise in later encyclicals, especially truth and its connection to freedom, particularly by handling the themes of sacrifice, redemption, and penance. These would play a central role in *Ecclesia de Eucharistia* (2003) and its anthropological analysis of modern social problems, which are also at the heart of the social encyclicals *Laborem Exercens* (1981), *Sollicitudo Rei Socialis* (1987), and *Centesimus Annus* (1991), where the central point is the dignity of man who is always an end rather than a means.

However, the main encyclicals to which Ratzinger made substantial contributions, and which remained most dear to his heart, were the three that dealt directly with doctrinal matters: *Veritatis Splendor* (1993), *Evangelium Vitae* (1995), and *Fides et Ratio* (1998). In the case of each of these, the prefect was convinced that it was essential to contextualize the document historically given their primary objective was to respond to a particular question at a specific moment in the life of the Church. Otherwise, they can be mistakenly viewed as mere theoretical exercises.

In *Veritatis Splendor,* John Paul II intended to confront the urgent crisis of moral theology in the Church, formulating his treatment in positive terms with the Christian faith at its core rather than by issuing a list of prohibitions. He widened the scope of the discussion to include an ethical debate of global proportions, which at the time was already a question of life or death for humanity. The cardinal prefect explained that the imitation of Christ and the principle of love were the guideposts for organizing the various individual elements of moral teaching and contrasting them with a positivistic way of thinking that was incapable of recognizing the good as such.

Ratzinger was deeply troubled by theologians insisting that "the good" meant nothing more than "better than *x*." He therefore emphasized that, if the basic criterion for judging moral actions were merely a calculation of its possible consequences, and if morality were based simply on whatever seemed more positive, then morality itself would collapse insofar as it would fail to account for the "good" in itself, and consequently Christianity could hardly be referred to as "the Way" with any consistency and integrity.

The cardinal prefect explained that, at the time, Pope John Paul II "made a distinctive turn to a metaphysical perspective, rooted in nothing other than faith in creation. Once more, by departing from faith in creation, he was able to bring together anthropocentrism and theocentrism and have them mutually reinforce one another: '… [R]eason draws its own truth and authority from the eternal law, which is none other than divine wisdom itself … the natural law is nothing other than the light of understanding infused in us by God' (*Veritatis Splendor,* 40)…. A real gem of the encyclical, both philosophically and theologically, is the long section on martyrdom. If there is no longer anything worth dying for, life itself has become empty. Only if there is an absolute good worth dying for, and an eternal evil that is never transformed into the good, is man affirmed in his dignity and are we protected from the dictatorship of ideologies."

Ratzinger stated that these were also the basic underpinnings of *Evangelium Vitae*, which was an expression of John Paul II's absolute respect for and unwavering service to the dignity of human life. Ratzinger explained: "Human life, whenever treated as a mere biological entity, turns into an object considered only through the lens of consequentialism. But the pope, with the faith of the Church, sees the image of God in man, in every man, however young or old, strong or weak, useful or seemingly useless. Christ, the very Son of God made man, died for all men. This confers infinite value upon every human being, an absolute and inviolable dignity."

The cardinal also felt it crucial to assert that "after all the cruel experiences of human abuse, even if the motivations seem lofty, those words were and are necessary. It is clear that faith is a defense of humanity. In the atmosphere of metaphysical ignorance in which we find ourselves, which then descends into moral atrophy, faith shows itself to be the human reality that saves. The pontiff, as a spokesperson of the truth, defends man from a specious morality that threatens to crush him."

Fides et Ratio stands as a sort of *summa* on truth. It represents the kind of thinking distinctive to John Paul II and Ratzinger, particularly because it goes to the heart of a serious problem—namely, the proclamation of the Christian message as a truth that can be recognized as definitive, especially in an age when it is considered an attack on tolerance and pluralism.

This is exactly the point at which the theme of human dignity enters the discussion, for "if man is not able to arrive at the truth, then everything he says and does becomes merely a matter of convention. If faith does not have the light of reason, then it is reduced to mere tradition and presents itself as nothing but pure arbitrariness. Here again, we see that faith defends man precisely as a human being, and the pope maintains that faith is called to encourage reason once more to seek the truth and to grasp it whenever it finds it. Faith is enervated without reason, and, without faith, reason atrophies."

It took an enormous amount of work to produce *Veritatis Splendor* and *Fides et Ratio,* and Ratzinger was the orchestral director behind them. When the initial draft was ready, members of the congregation were asked to give feedback, and theologians outside of the congregation also collaborated in giving advice based on their specific areas of theological competence. There was also close oversight on the part of the bishop and cardinal members of the congregation who offered their own opinions during *feria quarta* meetings. The prefect always shared his own thoughts about the document in writing so that his assessment of how things were proceeding and the proposed improvements made through collaboration would be clear to everyone.

The stylistic redaction of the document fell under the responsibility of Monsignor Paolo Sardi at the Secretariat of State before it went to John Paul II for final approval. Besides making sure that the prose was fluid and clear, Monsignor Sardi occasionally made his own suggestions regarding the document. When that happens, since the document contained subtle and important doctrinal points, any significant modifications must be referred back to the Congregation for the Doctrine of the Faith for subsequent approval.

The certainty of faith

Another magisterial beacon yielded by the Ratzinger-Wojtyła collaboration was the Declaration *Dominus Iesus* on the salvific unicity and universality of Jesus Christ and his Church, published roughly in conjunction with the Great Jubilee of 2000. This document arose from concerns voiced by some episcopal conferences and individual bishops about ecumenical relations with other Christians and religions in light of the coming celebrations of the Holy Year. The text found its form after careful study by numerous consultors, and a draft was later improved during various meetings of the cardinal and bishop members of the congregation at that time. The guiding principles of the document were drawn from *Dei Verbum* and *Lumen Gentium.*

Here is how Cardinal Ratzinger explained the content and meaning of the declaration: "In today's lively debate on the relationship between Christianity and other religions, it is increasingly asserted that all religions are equally valid ways for their followers to attain salvation. … A fundamental consequence of this way of thinking is that it compromises the central nucleus of the Christian faith, insofar as it substantially rejects the singular uniqueness of a historical figure, Jesus of Nazareth, which amounts to marginalizing God himself, indeed, the living God. … It is a position that maintains that any universal truth, binding and valid within history, brought to fulfillment in the person of Jesus Christ, and transmitted through the faith of the Church, is often a kind of fundamentalism that amounts to attacking the modern spirit and represents a threat against tolerance and freedom."

While emphasizing "esteem and respect for world religions and cultures that have objectively contributed to the promotion of human dignity and civic development," the cardinal also strongly affirmed that "the conviction that the fullness, universality, and completion of God's revelation are present only in the Christian faith does not consist in the presumed preference of the members of the Church, nor in the historical achievement of the Church on its earthly pilgrimage, but rather in the mystery of Jesus Christ, true God and true Man, present in the Church. Christianity's claim to salvific unicity and universality stems precisely from the mystery of Jesus Christ who continues to be mysteriously present in his Church, which is his Body and Spouse. That is why the Church is compelled by her very nature to spread the Good News among peoples."

Obviously, negative reactions to this declaration surfaced immediately. The cardinal commented on these frequently and somewhat ironically in order to soften the head-on blow: "[S]ince there are theologians trying to retain their popularity who consider it their duty to criticize everything that comes out of the Congregation for the Doctrine of the Faith, a barrage of assaults rained down on this Declaration, from which it was barely able to save itself."

What really bothered the cardinal, however, was the accusation that he had forced the hand of John Paul II to sign the declaration at a time when the pontiff was displaying signs of physical exhaustion and weakness. But in reality, it was Pope Wojtyła himself who, during a meeting with Cardinals Ratzinger and Re together with Archbishop Bertone, asked the prefect to prepare a speech for him that would give a brief synthesis of the document and express his unmitigated approval, which the pope subsequently read during the public Angelus on 1 October 2000.

The publication of the declaration also manifested the conciliarity and non-polemical side of the cardinal, who—as it was revealed in an interview—when he brought the document to the pope for his approval, asked if it were "air tight" and didn't leave too much room for misinterpretation: "I did not want to be too brusque with the document, and so I tried to express myself clearly but not heavy-handedly. After the pope read it, he asked me once more, 'Do you think it is clear enough?' I responded, 'Yes.' So it is quite amazing that, despite the Holy Father's concern that it may not be strong enough, there were still some theologians who maintained that the pope had prudently taken his distance from the declaration!"

Among the prefect's most important projects was the preparation of the Catechism of the Catholic Church, a work entrusted to him after a recommendation arose at the 1985 Synod of Bishops to undertake an organic and comprehensive presentation of Catholic faith and morals. Pope Wojtyła established a commission of cardinals and bishops in June of 1986 to prepare a document and appointed Ratzinger president. For six years, the prefect immersed himself in the intensive work of developing a text that would be of maximal use to the Christian faithful.

When the voluminous work was finally published in the autumn of 1992, some complained that the Church only wanted to tell people what *not* to do, as if she cared only about pointing out sins. Even though he considered these objections unmerited and disingenuous, he did accept them as an opportunity to intervene personally in the debate to explain that "the question of what, as men, we should do to make the world and ourselves just is an essential, never-ending question. In our own time, confronted with catastrophes and threats, we seek an authentic hope with a new passion as we pursue an answer to this fundamental question that regards each of us in a personal way."

Above all, Ratzinger wanted to emphasize that the catechism was an integral, unified text: "It is a grave mistake to read individual passages detached from their context of the confession of faith, the teaching of the sacraments, and prayer. In fact, there is a central claim that rings loud and clear throughout the entire Catechism: man is created in the image and likeness of God. Anything that is said about right conduct must be viewed through this central perspective. The ten commandments are nothing but an exposition of the ways of love, and we read them correctly only when we utter them together with Jesus Christ."

Ten years later, in 2002, a request was voiced at the International Catechetical Congress for a compendium of the catechism that would synthesize and highlight the most essential elements of the Church's confession of faith. Once more, Pope John Paul II entrusted the coordination of the project to Cardinal Ratzinger. When the cardinal signed the introduction to the work on 20 March 2005, he never imagined that he himself would present it officially on 28 June 2005 as pope!

3
The Darkness Falls Away

The electoral campaign goes pear-shaped

While John Paul II's health was declining during the initial months of 2005, Cardinal Ratzinger found himself thrust to the frontlines of several high-profile events. In addition to his duties as prefect of the most important congregation in the Roman Curia, Ratzinger was also serving as Dean of the College of Cardinals. He was, in fact, elected to this position on 30 November 2002 following Cardinal Bernardin Gantin's decision to return to Benin after his eightieth birthday.

When news of Monsignor Luigi Giussani's death had reached the cardinal on the morning of 22 February 2005, he was not expecting John Paul II to ask him to preside at the funeral scheduled to take place two days later at the Duomo in Milan. But the close, decades-long friendship between Ratzinger and the founder of Communion and Liberation probably motivated John Paul to extend the invitation to the cardinal prefect.

I had relayed the invitation to the cardinal after taking a phone call from Don Stanisław so that he could begin working on the homily at home that very afternoon. Truth be told, there were too many actors involved in that affair—Cardinal Dionigi Tettamanzi, Archbishop of Milan, wished to personally preside at the funeral, while Archbishop Stanisław Ryłko, President of the Pontifical Council for the Laity, wished to read a letter of condolence signed by the pope. Ratzinger, in his usual humility, avoided stepping on anyone's toes and limited himself to delivering the homily.

In fact, if there were any suspicion that this was a maneuver to launch a campaign in anticipation of an inevitable conclave, Ratzinger seemed to manifest his opposition to the idea by expressly making it clear to his supporters that he wished them to deny him rather than support him. He uttered words to this effect on live television during a *Rai* broadcast, as if saying: "Don't complain later that I didn't make it clear what I think about the idea!"

After affirming that "Christianity is not an intellectual system or a package of dogmas or moralism, but rather an encounter, a love story, an event," the cardinal warned against attempts to "transform Christianity into a moralism and moralism into a political system, or to substitute believing for doing.... [T]his would inevitably lead to particularism and a loss of criteria and proper direction, and finally to a system that would divide rather than build up." He concluded on a note of stark realism: "Whoever believes must also pass through a 'dark valley'—that is, the dark valley of discernment—and consequently through adversity, opposition, and ideological assaults."

Just one month later, on 25 March 2005, Cardinal Ratzinger's reflections served as the texts for the celebration of the Way of the Cross on Good Friday at the Colosseum, at which Pope John Paul sadly could not be physically present due to poor health. The ailing pope instead followed them on a television screen while embracing a crucifix in his private chapel within the apostolic palace.

Again, John Paul II personally chose Ratzinger to write the *Via Crucis* reflections, and the cardinal, after cordially accepting the invitation, dedicated himself to hours of intense prayer in order to compose the texts properly. He decided to seek no external input and to share the texts with no one. Reflecting back on this, I cannot help but grin when I remember an anecdote that Cardinal Angelo Sodano shared in a book-length interview entitled, *Ho scommesso sulla libertà* ["I bet on freedom"]: "I remember a private meeting with him [i.e., Ratzinger] in the eighties when I spontaneously decided to give him a piece of advice. At the moment, he showed no reaction, but at the end of the conversation, as I was taking my leave, he said to me in a good-natured tone but serious: 'Dear Don Angelo, remember: there is nothing worse than giving advice to someone who didn't ask for it.'"

The cardinal had always lived the liturgical celebrations of the Paschal Triduum with great fervor and devotion, all the more so since—as he often recalled—he was born on Holy Saturday (16 April 1927). "On Good Friday, our gaze is constantly fixed on the Cross; but on Holy

Saturday, we meditate on the 'death of God,' the day that expresses and anticipates the unimaginable event that characterizes our present age—that is, the feeling that God is simply absent, that the tomb encloses him, that he is no longer acting in the world, that he no longer speaks, so that there is no reason to even ask about his existence, but simply to go on in life without a moment's thought to such a question." These words come to us from his celebrated *Introduction to Christianity.* Similarly, commenting on a painting by William Congdon in *The Sabbath of History,* he tells us that, from the time of his youth, he had understood that "the message of the day on which I came into the world was linked in a special way with the Church's liturgical cycle; so that, from the very beginning, my life was molded by this unique intermingling of darkness and light, pain and hope, and the hiddenness and presence of God."

The reflections Ratzinger composed for the Way of the Cross that year are a snapshot of his thought as he responds to the most urgent questions pressing on the Church at that time. The media, obviously, only focused on a few aspects of his reflections, but even today the full text is worth reading and pondering. He took an all-encompassing approach to the meditations. He didn't aim to pull one or two pebbles from the Church's shoes (an Italian way of phrasing the act of ridding oneself of a nuisance) or to set up black and white scales. Much less did he try to be "ecclesiastically correct"—the dust clouds these meditations kicked up inside and outside the Church is proof enough of that.

The scalpel cuts deepest in the ninth station commemorating Jesus's third fall under the weight of the cross: "Should we not also think of how much Christ suffers in his own Church? How often is the holy sacrament of his presence abused, how often must he enter empty and evil hearts! How often do we celebrate only ourselves, without even realizing that he is there! How often is his word twisted and misused! What little faith is present behind so many theories, so many empty words! How much filth there is in the Church, and even among those who, in the priesthood, ought to belong entirely to him!" The cardinal was pouring out his heart with these words and, without knowing it, anticipating certain actions he would later take during his pontificate.

Other sections of the meditations pass sharp judgment on Christian behavior today and provoke a response from believers: "But we can also think, in more recent times, of how a Christianity which has grown weary of faith has abandoned the Lord: the great ideologies, and the banal existence of those who, no longer believing in anything, simply drift through life, have built a new and worse paganism, which in its attempt to do away with God once and for all, have ended up doing away with man." And: "Hearing Jesus reproach the women of Jerusalem who follow him and weep for him ought to make us reflect. How should we understand his words? Are they not directed at a piety which is purely sentimental, one which fails to lead to conversion and living faith? It is no use to lament the sufferings of this world if our life goes on as usual. And so the Lord warns us of the danger in which we find ourselves. He shows us both the seriousness of sin and the seriousness of judgement." All this leads to a passionate appeal: "Lord Jesus Christ, you let yourself be nailed to the Cross, accepting the terrible cruelty of this suffering, the destruction of your body and your dignity. You allowed yourself to be nailed fast; you did not try to escape or to lessen your suffering. May we never flee from what we are called to do. Help us to remain faithful to you. Help us to unmask the false freedom which would distance us from you. Help us to accept your 'binding' freedom, and, 'bound' fast to you, to discover true freedom."

I should make it clear that Ratzinger was always detached from all speculation of an eventual conclave. A Vatican journalist for the Italian network *Tg1*, Giuseppe De Carli, teased Ratzinger in 2004 by pointing out that he had already participated in two elections, so it wasn't unthinkable he might participate in a third. The cardinal wryly replied, "If I am still alive!" When asked by a Bavarian journalist in 1997 about the role of the Holy Spirit in the process of electing a pope, the cardinal replied: "The Holy Spirit does not simply lay hold of the situation. Rather, like a good teacher, he leaves the students a lot of space and a lot of freedom, but never abandons them. Therefore, the role of the Holy Spirit should be conceived in a more flexible way rather than as a force dictating who the next pope will be. Perhaps the only assurance we can have of the Holy Spirit is that the whole thing will not fall apart completely. There are plenty of examples of popes who, in hindsight, were probably each not the Holy Spirit's first choice…."

The challenge launched in Subiaco

As Dean of the College of Cardinals, Ratzinger was kept in the loop regarding John Paul II's declining health. After Easter in 2005, it was clear that the pope was facing his last days, so the cardinal asked me to clean up his schedule and cancel or reschedule any non-essential commitments. The only appointment that remained hanging and had been scheduled for some time was in Subiaco on April 1st at the Monastery of Saint Scholastica. Cardinal Ratzinger was to accept the Saint Benedict Prize for "his promotion of life and the family in Europe" and to deliver an acceptance speech on the topic of "Europe and the Crisis of Cultures."

Ratzinger had talked with the Secretary of State, Cardinal Angelo Sodano, about the commitment, and the latter encouraged him to go so as to avoid creating any rumors that might fly through the media if he cancelled. Just to be sure, Cardinal Sodano arranged a direct phone line between me and Monsignor Piero Pioppo, his own personal secretary, in the event that something important happened while we were away in Subiaco.

The cardinal had arranged his thoughts very carefully for the occasion, and his words are even more significant today than they were then. In particular, he declared, "[W]hat we are in need of at this moment in history are men who, through an enlightened and lived faith, render God credible in this world. The negative testimony of Christians who speak about God and live against him, has darkened God's image and opened the door to disbelief. We need men who have their gaze directed to God, and in God's own eyes learn what it is to be truly human. We need men whose intellects are enlightened by the light of God, and whose hearts God opens, so that their intellects can speak to the intellects of others, and so that their hearts are able to open up to the hearts of others. Only through men who have been touched by God, can God return among men."

At that time, Ratzinger was reflecting deeply upon the European situation, and he was particularly troubled by the emergence of "a culture that, in a way hitherto unknown to humanity, excludes God from public consciousness, whether he is totally denied or whether his existence is judged to be indemonstrable, uncertain, and so is relegated to the domain of subjective choices, as something in any case irrelevant for public life."

He was deeply concerned with a debate at that time over the preamble of the European constitution and whether it should contain any explicit mention of God or of the continent's Christian roots. "The reasons for this double 'No' are deeper than the arguments that have been advanced for it would suggest. They presuppose the idea that only radical Enlightenment culture, which has reached its full development in our time, is able to define what European culture is," he noted with dismay.

With the lucidity for which he was always known and respected, he explained that the "true contrast that characterizes today's world is not that between different religious cultures, but between the great religious cultures and the radical emancipation of man from God, from the roots of life. If we eventually find ourselves in a clash of cultures, it will not be because of the clash of the great religions—which have always been in conflict with one another, but which, in the end, have always managed to coexist—rather, it will be because of the clash between this radical emancipation of man and the major cultures of history."

This led to an intriguing proposal which—like a stone thrown into a still pool of indifference he seemed to describing—was particularly directed at the laity: "The Enlightenment attempted to define the essential norms of morality while claiming that they would be valid *etsi Deus non daretur,* even if God did not exist.... [T]he extreme attempt to fashion the things of man without any reference to God leads us ever closer to the edge of the abyss, to the total abolition of man. We therefore have good reason to turn the Enlightenment axiom on its head and say that even those who are unable to accept God should nonetheless try to live *veluti si Deus daretur*, as if God existed." Ratzinger would have several occasions to repeat and reformulate this message during his pontificate.

During the ceremonies in Subiaco, I always made sure to sit in a strategic position so that I could feel the phone vibrating in my pocket should we receive an important call. Sure enough, toward the end of the cardinal's speech, a call arrived from Monsignor Pioppo, who told me that there was yet another serious setback for the Holy Father and that the cardinal and I would do best to return home that evening rather than staying overnight to celebrate Mass at the monastery in the morning. Whenever we got into the car after an event like this, we usually chatted about how things went, but this time, the cardinal was consumed by his own thoughts, so the chauffeur and I remained in respectful silence.

The next day, I went into work at the congregation as usual, but in the middle of the morning I received a phone call from Don Mietek asking me to get the cardinal prefect on the phone. I then saw the cardinal rush out, so I presumed he was headed for the papal apartment. I neither saw nor heard from him further on that April 2nd. I was living at Casa Santa Marta at that time. During dinner, around 8:30 p.m., I noticed one of the priests from Poland suddenly get up from the dinner table with an anxious look on his face. It was at that moment I realized John Paul II was entering his last moments. I immediately went into Saint Peter's Square and it was there that I heard the announcement of John Paul II's death. I remained in the square, praying with the tens of thousands who had gradually gathered under the same window where John Paul II had appeared so many times to greet and bless the faithful.

I finally had a chance to speak on the phone with the cardinal on Sunday morning. He told me that he had been summoned to the pope's bedroom to receive a final blessing. During a period of *sede vacante,* all heads of dicasteries are immediately suspended from their positions, so the cardinal told me he would not be coming to the office as usual and that I should "play the postman" and bring any mail for him from the office to his residence, and to take his own letters to the post office for delivery. So, twice a day, I would go to his apartment at Piazza della Città Leonina 1, just to the right of the colonnade, where he had lived since he first moved to Rome.

As Dean of the College, his first task—as stipulated in John Paul II's Apostolic Constitution *Universi Dominici Gregis*—was to deliver the official news to his brother cardinals that the pope had died (and thereby to convoke the College of Cardinals), and to invite members of the diplomatic corps accredited to the Holy See and heads of state to the funeral rites. His closest collaborators in these tasks were Archbishop Francesco Monterisi, Secretary of the Sacred College of Cardinals, and his assistant, Monsignor Michele Castoro. I informally became the go-between for Cardinal Ratzinger so that he could maintain constant communication with them.

In light of the coming funeral, the cardinal diligently got to work on the homily he was expected to deliver. The emotional impact that John Paul II's death had on the world was evident from the interminable line of mourners who had flocked to Rome from every corner of the globe to render homage to a pope who had courageously led the Church into the third millennium. At one point, the line stretched more than three miles long. But no one seemed to mind the 24-hour wait just to get to the doors of Saint Peter's Basilica. This public outpouring of grief did not go unnoticed by Cardinal Ratzinger, who realized that he needed to apply his heart to his words much more than simply his head.

A couple of days later, he handed me a sketch of the text handwritten in pencil, which was then transcribed *via* computer by Sister Birgit Wansing (fondly known as "Suor Brigida"). The Cardinal explained that he preferred to initially write the homily in German to make sure his thoughts were expressed more clearly and accurately. As usual, the Italian version fell to Monsignor Damiano Marzotto, the *capoufficio* ["office manager"] of the Congregation for the Doctrine of the Faith.

A blessing from heaven

More than a million pilgrims arrived in the Eternal City for the funeral on the morning of 8 April 2005. Hundreds of millions more, hailing from more than eighty-one nations, watched the ceremony *via* a live broadcast carried by 137 television stations. The foreign delegation attending the funeral numbered 169 (including 10 monarchs and 59 heads of state), while the religious world was represented by 23 Orthodox Churches, eight Eastern Communions, three international Christian organizations, 17 non-Christian religions, and various representatives from the Jewish world.

During the procession, as the cardinals reached the altar, blustery wind gusts whipped through the square at nearly fifty miles per hour, the highest velocity recorded in Rome that year, billowing concelebrants' vestments and flipping the pages of the Book of the Gospels that rested on the bier. Many recognized this as a real "breath of the Spirit."

Cardinal Ratzinger structured his homily around a brief biographical sketch of Karol Wojtyła based on the Lord's invitation to Peter, "Follow me!" "This lapidary saying of Christ can be taken as the key to understanding the message which comes to us from the life of our late beloved Pope John Paul II. Today we bury his remains in the earth as a seed of immortality; our hearts are full of sadness, yet at the same time are full of joyful hope and profound gratitude.... In the first years of his pontificate, still young and full of energy, the Holy Father went to the very ends of the earth, guided by Christ. But afterwards, he increasingly entered into the communion of Christ's sufferings; increasingly he understood the truth of the words: 'Someone else will fasten a belt around you.' And in this very communion with the suffering Lord, tirelessly and with renewed intensity, he proclaimed the Gospel, the mystery of that love which goes to the end (cf. Jn 13:1)."

He ended the homily in an unusually lyrical manner, atypical for his style, but perfectly appropriate at such an intense moment. It was then that the tears of the crowd began to flow most copiously: "None of us can ever forget how in that last Easter Sunday of his life, the Holy Father, marked by suffering, came once more to the window of the apostolic palace and one last time gave his *urbi et orbi* blessing. We can be sure that our beloved Pope is standing today at the window of the Father's house, that he sees us and blesses us. Yes, bless us, Holy Father. We entrust your dear soul to the Mother of God, your Mother, who guided you each day and who will guide you now to the eternal glory of her Son, our Lord Jesus Christ. Amen."

According to the norms of a conclave, the Preacher of the Papal Household—in this case, Fr. Raniero Cantalamessa, O.F.M. Cap.—was to offer the first of two meditations on "the problems of the Church and the selection of a new Roman Pontiff" on April 14th. All the members of the College of Cardinals were invited to attend this event, even those over the age of eighty, whereas only the cardinal electors—i.e., those aged eighty and under—were permitted to attend the second meditation in the Sistine Chapel on April 18th, delivered by Cardinal Tomáš Špidlík.

Long excerpts of Fr. Cantalamessa's meditation were printed in the media. It is quite interesting to look back on these in light of Ratzinger's election since they unmistakably reflect certain aspects of Ratzinger's own perspectives on the Magisterium. Indeed, some commentators referred to them as "Cantalamessa's Ratzingerian encomium" since they bear such an uncanny resemblance to the man who would ultimately be elected pope—namely, the Cardinal Prefect Ratzinger.

Anyone who had studied Cardinal Ratzinger's thought at the time would have easily seen direct parallels between his teaching and specific points made by Father Cantalamessa in his reflection. I will try to demonstrate this extremely succinctly by confronting five particular passages from each man.

CANTALAMESSA	RATZINGER
"The Church must focus her efforts more narrowly on creating an alternative reality to the world; a community, perhaps smaller, that has discovered 'the law of the Spirit who gives life in Christ.'"	"There are Christians today who are 'cut off,' so to speak; who place themselves outside of this strange modern existence; who are attempting new forms of life; these communities obviously do not draw much public attention, but they are really doing something that points toward a future." (*Salt of the Earth,* 1997)
"Every pastoral initiative, every mission, every religious undertaking—even a conclave—can becomes a new Babel or a new Pentecost. It becomes a new Babel if everyone is seeking to assert himself, to make a name for himself; it becomes a new Pentecost if it seeks the glory of God and the coming of His Kingdom."	After the death of the Archbishop of Munich in 1976, people were already saying that Ratzinger would be made his successor. In the cardinal's opinion, "I couldn't take them very seriously given my health limitations and my lack of expertise in matters of governance and administration. I always felt that my life would be one of scholarship and I couldn't imagine anything else." (*My Life,* 1997)
"*Lumen Gentium* affirmed the core charisms at the heart of the Church. It seemed the Lord himself wanted to confirm this conciliar teaching because in the wake of the Council there was a rapid reawakening of these charisms."	"Then, all of a sudden, something happened that nobody expected. It was the Holy Spirit's turn to speak again. The faith began to flourish in the hearts and minds of young people not with 'ifs' or 'buts,' without any subversion or escapism, but lived in its fullness as gift, as a precious gift that brings new life." (*The Ecclesial Movements: A Theological Reflection on Their Place in the Church,* 1998)

"There are those who believe that it is possible—indeed, even necessary—to renounce the unicity of Christ in order to enter into a genuine dialogue with other religions. But to proclaim Jesus as Lord precisely means to proclaim his unicity. The great challenge confronting Christianity today—and the one that the new pope will have to confront—is to connect a faithful and convinced participation in interreligious dialogue with an unshakeable faith in the universal salvific meaning of redemption in Jesus Christ."

"To hold that there is a universal truth, binding and valid within history itself, fulfilled in the figure of Jesus Christ and handed down through the faith of the Church: this is considered a kind of fundamentalism today, an affront to the modern spirit, a threat to tolerance and freedom.... The respect and esteem the Church has toward other world religions, as well as for the cultures who have objectively enriched and promoted human dignity and the development of civilization, does not diminish the originality and unicity of the revelation of Jesus Christ, and in no way does it limit the Church's missionary duty." (*Presentation of the Declaration* Dominus Iesus*, 2000*)

"The present canonical formulation of the relationship between the pope and the bishops is *cum Petro et sub Petro.* Until now, the accent has been on the *sub Petro.* Perhaps the time has come to shift that accent to *cum Petro.* This would involve creating appropriate means to make this happen; means that will not draw their inspiration from outdated categories of the Catholic world. We can no longer reason within in terms of the ancient patriarchates."

"In its original sense, the primacy of the Bishop of Rome is not opposed to the collegial constitution of the Church. It is rather a primacy of communion which places itself within a Church that lives and understands as a community of 'communion.' This authoritative interpretation of episcopal collegiality is not simply for the sake of human utility (even if it requires it), but it because the Lord himself established—together with the ministry of the Twelve—the special ministry of the Petrine office.... I am always more doubtful whether this form (i.e., of patriarchates) has the capacity to organize and group large continental entities." (*The New People of God,* 1971; *God and the World,* 2001)

Ephemeral predictions

Whether due to the proverb "no prophet is accepted in his home country," or the certitude that Ratzinger would finally get his wish and return to the peace and quiet of his beloved theological studies, I must confess that we in the Congregation for the Doctrine of the Faith hardly thought it possible that our prefect would succeed Pope John Paul II. It is true that we considered him a strong candidate for the first rounds of voting since there were a good number of cardinals who knew him and his work and admired both. But we didn't think his name would last long due to the hostility anticipated in those who would have never appreciated the consistency of his thought and the firmness with which he articulated his theological positions.

We were even more certain that he would not assume the role of "pope maker" as the Austrian Cardinal Franz König was said to have occupied for the election of Karol Wojtyła in the second conclave of 1978. Ratzinger was never interested in participating in any curial alliances since he knew that to do so would mean forfeiting his freedom as an elector. Much less did he want to be the leader of such a faction, even though some of his brother cardinals—more or less indirectly—tried to coax him into taking on this role. Even when he felt inspired to vote for a certain candidate, he did so discreetly and freely, never attempting to create a consensus around that individual, but rather highlighting some specific gift or talent that that particular candidate possessed to help him carry out the responsibilities of the papal office.

There were various signs before and during the conclave of the fact that he himself was oblivious to the prospect that he might be elected. For example, I remember well when Bishop of Chieti-Vasto, Bruno Forte, brought him a copy of a book on the Holy Shroud of Manoppello that had just been published by *Famiglia Christiana.* On that occasion, the bishop kindly invited Cardinal Ratzinger to visit the shrine. The cardinal assured him that he would visit as soon as the conclave was over. Indeed, he kept his promise as Benedict XVI and visited the shrine on 1 September 2006. I also recall that on his 78th birthday on 16 April 2005, he assured the staff of the congregation once again that he could already taste his long-awaited retirement and return to academia.

But I must also say that I was not alone in my obliviousness to the eventual outcome of the conclave. For instance, during the Wikileaks affair, correspondence emerged from the United States Embassy located on Via Veneto affirming that the cardinal "did not have the support needed to gain the necessary two-third majority of the electors given the staunch opposition of factions who considered Ratzinger too rigid and firm in his commitment to Roman priorities!"

Thinking back on the days preceding the conclave, I remembered a headline in the *Corriere della Sera* that read: "The Trading Desk of the Vatican Insiders." I recently retrieved that issue from the archives to refresh my memory, and, now from a distance of twenty years, I am dumbstruck at how clueless the world of journalism was as to who would be the frontrunners.

On 4 April 2005, following the death of John Paul II, the headline read: "Eyes Turn to the Italian Tettamanzi and the African Arinze." On the next day: "Arinze in the Lead as the Star Rises for Maradiaga." And then on 6 April 2005, the prefect's name was thrown into the ring for the first time: "Ratzinger and the South American Team on the Rise." His name disappears for a week until the 13th and 14th when he is referred to as "the Dean" ("Eyes Turn to the Dean: Sodano on the Rise"), but then things take a sudden turn on the following day: "An Italian Pact (without Ruini) Against Ratzinger." Finally, on the day the electors entered the Sistine Chapel, the newspaper read: "The Dean is Favored: Sodano Stands in Third Place."

We had the opportunity to look back on those chaotic days when the current director of the *Corriere della Sera,* Luciano Fontana (at the time of the conclave he was vice-director to Paolo Mieli), and the opinion columnist Massimo Franco, came to visit the pope emeritus at the Mater Ecclesiae Monastery where we were living. The guests brought two statuettes designed by Emilio Giannelli. The first depicted the newly elected pope embracing a crowded Saint Peter's Square with open arms. The second depicted Benedict handing over the keys of the Church to Francis and saying, "*Mi raccomando...*" ["Be careful..."].

In our dinner conversation that evening about that day's encounter, Benedict XVI humorously recalled a comic that Giannelli had published on the front page of the Milanese newspaper on 20 April 2005, in which the newly elected pope, raising a menacing index finger to the crowd in the square below, threatened (with a play on words pronounced by a newly-elected John Paul II): "*E se sbaglio, guai se mi correggerete!*" ["And if I make a mistake, don't you dare correct me!"]. The members of the Memores community and I had a hearty laugh over that one!

In any case, in the days leading up to the conclave—held from April 4th to April 16th—it was Cardinal Ratzinger's responsibility to preside over the twelve meetings of the General Congregations of Cardinals and to convoke all the electors (cardinals under the age of eighty) to elect a new pope. The closed balloting sessions were scheduled to begin on April 18th. A daily pile of official documents needing the cardinal's signature was being forwarded from the Secretariat of State to my office at the Congregation for the Doctrine of the Faith. The cardinal himself was working, reading, and studying at home. As secretary, Archbishop Angelo Amato was taking care of the day-to-day business of the congregation, deciding what to forward to the prefect and what to deal with himself.

Every morning, I would wait for him downstairs in my car and drive him from his residence to the Synodal Hall in order to help him avoid the mob of reporters eager to squeeze something out of him. In those days he did everything possible to stay out of the limelight. I don't know if he had any visitors, and it didn't seem my place to ask, but my impression was that he neither hosted any brother cardinals at his place nor accepted any invitations to socialize and consult with them elsewhere. Indeed, he cancelled all appointments and asked me to cross them off the calendar.

A few days before the conclave was scheduled to begin, he asked me to accompany him as his personal assistant according to the provision made by *Universi Dominici Gregis:* "In order to meet the personal and official needs connected with the election process, the following individuals must be available and therefore properly lodged in suitable areas

… (including) an ecclesiastic chosen by the Cardinal Dean or by the Cardinal taking his place, in order to assist him in his duties" (46).

On Sunday afternoon, the 17th of April, I went to pick him up in my Golf and accompany him into Casa Santa Marta where the cardinals lodge during the conclave. After parking the car, I went to check into my room on the fourth floor, which, of course, was different from my normal room on the fifth floor. I didn't really have a specific job description, so I simply told him that I would be available and would not otherwise interrupt him. Every once in a while, if he happened to need something, he would ask for me.

The dining room was arranged with tables of eight at which the cardinals would sit and engage in informal conversation as they wished. The collaborators—masters of ceremony, confessors, and medical professionals—were seated at a long table on the side. We were able to observe most everything that was happening, but it was difficult to hear or understand anything since the din of 130 people murmuring in different languages came across as true "Babel."

If there were any doubt over Ratzinger's desire to pull himself out of the "papal race," the homily he delivered at the *pro eligendo Romano Pontifice* Mass on April 18th eliminated it. The firmness with which he expressed his convictions and lined up his battle horses seemed to assure that many of his brother cardinals would have done everything to avoid electing him. In fact, at that conclave, it would have taken only 39 votes to form a block that would have prevented the electors from reaching the two-thirds majority needed for a successful ballot.

One paragraph of Ratzinger's homily in particular caught the media's attention. Aldo Cazzullo dubbed it "Joseph's manifesto" in the *Corriere della Sera* the next day. Here is what the cardinal said in no uncertain terms in his last homily before becoming pope: "Today, having a clear faith based on the Creed of the Church is often labeled as fundamentalism. Whereas relativism, that is, letting oneself be 'tossed here and there, carried about by every wind of doctrine,' seems the only attitude that can cope with modern times. We are building a dictatorship of relativism that does not recognize anything as definitive and whose ultimate goal consists solely of one's own ego and desires. We, however, have a different goal: the Son of God, the true man. He is the measure of true humanism. An 'adult' faith is not a faith that follows the trends of fashion and the latest novelty; a mature adult faith is deeply rooted in friendship with Christ."

The black sweater underneath

I didn't have any major responsibilities during the first two rounds of voting on the afternoon of the 18th and the morning of the 19th. But I kept within eyesight of the cardinal, even though he never really needed my services. I therefore passed the time praying, reading, and chatting occasionally with the papal physician, Renato Buzzonetti, and with the Papal Master of Ceremonies.

I did notice some agitation among the cardinals at dinner on the 18th, probably because the first round of voting brought home to them the seriousness of their responsibility in electing the new pope. By lunch the next day, the atmosphere was more relaxed. Unexpectedly, as he was approaching the elevator to head back to his room, Cardinal Ratzinger summoned me and asked that I accompany him on foot to the Sistine Chapel. This was already unusual since he normally took the shuttle bus provided for the cardinals. I obviously obliged. The first round of afternoon voting was scheduled for 4:00 p.m., so he told me to meet him at the entrance of Casa Santa Marta at 3:30 p.m.

The weather was unpredictable (as is often the case in Rome), and as we walked down the Via delle Fondamenta that passes along the backside of Saint Peter's Basilica and is always a bit windy, I remember being engulfed by a gust of chilled, fresh air. The cardinal had mentioned to me how cold it was in the Sistine Chapel that morning, and he told me he decided to put on an extra sweater underneath his ceremonial red cassock and white surplice for the afternoon session.

Completely absorbed in his thoughts, he clearly preferred not to talk, so I was content just to walk by his side, occasionally sneaking a glance at his face and praying for him as best I could. Mentally, it was the longest and most exhausting walk I had ever taken with him. I had the distinct impression that we had reached a historic and dramatic moment, and I sensed that Ratzinger felt as if he were standing on the edge of a cliff.

It seemed we were completely alone except for a few members of the Swiss Guard and Gendarmerie Corps who were guarding the area to ensure the conclave would be conducted in utmost secrecy. After crossing the San Damaso courtyard and taking the elevator up to the *prima loggia*, we headed for the *Aula delle Benedizioni* where the cardinals gathered before entering the Sistine Chapel. There, I met Doctor Buzzonetti and we chatted for awhile, strolling through the *Sala Ducale*, the *Sala Regia*, and the *Aula delle Benedizioni*, all of which adjoin the Sistine Chapel. Several ceremonial assistants, confessors, and medical staff were doing the same.

To pass the time—which seemed like an eternity—I had brought some books and notes to read, and I happened to come across Cardinal Ratzinger's presentation of John Paul II's book of poetry entitled, *Roman Triptych: Meditations* (2003): "The contemplation of the Last Judgement in the epilogue of the second panel, is perhaps the part of the *Triptych* that moves the reader most. From the interior eyes of the Pope in a fresh way, there derives once again the memory of the conclaves of August and October 1978. Since I was also present, I know well how we were exposed to those images in the hour of the important decisions, how they challenged us and how they instilled in our souls the greatness of our responsibility. The Pope speaks to the Cardinals of the future conclave, 'after my death,' and says that Michelangelo's vision will speak to them. The word 'con-clave' imposes the thought of the keys, of the patrimony of the keys handed to Peter. To place these keys in the right hands: this is the immense responsibility of those days." I was immediately overcome by the realization that this was precisely what was happening behind those closed doors just a stone's throw away from me.

All of a sudden, at around 5:15 p.m., the silence of those grand halls adjacent to the Sistine Chapel was interrupted by light applause filtering through the doors. It didn't last long. We all looked at one another and understood that a pope had been elected. It then occurred to me that if indeed the 77 necessary votes had been obtained, we still had to wait while the rest of the ballots were accounted for and the procedures for authentication were carefully followed, let alone the need for the winner to voice his acceptance.

Twenty minutes later, we heard a second burst of applause through the closed doors and knew for certain the process was completed. In fact, within minutes, we heard the unmistakable sound of a key turning in the latch on the other side and saw the head of Atillio Nicora pop out (as last in the order of cardinal deacons, it was his responsibility to open and close the doors of the chapel). He must have enjoyed keeping us in suspense by assuring us that a pope had indeed been elected though he didn't reveal his name.

For some reason, the image of the black sweater that Ratzinger had put on beneath his official vestments flashed through my mind. As soon as I saw the Dean of Ceremonies, Monsignor Francesco Camaldo, who was also personally assigned to Ratzinger, I rushed over to him and pleaded: "If the new pope is Ratzinger, please make sure that His Excellency the Master of Ceremonies [i.e., Piero Marini] asks him to take off his sweater underneath or at least to roll up the sleeves so that it doesn't show." He assured me that he would, but unfortunately he forgot about it in the hustle and bustle of getting things ready for the presentation of the new pope. Hence the rest of the world caught an unmistakable glimpse of those dark, floppy sleeves underneath the sheer white vestments as the new pontiff stepped onto the balcony.

Excitement soared. Sitting beneath Michelangelo's imposing Last Judgment, I could partially make out the white clad figure seated on a throne, but I still couldn't tell who it was since the cardinals were crowding around him and rendering their acts of obedience. Yet soon the whispers started to fly: "Ratzinger, Ratzinger, Ratzinger … Benedict, Benedict, Benedict…." Then through a mist of confusion and apprehension it all suddenly became clear to me. I felt a flood of emotions and a little anxiety rush into my heart.

When I heard the name "Benedict," I clearly recognized it as a reference to the saint of Norcia rather than to Ratzinger's twentieth-century predecessor, Benedict XV. Just a few days before heading for Subiaco, Ratzinger had said to me, "We need more men like Benedict of Norcia who, in a time of dissipation and decadence, threw himself into extreme solitude. That was precisely how, after a slew of purifications, he was able to re-emerge into the light and establish a monastery on a hill literally full of ruins—Montecassino—and draw the strength he needed to build a new world."

During one of his first general audiences on 27 April 2005, he explained in more detail how he drew inspiration from the saint of Norcia and the extraordinary pope of the twentieth century: "I wanted to be called Benedict XVI in order to create a spiritual bond with Benedict XV, who steered the Church through the period of turmoil caused by the First World War. He was a courageous and authentic prophet of peace and strove with brave courage first of all to avert the tragedy of the war and then to limit its harmful consequences. Treading in his footsteps, I would like to place my ministry at the service of reconciliation and harmony between persons and peoples, since I am profoundly convinced that the great good of peace is first and foremost a gift of God, a precious but unfortunately fragile gift to pray for, safeguard and build up, day after day, with the help of all. The name 'Benedict' also calls to mind the extraordinary figure of the great 'Patriarch of Western Monasticism,' Saint Benedict of Norcia, Co-Patron of Europe.... [H]e is a fundamental reference point for European unity and a powerful reminder of the indispensable Christian roots of his culture and civilization."

As things began to settle down in the Sistine Chapel, Substitute Leonardo Sandri, Secretary for Relations with States Giovanni Lajolo, and Prefect of the Papal Household James Michael Harvey got in line. The papal physician, Doctor Buzzonetti, and I slipped in right behind them. When I finally stood face-to-face with Pope Benedict, I could see the emotional drain the process had taken on him, so I kept my words short and spoke in our native German: "Holy Father, a heartfelt congratulations on your election as the Successor of Peter. I am completely at your service. You can count on me *in vita et in morte*." It was far from a polished speech, but he instantly sensed my emotions and simply replied, "Thank you. Thank you."

In the vineyard of the Lord

At 5:50 p.m., we could hear the roar of the crowd in Saint Peter's Square as they witnessed the white smoke rise from the chimney signaling a successful ballot. At 6:43 p.m., they intently listened to the voice of Cardinal Protodeacon Jorge Arturo Medina Estévez as he officially announced the identity and name of the newly elected pontiff. As the processional line formed to head to the balcony, I could see that Benedict XVI was getting his color back as he smoothed out his new white vestments.

The tension was slowly lifting from the *loggia*, and Benedict's voice calmly delivered his first greeting and blessing to the crowd at 6:48 p.m.: "Dear Brothers and Sisters, after the great Pope John Paul II, the Cardinals have elected me, a simple and humble labourer in the vineyard of the Lord. The fact that the Lord knows how to work and to act even with inadequate instruments comforts me, and above all I entrust myself to your prayers. Let us move forward in the joy of the Risen Lord, confident of his unfailing help. The Lord will help us and Mary, his Most Holy Mother, will be on our side. Thank you."

As I was going through some documents in Benedict XVI's personal archive, I noticed that the words of his first greeting resembled some of the phrases Paul VI used in the papal bull of Ratzinger's appointment to the Archdiocese of Munich and Freising in 1977: "In the Spirit, we look toward you, our beloved brother. You have been endowed with extraordinary gifts of the Spirit and you are a fine teacher of theology.... We now ask you: Work in the vineyard of the Lord."

After greeting the crowd once more with a somewhat awkward hand gesture (he simply wasn't accustomed to this ritual), the pope headed for the elevator with Cardinal Angelo Sodano, vice-Dean of the College of Cardinals, and they descended together to the San Damaso level where an automobile bearing the traditional "SCV 1" license plate was waiting for him. Pietro Cicchetti, who would become his trusted driver for many years, was behind the wheel. Benedict XVI accepted the invitation to take his proper place in the back seat on the right, and, finding me in the crowd, gestured that I should take my place to his left.

When he entered the dining room at Casa Santa Marta, the cardinals joined their voices in the traditional *Tu es Petrus* and *Oremus pro Pontifice,* boisterously intoned by the unmistakable baritone of Salvatore De Giorgio, Archbishop of Palermo. Seated with the newly elected pontiff were Cardinals Sodano and Medina Estévez, as well as the *camerlengo*, Eduardo Martínez Somalo. The celebrations consisted of little more than a cordial toast since Pope Benedict wanted to retire to his room and work on the Latin homily that he was supposed to give the next morning in the Sistine Chapel during a concelebrated Mass with the electors who had chosen him.

The Secretariat of State had prepared a draft of the homily ahead of time, subsequently customizing it to the voice of the newly-elected pope once they knew who it was. But Ratzinger did not deny himself the desire to enliven and personalize it by including his own feelings regarding what had just happened during those intense hours. He candidly spoke of two contrasting sentiments: "On the one hand, [I feel] a sense of inadequacy and human apprehension as I face the responsibility for the universal Church, entrusted to me yesterday as Successor of the Apostle Peter in this See of Rome. On the other, I have a lively feeling of profound gratitude to God who, as the liturgy makes us sing, never leaves his flock untended but leads it down the ages under the guidance of those whom he himself has chosen as the Vicars of his Son and has made shepherds of the flock."

With a moving reference to his predecessor, John Paul II, he said, "I seem to feel his strong hand clasping mine; I seem to see his smiling eyes and hear his words, at this moment addressed specifically to me, 'Do not be afraid!'" He begged the Lord "to compensate for my limitations so that I may be a courageous and faithful Pastor of his flock, ever docile to the promptings of his Spirit. I am preparing to undertake this special ministry, the 'Petrine' ministry at the service of the universal Church, with humble abandonment into the hands of God's Providence."

He also stressed that "the Church of today must revive her awareness of the duty to repropose to the world the voice of the One who said: 'I am the light of the world. No follower of mine shall ever walk in darkness; no, he shall possess the light of life' (Jn 8: 12). In carrying out his ministry, the new Pope knows that his task is to make Christ's light shine out before the men and women of today: not his own light, but Christ's." The pope "is entrusted with the task of strengthening his brethren (cf. Lk 22: 32)."

The homily he delivered at the inauguration of his Petrine ministry on April 24th was even more significant. He dared to bare his soul to all humanity, not as an expression of false modesty or feigned humility, but precisely to orient his pontificate toward what he thought to be the highest priority: "And now, at this moment, weak servant of God that I am,

I must assume this enormous task, which truly exceeds all human capacity. How can I do this? How will I be able to do it? All of you, my dear friends, have just invoked the entire host of saints, represented by some of the great names in the history of God's dealings with mankind. In this way, I too can say with renewed conviction: I am not alone…. My real program of governance is not to do my own will, not to pursue my own ideas, but to listen, together with the whole Church, to the word and the will of the Lord, to be guided by Him, so that He himself will lead the Church at this hour of our history."

At the core of his homily was an explanation of the two signs that liturgically represent the inauguration of his Petrine ministry. The pallium, a circular vestment with two strands of wool hanging in front and back, "may be considered an image of the yoke of Christ, which the Bishop of this City, the Servant of the Servants of God, takes upon his shoulders. God's yoke is God's will, which we accept…. [T]he lamb's wool is meant to represent the lost, sick or weak sheep which the shepherd places on his shoulders and carries to the waters of life." The gold ring is called the "Fisherman's Ring" because "Peter's call to be a shepherd … comes after the account of a miraculous catch of fish: after a night in which the disciples had let down their nets without success, they see the Risen Lord on the shore. He tells them to let down their nets once more, and the nets become so full that they can hardly pull them in…. Today too the Church and the successors of the Apostles are told to put out into the deep sea of history and to let down the nets, so as to win men and women over to the Gospel—to God, to Christ, to true life." Indeed, the figure of Peter tossing his nets into the sea is inscribed on the face of the ring.

But sadly, in this case too, the press decided to isolate a single sentence: "Pray for me, that I may not flee for fear of the wolves." Admittedly, these are unsettling words, but I can assure you that they were not meant to convey any specific fear about the future of his pontificate or the problems he was obviously aware of, such as clerical sexual abuse or the Vatican's financial troubles. Rather, they were meant to reflect a strong and paradoxical image employed by one of his heroes, Saint John Chrysostom, a fourth-century Doctor of the Church, who addressed a series of homilies against the vices and nefarious deeds of his time. In fact, during his general audience of 26 October 2011, he cited Chrysostom's commentary on the Gospel passage in which Jesus sends his disciples "like sheep among wolves" (Lk 10:3). The "golden-mouthed" saint wrote, "For so long as we are sheep, we conquer: though ten thousand wolves prowl around, we overcome and prevail. But if we become wolves, we are worsted, for the help of our Shepherd departs from us."

Schönborn's letter

Unsurprisingly, there were rampant speculations after the conclave about how the voting process unfolded. Only one thing is certain: historically, this was a quick conclave. Only four rounds of voting were needed to elect Benedict XVI (the same number needed for John Paul I in 1978). In the last century, only one conclave has been briefer: Pius XII was elected on the third *scrutinium* in 1939. Otherwise, conclaves have ranged from five rounds—as for Paul VI in 1963 and Francis in 2013—to seven (Pius X in 1903), eight (John Paul II in 1978), ten (Benedict XV in 1914), eleven (John XXIII in 1958), and fourteen (Pius XI in 1922).

There were many indiscreet leaks concerning the voting, but all of them support the claim that Ratzinger's name was put forward from the very beginning. In his memoir entitled *On the Outskirts of Jericho,* this is how Cardinal Julián Herranz tells the story: "Why were the two-thirds necessary for Ratzinger obtained so quickly? Some reports have correctly identified a fourfold reason: his intellectual prestige as a first-class theologian; his institutional experience as Prefect of the Congregation for the Doctrine of the Faith and Dean of the Sacred College; his familiarity with the Roman Curia after having worked at the Holy Office and having served on several other congregations for many years; and his closeness and fidelity to Karol Wojtyła, who, in turn, had clearly trusted him. But I would dare add one further criterion: his spiritual reputation as a priest with a deep interior life and a habit of contemplation, as well as his vibrant apostolic spirit. John Paul II admired Ratzinger's willingness to bring the teaching and love of Christ to every areopagus throughout the world."

In an interview with biographer Peter Seewald, Benedict explained that, during the period preceding the conclave, he was struck by the fact that "many cardinals, so to speak, were imploring whomever was elected to take up the cross and accept, even if he didn't feel up to the task; to yield to the two-thirds majority as a sign that that man was the right choice. It was a matter of spiritual duty, they said. They then tried to convince me in all seriousness by saying that if the majority of cardinals expressed their conviction that I was the right choice, then their voice must clearly imply that it was the Lord's will that I accept."

During an audience with German pilgrims on April 25th, Benedict explained the final moments before his election in more detail: "When, little by little, the trend of the voting led me to understand that, to put it simply, the axe was going to fall on me, my head began to spin. I was convinced that I had already carried out my life's work and could look forward to ending my days peacefully. With profound conviction I said to the Lord: Do not do this to me! You have younger and better people at your disposal, who can face this great responsibility with greater dynamism and greater strength. I was then very touched by a brief note written to me by a brother cardinal. He reminded me that on the occasion of the Mass for John Paul II, I had based my homily, starting from the Gospel, on the Lord's words to Peter by the Lake of Gennesaret: 'Follow me!' I spoke of how again and again, Karol Wojtyła received this call from the Lord, and how each time he had to renounce much and to simply say: Yes, I will follow you, even if you lead me where I never wanted to go. This brother cardinal wrote to me: Were the Lord to say to you now, 'Follow me,' then remember what you preached. Do not refuse! Be obedient in the same way that you described the great pope, who has returned to the house of the Father. This deeply moved me. The ways of the Lord are not easy, but we were not created for an easy life, but for great things, for goodness. Thus, in the end I had to say 'yes.'"

It was Cardinal Christoph Schönborn who wrote those words to Cardinal Ratzinger. Schönborn had known Ratzinger since 1972, when, as a young Dominican, he went to Regensburg to study under the professor, and he remained close to him through a tight-knit group of former disciples. In fact, aside from childhood friends, Schönborn was one of the few who was accustomed to using the informal Italian *tu* when addressing Ratzinger. The others were Cardinals Cordes, Kasper, Meisner, and Müller. But Ratzinger was always addressed with the formal

Lei by Amato, Bertone, Comastri, Ruini, Scola, Sodano, and Vallini, even though he had regular exchanges with them both as cardinal and as pope.

There are various reports—all of them fantastical—regarding the exact words Ratzinger used when asked by the vice-Dean, Cardinal Sodano, if he accepted the election. None of these stories—from Cardinal Michele Giordano's *"propter voluntatem Dei accepto"* to Cardinal Cormac Murphy-O'Connor's more complex, "No, I cannot. I accept it as God's will"—are consistent with Ratzinger's personality. On this point, I couldn't be more precise since I asked the pope himself. He told me he said nothing more than *"Accepto"* ("I accept" in Latin); and when asked his name, he responded simply, *"Benedictus."*

The moment of his acceptance also marked the end of a long-standing prejudice: four centuries had passed since a head of the Holy Office had been elected pope. The last had been Camillo Borghese (1552–1621), elected as Paul V on 16 May 1605, who had been in charge of the Roman Inquisition for two years. By a unique coincidence, the last Dean of the College of Cardinals to be elected pope was, like Ratzinger, in charge of the congregation: Gian Pietro Carafa (1476–1556), who was elected as Paul IV on 23 May 1555 at age seventy-nine.

Many have wondered how Ratzinger himself had cast his vote. Personally, I think the answer may be found in the report that Cardinal Giacomo Biffi, the Archbishop of Bologna from 1985 to 2003, received one vote in every single *scrutinium.* According to Vatican expert Francesco Grana, after the third round of voting, Biffi had a playful exchange with the Archbishop of Naples, Michele Giordano. Biffi said, "If I find out who dared to vote for me, I'll slap him." Giorando responded, "We are very close to electing a new pope and it's pretty clear that he's the one who keeps voting for you. So, are you quite sure you want to slap the pope?"

Actually, Ratzinger knew Cardinal Biffi quite well, mostly from his active participation in meetings of the Congregation for the Doctrine of the Faith, of which Biffi was a member. Ratzinger had read several of his books and appreciated deeply the opinions he offered during the *feria quarta* gatherings. As an expression of his esteem for the Archbishop of Bologna, Ratzinger invited him to preach the spiritual exercises for the

Roman Curia in 2007, making Biffi the only cardinal to have performed this function twice, the other being in 1989 for John Paul II. On the first anniversary of Cardinal Biffi's death, Benedict XVI offered a moving message for the commemorative book prepared for the occasion in 2016: "I will always remember Cardinal Biffi as an exemplary pastor of the Church in tempestuous times. There was no gall in him whatsoever. He was a man of extraordinary courage without any concern for being popular or unpopular. He was directed by nothing but the light of truth that appears to us in the person of Jesus Christ. His penetrating intelligence and cultural and theological formation, together with his good sense of humor, were so attractive precisely because he dedicated himself completely to the Lord's service, and therefore to the service of his fellow men. My greatest wish is that the Church of God never lacks men such as this one."

The secret diary and other polemical accounts of the conclave

In the days following the election, a friend of mind remarked—with a hint of bitterness that probably reflected the sentiments of some within the conclave—that the cardinals preferred "a safe bet" over someone "new who would charge ahead." Be that as it may, I think it is true that after the dense magisterial teaching set forth by John Paul II, who reigned for twenty-seven years, it was time for a period of assimilation. A good successor would foster a fuller understanding of Wojtyła's teaching and bring it to completion. And who else could it possibly be but Ratzinger, his closest theological collaborator?

Over the next few months, various reconstructions of the balloting began to emerge, but none caused as much ruckus as that composed by an unidentified cardinal and published by Vatican reporter Lucio Brunelli, claiming that, in the end, Ratzinger had gained 84 of the 115 votes. Personally, judging from the joy I saw on the faces of virtually all the cardinals as they exited the chapel, I think this is an underestimation. The congratulatory conversations I heard between Pope Benedict and the cardinals in the days following the conclave—in addition to various public declarations surrounding the developments of the conclave—give me the same impression. My guess is that among Ratzinger's staunchest supporters were Columbian Alfonso Lópes Trujillo, Chilean Jorge Medina Estévez, Spanish Cardinals Julián Herranz and Antonio María Rouco Varela, German Joachim Meisner, Austrian Christoph Schöborn, Nigerian Francis Arinze, and the Indian Ivan Dias. But there were undoubtedly many others who were likewise in favor of Ratzinger.

As to the author of that secret diary, journalists have proposed several names, including Brazilian Cláudio Hummes (with the intention of making it clear for posterity that Bergoglio also received a significant amount of votes), Italian Mario Francesco Pompedda (Vatican reporter Sandro Magister wrote that "several indiscreet voices have revealed that Pompedda is the author of the diary," even though it is unlikely Pompedda would have made the mistake of referring to Cardinal Ruini as the "Apostolic Vicar" rather than the "Vicar General" of the Diocese of Rome), Portuguese José Saraiva Martins (whose voice seems to come through when he writes that he himself "was one of the possible candidates on the next day," but was criticized by Cardinal Martini for campaigning), Belgian Godfried Danneels (who boasted that he had participated in the 1999 meeting of the "Sankt Gallen group" to discuss some possible progressive reforms in the Church with other cardinals including Martini, Silvestrini, Kasper, Lehmann, and Murphy-O'Connor). Obviously, as some journalists surmised, there are hints that the "diary" might be nothing more than a text fabricated to raise certain suspicions and suppress others.

I must confess that within the peaceful confines of the Mater Ecclesiae Monastery, I occasionally tried to pick Pope Benedict's brain on the topic of the secret "diary," but he limited himself to suggesting that, if a cardinal were behind it, it was a brash decision to make it public and he would have to grapple with that decision in his own conscience. He never gave a hint as to who he thought was behind it, and refused to deny or confirm any of my guesses. "But *someone* must have said *something,*" I insisted. But to this he never even said as much as, "I suppose."

In any case, there was no shortage of intrigue, misinformation, and sensational speculation regarding the conclave. In my free time, I read a lot of books that promised to reveal some secret or reconstruct the events surrounding the election of Cardinal Ratzinger. But I always came away with the impression that the author had a prejudiced view or agenda to advance at all costs, even when evidence for such positions was completely lacking. I do not want to belabor the point, so I will limit myself to three different examples.

The first is, quite frankly, utterly absurd. In *The Pope's War: Why Ratzinger's Secret Crusade Has Imperiled the Church and How It Can Be Saved,* Matthew Fox, an ex-Dominican, writes, "An 'addiction to power' seems to be a particularly Ratzingerian problem, as illustrated in the following true story. A few years ago, I was talking with an American theologian who had studied under Ratzinger when he received his doctorate in theology at a German university. He knew Ratzinger well, and he was so upset by what Ratzinger was doing as chief inquisitor—silencing and expelling theologians right and left—that he made a special trip to Rome to confront him. Ratzinger did meet with him, and they had a serious exchange in German. On exiting the Vatican, this former student of Ratzinger's shook his head and said in disgust, 'It is all about the pursuit of the purple.'"[3] Now, considering that the prefect came to Rome in 1981 and had already been a cardinal for at least four years before this anonymous ex-student met him in Rome, there seems to be some serious confusion about the timeline of this Ratzinger figure so "addicted to power."

Vatican reporter Marco Politi, in a book entitled *Crisi di un papato* ["A Pontificate in Crisis"], makes this specific accusation: "Those in favor of a dug-in, defensive Church do not even want to have a public discussion about the future pope. Danneels opened a press conference just in time at a religious institute not far from the Via Aurelia before the axe fell on such events. Cardinal Danneels probably heard a rumor that these kind of informational sessions would be squashed because he ended the press conference with this quip: 'Freedom of speech is a fundamental human right.' At the plenary meeting of the cardinals on the day after the funeral of John Paul II, the vote passed to approve a resolution—supported by Ratzinger—to hold the cardinals to silence." On April 7th, it was indeed announced at the General Congregation that the cardinals had decided to observe strict silence with the press from the

3 Matthew Fox, *The Pope's War: Why Ratzinger's Secret Crusade Has Imperiled the Church and How It Can Be Saved* (Sterling Ethos, 2012), p. 132.

day of the John Paul II's funeral until the end of the conclave on April 18th. John Allen, Jr., makes it clear in *The Rise of Benedict XVI* that Cardinal Godfried Danneels himself clearly stated that the decision to keep silence was anything but a top-down command: "Ratzinger had said in the General Congregation meetings that it was a 'human right' of cardinals to speak to whomever they chose. Other cardinals confirmed this account. Instead of an explicit ban, therefore, the cardinals struck a sort of gentleman's agreement among themselves to be discreet."[4]

In a book-length interview entitled *Confession d'un cardinal,* in which French author Olivier Le Gendre traces the details of an anonymous cardinal's personal diary (who seems to be Cardinal Achille Silvestrini despite numerous biographical inconsistencies), there is a claim that 35–40 votes went to Cardinal Jorge Mario Bergoglio: "This is something to keep in mind for the future in the event that Benedict XVI's pontificate does not last long." However, Austen Ivereigh, in his biography of Pope Francis entitled *The Great Reformer,* states unequivocally that Bergoglio was "so upset by [the 'secret diary's'] picture of him as an anti-Ratzinger blocker or stalking horse.... Bergoglio was annoyed enough to tell journalists he was 'confused and a bit hurt' by 'these indiscretions,' which he said have given a false picture."[5]

4 John Allen, Jr., *The Rise of Benedict XVI: The Inside Story of How the Pope Was Elected and Where He Will Take the Catholic Church* (Doubleday, 2005), p. 71.

5 Austen Ivereigh, *The Great Reformer: Francis and the Making of a Radical Pope* (Henry Holt, 2014), p. 286.

4
The Family (Pontifical and Otherwise)

Bavarian roots

There is a passage in the book-length interview *Light of the World* that I think perfectly expresses how Joseph Ratzinger, as man and pope, perceives friendship and its importance both to his immediate family and the spiritual family he created with his closest collaborators: "The Pontifical family is extremely dear to me. Visits from old friends are also of the highest priority. In general, I am happy to say that I don't spend my days surrounded by an artificial courtly retinue. I rather prefer to live in as normal a way possible with lots of direct, personal interaction, and to conduct my daily affairs in as healthy a way as possible."

Ratzinger's strong attachment to familial bonds is rooted in the story of his own family going back to the early twentieth century, to the time when his father was finally able to marry at an advanced age as things began to calm down after the Great War. The forty-three-year-old Joseph was joined in matrimony to the thirty-six-year-old homemaker, Maria Peintner, on 9 November 1920. Their firstborn, a daughter they named Maria, came into the world on 7 December 1921, and their first son Georg was born on 15 January 1924. The future pope, Joseph (as his name was recorded in the baptismal registry rather than the more traditional spelling "Josef") was born on 16 April 1927.

The calling of both sons to the priesthood entailed a significant economic burden on the family since their seminary tuition could hardly be covered by their father's meager pension, even with subsidies available from the diocese. So, both mother and sister went to work to help raise tuition money, the former as a cook at the Reit im Winkl hotel, the latter at an office in Traunstein.

This was just one of the many reasons that both Joseph and his brother Georg—both of whom were ordained to the priesthood on 29 June 1951—were always extremely grateful to their parents (Joseph died in 1959 and Maria in 1963) and to their sister, Maria. In his autobiography, *My Life,* the cardinal confesses that "my mother's generosity was constant, and it was always for me a concrete sign of the faith she nourished daily. I cannot think of a more persuasive proof of Christian truth than the transparent, sincere humanity that my parents had precisely because of their belief in Christ." In regard to his sister Maria, Ratzinger writes, "her presence, her way of living, and her humility created a climate of a shared faith, the faith we both grew up with, which matured in us and grew stronger year after year."

Maria never married and, after becoming a third-order Franciscan at twenty years of age and taking the name "Clare," she accompanied her brother wherever he went, caring for his domestic needs in his various residences, including in Rome. She died from a stroke on 2 November 1991 while traveling to Ziegetsdorf, and is buried there in the family tomb with her parents. The commemorative card distributed at her funeral reads: "For thirty-four years, she served her brother Joseph with tireless dedication, generosity, and humility on every step of his journey."

Cardinal Schönborn shared a touching story about Joseph and Maria: "Cardinal Ratzinger had a mild stroke in September of 1991. He went to the hospital, but it was nothing serious and he recovered quickly. A little over a month later, his sister Maria had a terrible stroke and died on the same day. We were all extremely concerned because we didn't know how the cardinal would have dealt with this terrible loss. The day after the conclave in which he was elected, the new pope—my dear professor and friend—now dressed in white, came into the dining room at Casa Santa Marta for breakfast. After greeting one another, I said, 'Holy Father, yesterday, when you were elected, I couldn't help but think that your sister asked the Lord to take her life instead of her brother's.' He responded, 'Yes, I think so.' Of all our interaction, this encounter remains the most moving."

I never knew Maria personally since she passed away well before my arrival in Rome. But on various occasions, both as cardinal and as pope, Ratzinger remembered her with deep affection and I clearly understood the unique bond they shared as siblings. It pained him deeply that he was not able to make it to her bedside for a final farewell before she died.

Her death was in fact at the center of one of the most emotional moments toward the end of Benedict's life. The pope emeritus desperately wanted to visit his brother Monsignor Georg as he neared the end of his life in Regensburg. Georg had planned to visit him at the Vatican in 2020, but COVID made it impossible. He subsequently fell ill and his condition was worsening when Benedict finally realized that the situation was critical. Unfortunately, the pope emeritus himself was having severe eye and ear problems, which his ENT specialist had diagnosed as an acute form of herpes zoster ("shingles" or, as the Italians call it, "Saint Anthony's Fire"), which blurred his vision and caused intense pain to his trigeminal nerve (the doctor believed it to be a symptom of severe stress). On top of this were issues with mobility, as Benedict was confined to a wheelchair at the time. Given his condition, Doctor Patrizio Polisca, who had been his personal physician since 15 June 2009, together with the other specialists, counseled against extensive travel. Benedict, however, was insistent, and he turned to Pope Francis for help, for the latter had told him that he would do anything he could to assist his predecessor when in need. Thanks to the assistance of the Italian Air Force and the Bavarian government, who helped with both flights and ground transportation, Benedict was able to visit his brother from 18–22 June 2020, just days before Georg's death on July 1st.

When Georg Ratzinger was made an honorary citizen of Castel Gandolfo on 21 August 2008, Pope Benedict XVI had this to say about his older brother: "From the beginning of my life, my brother has always been for me not only a companion, but also a trustworthy guide. For me he has been a point of orientation and of reference with the clarity and determination of his decisions. He has always shown me the path to take, even in difficult situations…. My brother has pointed out that since then, we have arrived at the last stage of our lives, at old age. The days left to live progressively diminish. But also in this stage my brother helps me to accept with serenity, with humility, and with courage the weight of each day."

It was a heavy loss for Benedict when his brother Georg died, but he also told me several times that he felt consolation from the Lord that Georg was safely in the Father's embrace. The pope emeritus also had frequent occasion to recall the living presence of his dear brother whenever he listened to recordings of the *Regensburger Domspatzen*, the choir Georg faithfully conducted for many years.

With the Introduction *under my arm*

My first encounter with Ratzinger, as for many people, came through his book *Introduction to Christianity*. He wrote it in 1968, but I only learned of it in 1974 on the threshold of my eighteenth birthday. My pastor recommended it to me as a way of gaining insight into my own personal situation because I was just starting to consider the idea of entering the seminary, even though I was still relishing the peace of everyday life in Riedern am Wald, a small village in southwest Germany with a few hundred inhabitants.

My father, Albert, was a blacksmith, and my mother, Gertrud, a homemaker. I was the firstborn of five children (two brothers and two sisters). I was not very wise in the ways of the world, and a little rebellious in my youth, sporting long, curly hair and exuding an air of nonconformity. I listened to a lot of rock music, especially the Beatles, Pink Floyd, and Cat Stevens, but I also liked our traditional music, and played the clarinet in our village band. Ratzinger and I talked about music sometimes, and while listening to him play the piano, I assured him that he did very well never to have quit practicing. I, unfortunately, having given up the clarinet when I entered the seminary, found it impossible to pick it back up again, both because I was out of practice and because I ideally needed a small ensemble to make it worth playing again. When I was young, my dream was to become a stockbroker and make a lot of money. In the meantime, I was an ordinary high school student, scraping together whatever spare change I could earn by delivering mail on my bicycle. I also played a lot of sports—skiing, soccer, and later tennis, too.

I started to read Ratzinger's book just to avoid disappointing my pastor. But as I read the preface, I couldn't help but detect the enthusiasm of the young, forty-year-old professor at Tubingen as he explained the intent of the text: "…[T]o help understand faith afresh as something that makes possible true humanity in the world today, to expound faith without changing it into the small coin of empty talk painfully laboring to hide a complete spiritual vacuum."

It was not an easy read, I admit, but I had little doubt that the author was tackling difficult and subtle questions, beginning with man's current situation in confronting the problem of God. But the stories that Ratzinger had inserted here and there—such as the foolish Hans who constantly traded his property for something worse, or the clown who tried in vain to convince the townspeople that there was a fire—helped me to see that the author was also a highly spirited man, gifted with the ability to boil down his reflections to the most fundamental themes of the Christian faith.

When I passed the *esame di maturità* (exams proper for students leaving high school), I was unsure which path to follow at the university, so I thought about studying theology and philosophy at Freiburg im Breisgau. At the same time, I decided to enter the diocesan seminary, where I discovered that *Introduction to Christianity* was required reading: a few pages were assigned every week, leading to a dialogue between students and teachers concerning its meaning. With the help of my instructors, I was able to understand Ratzinger's teaching much more easily, and from then on Ratzinger's way of approaching theology became a doctrinal compass, central to my own intellectual formation.

I read the book a third time shortly before my priestly ordination when I was working at a local parish and leading a study group through the Creed, using the *Introduction* as a guide. I read the book yet again during a week of spiritual exercises in 1999. This time, I could hear the cardinal's voice reciting the text in my head, given that I had been working at the congregation for some years already and had grown accustomed to interacting with him. That third encounter with the text was significantly different from the previous two, given that I was much more mature and the reflections appealed to my heart and soul in a more direct and personal way, providing much needed nourishment for my spiritual life.

In short, every rereading of the text has plunged me deeper into the fundamental question posed by Ratzinger: "What is the meaning of significance of the Christian profession 'I believe' *today,* in the context of our present existence and our present attitude to reality as a whole?" I was increasingly convinced in my reading that "every human being must in some way take a position within the realm of fundamental decisions, and no one can do so outside of the form of some kind of faith." I am reinvigorated and encouraged by description of the fundamental Christian choice, when he explains that "to believe in a Christian way means to abandon himself in trust to the meaning that sustains me and the world; it means accepting him as the firm foundation upon which I can stand without any fear. Christian faith is an encounter with the man Jesus, and in that encounter the believer perceives the meaning of the world in a personal way."

I was ordained to the priesthood on 31 May 1984, the Solemnity of the Ascension of the Lord, by Archbishop Oskar Saier, Ordinary of the Archdiocese of Freiburg im Breisgau. A few months later I read the German translation of a dialogue between Ratzinger and author Vittorio Messori, published in English under the title *The Ratzinger Report.* I was struck by the ease with which the prefect could talk about many problems both within and external to the Church, even to the point of criticizing some of the results of the Second Vatican Council, particularly with regard to the liturgy and pastoral theology.

I remember when I bought that book, I took it with me on a weekly hike into the Black Forest, something I did every Tuesday when I was free from teaching assignments and the pastor excused me from parochial duties. I brought a sandwich and something to drink and found a nice, shady space in the woods to read in peace. I didn't return to the rectory until late—I was utterly absorbed in the book until darkness fell.

After two years as associate pastor, I was sent to Munich in Bavaria to study canon law at the Ludwig Maximilian University. At the beginning, I wasn't enthused in the least by the topic, but I gradually understood the meaning and scope of canon law, such that after I had completed my licentiate and my doctorate, I reentered the diocese in 1993 and became a personal assistant to Archbishop Saier while serving as vicar of the cathedral.

In the Fall of 1994, I was told that the nuncio in Germany had asked the archbishop to release me for service in the Roman Curia since they were in need of a specialist in canon law. Archbishop Saier, of course, was not excited about the idea of losing me and he tried to block it. But the Vatican authorities persisted in their request for two specific reasons. First, the Archdiocese of Freiburg, second only to Cologne in number of baptized Catholics in Germany, had never released a priest for service at the Holy See; secondly, by turning to Archbishop Saier personally (who had expressed reservations about the Vatican Curia), they were suggesting that it wasn't really his place to complain about Roman centralism if he weren't willing to offer the manpower to help ameliorate the situation.

In fact, this attitude toward the Roman Curia was fairly widespread in my archdiocese, as Ratzinger himself suggested in the interview with Vittorio Messori: "From my viewpoint in Germany, I had looked at the workings of the Roman Curia with a dose of skepticism, or at least with some indifference and a bit of impatience. But after I arrived to work there, I recognized that the Curia is better than its reputation. For the most part, it is comprised of people who work with an authentic spirit of service. It could hardly be otherwise given the modest stipend, which in many parts of the world is barely at the level of sustenance. Add to this the fact that the work is not so gratifying, given that, for the most part, it consists of anonymously preparing documents and interventions that are ultimately signed or delivered by some higher-up on the totem pole."

Thus, on 7 January 1995, I was introduced to the Cardinal Antonio María Javierre Ortas, Prefect of the Congregation for Divine Worship and the Discipline of the Sacraments, who informed me that I would be working in the disciplinary section, which at that time was concerned mainly with the laicization of priests who had requested a dispensation from celibacy, as well as marriage cases of *ratum et non consummatum*. This was not particularly thrilling employment because my daily work was bogged down in documentation from people in a moment of existential crisis, who were disappointed in their vocational decision and uncertain about their futures. But I found consolation in the fact that it was only a three-year appointment, a term limit Saier was quite happy with, and he would be ready to welcome me back to the archdiocese when it was over.

An unlimited period of renewal

At that time, I was living within the walls of the Vatican at the Teutonic College, situated between the Paul VI Audience Hall and the left side of the Vatican basilica. Daily Mass was celebrated in the ancient church of the Archconfraternity of Our Lady at 7:00 a.m., and Cardinal Ratzinger was the normal celebrant there on Thursdays. He would usually stay at the college for breakfast. When I was first introduced to him, I had the opportunity to tell him that I had studied in Munich and offered my pastoral service to the Parish of Saint Peter, the oldest church in the city and well known to the cardinal. Week after week, our conversations continued. He became more familiar with my work at the Congregation for Divine Worship and the Discipline of the Sacraments and was interested to learn more about my previous studies.

Sometime in mid-September of 1995, at the end of Mass, he asked me to come visit him at the Congregation for the Doctrine of the Faith because he wanted to speak with me. I didn't know what to think, so I called the secretary of his congregation, Monsignor Josef Clemens, to make an appointment with him and—given he already knew Ratzinger well—I asked if he had any idea what Cardinal Ratzinger wanted to speak to me about. He said he hadn't a clue. So, I was a little nervous when I entered the prefect's study because I was honestly afraid that I had gotten into some sort of trouble. But he welcomed me cordially and explained that one of the German-speaking staff members was about to return to his diocese, and he needed someone to replace him. He thought my background well-suited for the job, so he wanted to know if I would be willing to transfer to his congregation.

I obviously expressed enthusiasm about the prospect, but I had to tell him that everybody had to be on board with the idea, including the prefect of the congregation for which I was working and my archbishop. Ratzinger spoke personally with Javierre Ortas, while I wrote to Saier, who responded that he didn't feel he could oppose the wishes of the Prefect of the Congregation for the Doctrine of the Faith, though the three-year term would remain in place. So, in March of 1996, I was transferred to the Holy Office and assigned to the doctrinal section, which deals with material touching on the promotion and safeguarding of doctrine in faith and morals.

I quickly found myself at home in the work, given the dynamic with colleagues and relationships with my superiors were both excellent. My main task consisted of helping to prepare drafts of responses to the numerous letters received by the congregation in regard to issues that arose in various parts of the world, as well as the documents that the congregation was involved with in conjunction with the other dicasteries in the Roman Curia.

In 1997, I received another exciting request from Monsignor Juan Igancio Arrieta, then Dean of the Canon Law Faculty at the Pontifical University of the Holy Cross (*Santa Croce*), who offered me a teaching position. We had gotten to know one another precisely through the congregation since he was often consulted on various juridical issues that came to us. So, I immediately turned to Cardinal Ratzinger to see if he would consent to the request. His only concern was whether I felt that I could continue to keep up with the work in the congregation while taking on the task of teaching. When I assured him that I could, he simply said, "All right then, go ahead."

As I approached the end of my three-year term, my archbishop felt somewhat obliged to defer to the wishes of Cardinal Ratzinger about my future, so he said that if the prefect were to ask for the customary five-year extension, he would agree to it. Toward the end of March in 2001, Ratzinger sent an official letter to Saier thanking him for allowing me to serve for three years and asking if he would be willing to renew my appointment for another five, to which the archbishop agreed. That set the stage for me to assume Monsignor Clemens's duties as personal secretary to the prefect in 2003. The election of Cardinal Ratzinger to the papacy occurred in the midst of my five-year mandate, so my archbishop felt there was no need to revisit the issue after that.

My appointment as personal secretary involved a completely different set of tasks. It was my responsibility to handle the heavy correspondence of the prefect and to keep track of his appointments. From day one, he gave me complete reign over opening his mail and handling his schedule, the latter of which we both had simultaneous access to so that we could both review the following day's agenda. If any routine letter needed no specific attention from the cardinal, I would draft a response myself or ask one of the staff members to do it such that I would have something specific to propose for the cardinal's final approval. When requests were submitted for meetings, I would summarize them in memos, highlighting main points and label them as institutional or private issues.

I was living at Casa Santa Marta during this time, and the cardinal would occasionally join me for lunch there. But our longest periods were spent together whenever traveling on official congregational business—to conferences, or to liturgical celebrations, where I would serve as Ratzinger's master of ceremonies. Our warm relationship matured over time. Until the very end, he always referred to me as "Don Giorgio" (actually pronounced in his thick, German accent as "Don Chor-choh"), even though he never used the informal Italian address of *tu* with me. Even in retirement, following his typical sense of respect, he continued to use the formal *Lei*, just as he did with the Memores sisters.

I must confess that I was very moved when, as Benedict's condition was weakening, he asked me read him a homily he had given as a deacon to a group of children in Freising on 23 April 1950, precisely on the feast of my patron saint, George (also the name of Ratzinger's older brother): "The dragon is a terrible nightmare for the whole human race. We tremble before it. It is the frightful force we call 'the devil.' Whoever arms himself with shield and sword has nothing to fear because God's weapons are stronger than the dragon. Saint George is not just someone we admire; he reminds us what we must do. He teaches us that there is indeed a dragon and that we are all called to be the one to kill it."

Ratzinger was accustomed to arriving at the Holy Office precisely at 9:00 a.m. after Mass and praying the breviary, both of which he said at home. He always came prepared, having studied whatever documents I had given him the previous afternoon. When he arrived at work, we would joke around about how he felt that day, and to do this we playfully used the five-point grading system of the pontifical universities: *summa cum laude, magna cum laude, cum laude, sufficit,* and *non sufficit* (when things were really going badly). That didn't happen very often, but even if his response were *sufficit*, it was a sign to spare him of any heavy or unpleasant task that day. His response always had something to do with how he had slept the previous night since he was a light sleeper. Pope

Francis once mentioned that he only slept six hours at night, but he slept like a rock. Benedict tweaked a smile and replied, "This is a gift that your predecessor, unfortunately, never had!"

Day-to-day service

The evening Cardinal Ratzinger was elected and I found myself standing next to the pope, I suddenly realized that no one teaches you how to be a papal secretary. There is no manual and no course of study. In the blink of an eye, you find yourself catapulted from the back seat to the front row. It was the closest thing to the experience my brothers and friends have described to me of holding their newborns for the first time, not knowing what to do, and even afraid of injuring the infant.

At the beginning of my service, Don Mietek was a great help. He stood by my side as a sort of "second secretary" for couple of years. It was Cardinal Marian Franciszek Jaworski who recommended him to Benedict and who also received him as his Coadjutor Archbishop of Lviv of the Latins on 16 July 2007. Don Mietek would later succeed Cardinal Jaworski on 21 October 2008. I had to learn a lot of things quickly, from managing relations with the Secretariat of State to coordinating the pope's schedule with the Prefect of the Papal Household and the Pontifical Master of Ceremonies. There were also small but no less important details, such as the logistics of the papal apartments and more mundane practical matters, such as making sure that everything worked in the papal study for the pope to appear from the window to deliver his Angelus address on Sundays!

The days seemed endless. I woke up at the same time as Pope Benedict—around 6:00 a.m.—and started the day with Mass, meditation, and the breviary. After breakfast, I handled the internal correspondence that arrived in huge, black leather mailbags, all bent out of shape due to the sheer weight, as Benedict went into his study to review important documents and read several international newspapers. I would meet him in his study a half hour later to update him on any important matters and to inform him about the appointments he had scheduled for the day. I would then accompany him to the second *loggia* for private audiences or to one of the other rooms for larger audiences. The rest of the morning was spent in other appointments and responding to telephone calls and mail.

After the customary Italian midday meal at 1:30 p.m., we would take a stroll on the terrace, protected from the gaze of tourists by ivy archways that blocked the line of sight from the dome of Saint Peter's Basilica to our apartments. After a brief nap, I would go through more mailbags that had been placed on my desk in the meantime, selecting documents that had to be personally reviewed and signed by the pope. Before the so-called *udienze di tabella* with the principal Vatican officials that took place every day around 6:00 p.m., I would inform the pope about the most pressing matters that needed attention, taking notes on how he wanted me to respond. Weather permitting, we would have a car take us for the short ride to the Vatican Gardens at about 6:45 p.m., getting out at the Lourdes Grotto for a short rosary walk. If the weather was bad, we would go to the hanging garden on the top floor where there was a wonderful panoramic view of Rome.

This was the moment when we could finally have a light chat, so I would tell him about the letters he received by schoolchildren from all over the world, decorated with crayons and brimming with curiosity: "When the pope is at home alone, does he take off his white robe and wear overalls or a nightgown? I heard that he likes the *Camillo e Peppone* movies. Is that true? Are his red shoes really made by Prada?" Now, I can finally give you some answers: No, Benedict always wore his white cassock because Don Mietek said that that was John Paul II's custom, so Benedict decided to do the same; Yes, Benedict was such a fan of the *Camillo and Peppone* films that the pastor and mayor of Brescello—the "descendants" of the main characters in Guareschi's films—attended a general audience at the Vatican in January of 2011 and gave the pope a boxed-DVD-set of the movies; No, the shoes were not made by Prada. This rumor probably started because the color red is so closely associated with Prada's line of products, inspiring the magazine *Esquire* to grant the "most elegant accessory" award to the pope in 2007.

Supper was served at 7:30 p.m., after which we usually watched the news on television. Benedict would then retire to his room for some personal reading and prayers, while I would go back to the office or bedroom on the upper mezzanine and finish any remaining tasks. On

Sunday, we would sometimes watch classic films (he particularly liked *Don Matteo*) or listen to classical music (mostly Mozart, Bach, and Beethoven), and sometimes he would play a piece on the piano himself (he was particularly fond of Schubert and Mozart).

It didn't take long for me to realize that I couldn't keep up such a frenetic pace. It is one thing to start a race in pole position and another to complete all the laps and make it to the finish line. Perhaps I had to exhaust myself before recognizing my limitations and finding the right pace to complete the day's work. I was particularly overwhelmed by the endless requests for private audiences and other appointments, all of which on the surface seemed to be reasonable: "Please just make this one exception"; "The pope and I go a long way back"; "I know he would love to reconnect," and so on. I know I must have disappointed many people—even if they had good reasons to make the request—by drawing boundaries around the pope, but it was precisely my duty to safeguard his time and space and to relieve him of undue pressures.

I recently found an old notebook in which I jotted down some thoughts for practical living. I was struck to find these words: "The cleaner a glass window is, the more it serves it purpose. If a window gets dirty or cracks, it's still a window, but it doesn't function as it's supposed to. And I must frankly admit that I have considered, do consider, and will always consider my role, my service, to be that of a window: I must allow the sun to come through, but I myself—inasmuch as possible—must remain invisible. The less a window is seen, the better it is. I wouldn't call this my motto *per se*, but rather the principle upon which I base my role as personal secretary to His Holiness. I will always try to act upon that principle, every day, throughout the day, with my heart, mind, soul, and all my strength."

Inside the papal apartments

One of the most vivid memories I have in the wake of the conclave was the ceremonial entry into the papal apartments on 20 April 2005, the day following Benedict's election. We ascended the *scala nobile* [the "noble staircase"] to the *terza loggia* [the "third story"] of the apostolic palace, where *camerlengo* Martínez Somalo cut the seals that he had placed on the door following the death of John Paul II. Benedict XVI was well acquainted with the apartments since he had spent much time there with his predecessor, but his initial steps into that space as pontiff were nevertheless timid, as if he did not want to break the equilibrium that had been established in that space during the quarter-century reign of Pope John Paul II. As Benedict later told me, crossing that threshold into the apartments filled his mind with countless memories that seemed to make John Paul reappear before him.

Once inside, we realized that the apartments smelled like a hospital ward, given that the windows had been closed for a long time and the carpets had absorbed the odor of the medications John Paul II had been taking during his agonizing illness. It was clear that we couldn't move in right away, especially since—as the technicians explained—there had been no maintenance work for over ten years, to the point that there were two electrical systems of differing voltage, and the ceiling had been outfitted with reservoirs to catch water leaking from the pipes.

Therefore, we made a visit to the *Torre di San Giovanni* (Tower of Saint John), which, during the pontificate of John XXIII, had been restored for the purpose of giving guests of honor a comfortable place to stay. Unfortunately, it was too humid, and the small, round spaces that made up the levels of the tower were simply too inconvenient. So, the choice was made for us: Benedict would temporarily move into the so-called "patriarchal apartment" at the Casa Santa Marta (the one Pope Francis decided to live in after his election in 2013 and numbered "201"), while I would stay in the smaller adjoining apartment.

We stayed at Casa Santa Marta until April 30th. I remember the date well since it happens to be the feast of Pius V, patron of the Holy Office. Within those ten days or so, the workers deep cleaned the papal apartments in the apostolic palace so that we could move in and begin organizing ourselves over the next couple of months.

Paolo Sagretti, director of the Floreria (i.e., the Vatican division responsible for—among other things—renovations of Vatican building spaces), explained to us that Pope Paul VI preferred a transparent, light-gray color for the draperies and upholstery, and John Paul II had no special requests, so it had been a long time since any redecorating had been done. Benedict requested that the carpets be removed and the splendid,

16th-century marble floors be restored, giving the apartments a fresh glow. He also asked for minimal restoration to the walls, upon which were hung several extremely fine paintings.

He asked that his favorite desk—which he had been using since his professorial days in Germany—be moved to his study, as well as the books from his private library that were still at his former apartment in Piazza della Città Leonina. He continued to make regular use of those books as pope (as he also did during his retirement, so that the same books were moved to the Mater Ecclesiae Monastery within the Vatican Gardens after his resignation). Benedict often remarked that he felt he was in the presence of friends whenever surrounded by his favorite books. Yet he never felt an undue attachment to them, asking that they be donated if anyone ever decided to move into the monastery after him. In fact, there was even a table at the Holy Office reserved for books Ratzinger wanted to give away, and the staff freely helped themselves whenever they saw something of interest.

We spent 11–28 July 2005 at Les Combes in Valle d'Aosta for some rest and relaxation. At the Angelus address there on July 17th, Benedict expressed heartfelt gratitude to the locals for the opportunity to stay with them, describing the experience as a "providential gift of God after the first months of the demanding pastoral service that divine Providence has entrusted to me." Indeed, it had been an intense period, made all the more stressful by a series of terrorist attacks across the globe: the Egyptian ambassador in Iraq, after being abducted, was killed on July 2nd; fifty-two people died in a terrorist attack in London on July 7th (in addition to 21 bombings in the same city without victims); five died in Netanya (Israel) on July 12th; Bishop Luigi Locati was assassinated in Kenya on July 14th; five were killed in Kusadasi (Turkey) on July 16th; eighty-eight died in Sharm el-Sheikh in Egypt on July 23rd; and two Algerian diplomats were assassinated in Iraq on July 27th. Not long after, on August 16th, the founder of the Taizé community, Brother Roger Schutz, was killed at the hand of a mentally disturbed woman during the recitation of vespers. Incidentally, Pope Benedict had received a letter from Brother Roger that very morning in which he expressed his desire to come to Rome to meet him, assuring him that "the community of Taizé wishes to walk in communion with the Holy Father."

Upon our return from the mountain village in Valle d'Aosta, we immediately went to the papal summer residence in Castel Gandolfo, where we stayed until the end of September. When we finally returned to Rome, we found that all the work on the papal apartments had been completed in record time. Pope Benedict was so grateful that he held a private audience for the workers who carried out the renovations. He told them he was convinced, "since I had a small house built in Germany, that anywhere else this work would have taken at least a year and probably more. I can only marvel at what you have done, especially in restoring the beautiful marble floors. I particularly like the new library and the marvelous antique ceiling. Now, I can only say 'thank you' for all of this, for your inspiring work. In giving your all, you have encouraged me to give my all, even at this late stage in my life."

The apartments were configured to facilitate the pope's work and that of the pontifical family. After entering the apartments from the *scala nobile*—where a member of the Swiss Guard was stationed around the clock—there was a small atrium with an elevator. Every evening, one of the higher-ranking Vatican authorities would be welcomed into the pope's private library for an *udienza di tabella*: on Monday, the Secretary of State; on Tuesday, the Substitute for General Affairs; on Wednesday, the Secretary for Relations with States; on Thursday, the Prefect for the Congregation for the Evangelization of Peoples; on Friday, the Prefect for the Congregation for the Doctrine of the Faith; and on Saturday, the Prefect for the Congregation for Bishops. Out of respect for his role, I would accompany the Secretary of State personally from his apartment on the first *loggia* up to the papal apartments via the *nobile* elevator, while the others came on their own, ringing the doorbell to the apartment when they arrived, signaling me to go and welcome them.

A doorway led from the atrium to the private library facing Saint Peter's Square. Also facing the square were a smaller study, the personal secretary's room (across from which, toward the interior, was a chapel), and the pope's private study with the bed in the corner. On the side facing Porta Angelica was a bathroom, a more reserved library (which had been set aside for John Paul II's personal physician in the Polish pope's latter years), a smaller room, the dining room, kitchen, and the personal rooms of the Memores sisters.

The so-called "Sixtus V elevator" was also located in this northwest corner, giving direct access to the courtyard of the same name. Use of this elevator was absolutely restricted to those possessing a key to open the door and operate the mechanism, and the master key was under the strict control of the Gendarmeria. Just as during John Paul II's pontificate, the only people equipped with a key were the members of the pontifical family.

The Sixtus V elevator stopped at the Secretary of State's apartment on the first *loggia*, and on the second *loggia* to allow the pope access to the library for audiences when they were held there. It also could take one to the fourth floor where there were rooms for secretaries and special guests, as well as to the roof terrace constructed under Paul VI, where there was a brick structure we called the *chalet*. It was furnished with the old tube television that Pope Paul VI had used to watch the Apollo 11 moon landing on 20 July 1969. It also had a small kitchen and a color television that had been a gift to Benedict XVI. We all gathered to eat there on Sunday evenings. There was also a small hydro-massage pool there that had been installed under Paul VI, but we never used it.

The three butlers

Fortunately, I had a reliable assistant for conducting the day-to-day affairs of the pontifical household—namely, Angelo Gugel, who had worked at the Vatican from 1955 to 1978 and had been personally selected by Pope John Paul I as his butler. Gugel had been the future pope's chauffeur at the Second Vatican Council. While he was Bishop of Vittorio Veneto, Luciani became good friends with the Gugel family and often went to their house for dinner.

After Pope Luciani died, Pope Wojtyła re-appointed him, and he appeared in countless photographs with Saint John Paul II throughout his pontificate. Gugel told me that, at the beginning of John Paul II's pontificate, the pope would recite his Italian speeches to him so that he could make sure he was placing his accents correctly. Gugel loved to tell stories, such as when President Sandro Petrini was seated next to the pope at dinner and out of fear of offending the pope refused to admit how good the *strozzapreti* pasta tasted (the word means "priest choker")!

Gugel was the only one who knew how to operate the old safe in the library, so he showed me how to open and close it. Don Stanisław Dziwisz had hastily handed over the two keys and the combination in June (there was also a smaller safe in the pope's private study for personal items, but Benedict never used it). Having served as John Paul II's personal secretary for twenty-six years, Don Stanisław had two concise pieces of advice for me: "First of all, you must be his castle: protect him from anything that could crush him. Secondly, find the right working pace; use your mind, your heart, and even your nose to keep every situation under control: the whole world is now his best friend and everyone will want something from him."

The safe was full of odds and ends, dating back to John Paul II's predecessors: episcopal rings, pectoral crosses, commemorative coins minted during earlier pontificates. It took a long time to sort through it all and make a complete inventory, but we finally did it with the help of notes accompanying many of the objects to trace them back to the original donor.

Don Stanisław also handed me an envelope with the account numbers and most recent bank statements for the account at the IOR[6] in the private secretary's name, which was solely for the pope's use and managed by the secretary. This account was funded exclusively with donations to the pope's personal works of charity, and was drawn from only when Benedict XVI wanted to intervene in certain matters.

Finally, Don Stanisław showed me a small chapel on the mezzanine level of the fourth floor that had been set up by Monsignor Pasquale Macchi during the reign of Paul VI. An enormous quantity of relics was inside, mostly in a disordered state, primarily dating back to the numerous beatifications and canonizations done under John Paul II. There were also a number of chalices and liturgical vestments there, most of which Benedict eventually entrusted to Don Stanisław so that they could be preserved as memorabilia from the saint's life.

Gugel celebrated his seventieth birthday precisely on the day of Pope Benedict's election, the age of mandatory retirement according to Vatican norms, but the trusted butler agreed to stay on for a few more

6 Istituto per le Opere di Religione, often referred to as the "Vatican Bank."

months in order to help with the transition to the new pontificate. In the meantime, we began to search for someone to replace Gugel. It seemed like the best suggestion came from Archbishop James Michael Harvey, who recommended Paolo Gabriele, a Vatican employee originally hired in the Secretariate of State as part of the custodial staff.

Gabriele occasionally served as a waiter at Archbishop Harvey's personal residence. Harvey, who himself was first head of the English section and then assessor under John Paul II, was impressed with Gabriele's professionalism. When Archbishop Harvey was promoted to head the pontifical household in 1998, he asked Gabriele to replace another staff member who had reached retirement age. Gugel shadowed him in the papal apartments for a training period, but he wasn't entirely satisfied with his performance. Yet there didn't seem to be any viable alternatives at the time, and, in hindsight, perhaps it was a mistake not to have prolonged the search.

After Gabriele had been convicted of misdemeanors for divulging classified documents in 2012 and sentenced to eighteen months in prison, he was replaced with Sandro Mariotti (we called him "Sandrone" because of his imposing stature). Mariotti, after a long career in the Vatican Floreria, had been Gabriele's replacement in the papal antechamber when the latter was officially promoted in 2007. I was struck by his honest response when I proposed the appointment to him: "I don't have any special training; I'm a normal employee. You need someone better for the job." So, I gave him two weeks to think about it and discuss it confidentially with his family and friends, and he even made an appointment to discuss it with the pope himself. Mariotti finally accepted and continued in the same capacity under Pope Francis.

Archbishop Harvey also helped to find an adjunct secretary to replace Don Mietek. He recommended Monsignor Alfred Xuereb, who had been working in the prefecture of the pontifical household since 2003. As an antechamber prelate, Monsignor Xuereb was responsible for accompanying guests to personal audiences with the pope on the second loggia. Pope Benedict got to know him well when he was cardinal prefect, especially since Xuereb spoke German and was well respected for his courtesy and discretion. Among other things, it was Monsignor Xuereb's responsibility to insert paper slips with prayer requests from all over the world into a special box kept next to the pope's kneeler in the chapel.

I was moved by the testimony Monsignor Xuereb gave after Benedict's resignation: "What struck me most about Pope Benedict was that a few days after receiving a prayer request, he would ask me, 'Have you heard from Mr. or Mrs. so-and-so (he would always remember the last name) that you told me about?' Sometimes, I would sadly have to tell him that the person died, and I was always struck by his reaction. The rest of us wouldn't have given much thought to the matter after that, but Pope Benedict would always recite a prayer for that person—'Eternal rest grant unto him,' etc.—and then invite me to pray too. It wasn't only his memory that was so impressive, but his presence. Even with a million things on his mind, he considered prayers for the sick, the dying, and the deceased to be an indispensable part of his pastoral ministry."

Other members of the pontifical family

Don Mietek continued to live in the same room where he was living while serving Pope John Paul II, located on the fourth-floor mezzanine (Don Alfred took over the same room when he succeeded Don Mietek). I lived in the room where Don Stanisław had once lived. The pope's brother, Monsignor Georg, often stayed in a guest room on the same floor. In the first months of Benedict's pontificate, Mrs. Ingrid Stampa lived on the same floor. She had served as Cardinal Ratzinger's housekeeper for about fifteen years.

A few weeks after the death of Ratzinger's sister in November of 1991, Doctor Renato Buzzonetti—who had served as John Paul II's personal physician and continued in the same capacity under Benedict—mentioned that, if the cardinal were looking for a housekeeper, he knew a German lady in her forties who might be a good fit. Ms. Stampa, a former and esteemed teacher of the viola in Germany, had moved to Rome to take care of Archbishop Cesare Zacchi, President of the Pontifical Ecclesiastical Academy, until his death on August 24th of that year.

Cardinal Ratzinger deemed her to be a good solution for his housekeeping needs, so he contacted her and she agreed. Ms. Stampa was a constant presence in Ratzinger's daily life, and later took on the same duties for Monsignor Paolo Sardi (who later became archbishop and cardinal), who knew her from her attendance at his daily Mass in Saint Peter's Basilica.

I didn't have much personal interaction with Ms. Stampa until I became the cardinal prefect's personal secretary in 2003, at which time I discovered that she indeed had a strong personality. The problem was that she was highly opinionated to the point that the cardinal would often give in to her wishes just to maintain peace. Benedict's most authoritative biographer, Peter Seewald, wrote that this personality trait eventually would turn out to be his "Achille's heel." Seewald writes that "in general, Ratzinger did not trust people easily, but he also did not reject those whom divine Providence placed in his path. The problem was that he subsequently tended to act meekly around anyone with a powerful personality who tried to get involved in business outside of his or her sphere of competence to the point of this inflicting a sort of psychological violence on the cardinal. Cardinal Ratzinger also had a strong sense of loyalty that sometimes got in the way of reproving others when necessary."

At a certain point, when we first began to inspect the papal apartments with the technicians, Ms. Stampa sharply intervened with an opinion about the arrangement of the rooms: "We must switch the bedroom with the private study because Benedict needs more space and light to do his work." Monsignor Paolo De Nicolò, Head of the Pontifical Household, and Mr. Sagretti, chief engineer, looked at one another with great surprise at her boldness and tried to explain to her that the pope's personal study was conveniently located near his private secretary's, that the pope delivered the traditional Angelus address from his study on Sundays, and that the bathroom was conveniently adjacent to the bedroom. Ms. Stampa continued to insist, so De Nicolò finally responded, "Fine, we'll think about it and then make a proposal to His Holiness." They knew her idea was unreasonable so it didn't go any further.

A jealous streak began to emerge in her with regard to the papal entourage, as she thought it was supplanting her role. Her envy may have been rooted in her relationship with Josef Clemens, who was hoping to be reappointed as Benedict's personal secretary.

Personally, I had already felt some jealousy from Clemens since I had replaced him as the cardinal's personal secretary. Even after he had been promoted and assigned to another congregation, he tried to maintain a role in prioritizing Cardinal Ratzinger's commitments and had become brusque with me, even though we had been friendly with one another prior to that. I had a confirmation of this change in attitude when I was practically the only one at the Congregation for the Doctrine of the Faith who did not receive an invitation to his episcopal consecration!

Right after Benedict's election, I caught wind of his low opinion of me, but I didn't pay much attention to it. In any case, I kept my ears open to protect the pope from any power plays, especially if they involved an old friendship that preceded Ratzinger's election. One thing I can say for sure is that there was no public animosity between Clemens and me, despite rumors to the contrary. There were even far-fetched stories about Clemens and I coming to blows and my refusal to give him my cell phone number. The fact is that he didn't need my number since Benedict himself gave Clemens the number to his private line in the papal apartments—a phone only he picked up. Ratzinger never owned a personal cell phone, and if he needed one, he would use mine or the adjunct secretary's. Aside from high-ranking Vatican authorities, only a few Italian and German friends knew his personal number. He used a separate line for his brother Georg since they often called one another just to say hello.

After becoming pope, Ratzinger graciously accepted the invitations Clemens extended three or four times a year to dine at his house on special occasions, such as his patronal feast day (name day), his birthday, and on other holidays, just as he did when still prefect. But Clemens made the terrible mistake of bragging publicly about those dinners, at which Ms. Stampa and Archbishop Sardi (and a few others) were also present. Clemens even boasted that the pope deeply appreciated these gatherings since—according to Clemens—"it was the only place where the pope could open his heart and breathe, while everything was a bit oppressive at home." When Benedict found out about what Clemens had said, he wrote him a personal letter in his elegant but straightforward style, requesting that he observe respectful silence about past engagements and furthermore communicating his decision to decline any future invitations.

In 2003, Ingrid Stampa had to leave Rome for a few months to take care of her ailing mother. Carmela Galiandro, a member of the Memores Domini of the Communion and Liberation movement, stepped in to take care of the cardinal's housekeeping needs. Ratzinger was impressed with her, so in the first months of his pontificate, he wrote—*via* the Substitute, Archbishop Sandri—to the President of Communion and Liberation, Don Julián Carrón, asking if there were four members of the Memores community available to take care of the papal apartments. In addition to Carmela, they were Loredana Patrono, Cristina Cernetti, and Manuela Camagni. Manuela sadly died tragically on 24 November 2010. She had gone with friends to a gathering of the Memores on Via Nomentana and was struck by a car while crossing the street. She was immediately found to be in grave condition and, despite an emergency surgical procedure she died shortly thereafter. By the time I arrived, I could do no more than impart a final blessing in the morgue at the Policlinico hospital.

Benedict, deeply saddened by this tragic accident, asked me to represent him at Manuela's funeral in San Piero in Bagno in Romagna on November 29th. There I read a personal message he penned for the occasion, which included these moving words: "I have been greatly blessed by her presence and service in the papal apartments for the last five years, where we live as a family. I therefore wish to thank the Lord for the gift of Manuela's life, her faith, and for the generous response to her vocation. Her unexpected loss—and the terrible way it happened—have brought on us an immense sorrow that only faith can heal."

Pope Benedict celebrated a Mass of remembrance for her in the Pauline Chapel on December 2nd, at which he recalled that Manuela had mentioned she would celebrate thirty years with the Memores Domini community on November 29th, which happened to be the exact day of her funeral. Benedict added, "she said this with great joy, preparing herself internally to celebrate these thirty years of walking with the Lord in communion with her spiritual friends.... Manuela was not one of those who forget the importance of remembering. She lived precisely with a living memory of the Creator, in the joy of his creation, seeing God shine through every aspect of creation, even in the simple details of our daily lives. She knew that this living memory—which involves the present and the future—was the key to joy."

Though impossible to replace, Manuela was succeeded by Rossella Teragnoli, who continued to bless us with her presence when we all moved to the monastery after Benedict's resignation. She was assigned to care for the secretaries' rooms and their wardrobes, while Cristina, from Le Marche, was responsible for the sacristy and chapel. Loredana, from Puglia, kept busy in the kitchen, while another native of Puglia, Carmela, loved to bake sweets and took care of the pope's wardrobe. During the day—both while we were still in the papal apartments and at the monastery—Sister Birgit Wansing, a member of the Schönstatt community, would come and serve as the pope's typist, a job she had been doing since 1984. An occasional visitor to our household was Christina Felder, a member of the spiritual family "The Work," who cared for Monsignor Georg Ratzinger whenever he came to visit.

5
Stumbling Blocks within the Vatican Bureaucracy

Decisions at every turn

From the very first days of the pontificate, I recognized the enormous weight of responsibility that rests on the pope's shoulders when it comes to episcopal and other appointments, since the final decision is ultimately his. There are more than 3,000 ecclesial jurisdictions throughout the world, nearly 200 papal representatives in diplomatic posts, yielding a total of about 4,000 active bishops, including diocesan, auxiliaries, and nuncios; not to mention the various offices of the Roman Curia carrying out both the pastoral and spiritual activities of the Holy See, as well as the Church's administrative and charitable works, all at the service of 1.3 billion Catholics scattered across the globe spanning every cultural, economic, and social background.

Article 18 of John Paul II's Apostolic Constitution *Pastor Bonus* (1988) specifies a wide range of decisions that fall within the purview of the pope (provisions that were essentially confirmed by *Predicate Evangelium* in 2022): "Decisions of major importance are to be submitted for the approval of the Supreme Pontiff…. The dicasteries cannot issue laws or general decrees having the force of law or derogate from the prescriptions of current universal law, unless in individual cases and with the specific approval of the Supreme Pontiff. It is of the utmost importance that nothing grave and extraordinary be transacted unless the Supreme Pontiff be previously informed by the moderators of the dicasteries."

Benedict didn't take these decisions lightly. He took Saint Bonaventure as his model, who wrote that "to govern does not mean simply 'to do,' but rather the think and to pray." Benedict noted that all of his decisions were the result of reflection and thought illuminated by prayer. He knew well that, humanly speaking, it was extremely difficult to judge persons and their qualities since "no one can read the heart of another man."

Another significant passage that reveals Ratzinger's approach to decision-making can be found in a speech he gave on 27 February 2000 to a group of scholars at an international congress on the implementation of the Second Vatican Council: "Let's take a moment to ponder our central theme—that is, fundamental human rights. This theme does not imply that the Church must not also talk about how to order itself rightly and how to assign responsibility. There will always be imbalances that need correction. There is certainly a natural tendency to Roman centralization, which, when it occurs, must be shown for what it is and corrected. But this issue should not distract us from the Church's true and proper task: she must not primarily speak about herself, but about God, and in order to do that in an authoritative way, she must also practice a spirit of intra-ecclesial self-correction, which should be guided by discussions about how to correlate what she says about God and her common service. In short, it is no accident that within the tradition of preaching the Gospel these words of Jesus constantly reemerge: 'The last shall be first, and the first shall be last,' as if he were holding up a mirror in which everyone could see himself better."

Although it is true that Pope Ratzinger did not have a particular affinity for governance, one thing should never be forgotten: Cardinal Ratzinger, practically from his first days in Rome, was a member of the Congregation for Bishops, and, almost every Thursday, he participated in a *feria quinta* meeting in the *Sala Bologna* to discuss episcopal appointments. He looked at every dossier concerning candidates for the episcopate, and on many occasions, he served as *ponens* (i.e., the cardinal who highlighted the characteristics of those identified for possible nomination to a specific diocese), and he thus accumulated a wealth of experience and knowledge about those who were nominated and those who were not.

As pope, Ratzinger diligently prepared for his weekly Saturday meeting with the head of the Congregation for Bishops, carefully studying documentation that he had received several days in advance. He would listen attentively to the cardinal prefect (who was Giovanni Battista Re until 2010 and later Marc Ouellet), who would explain the various vacancies to His Holiness and then convey the names of the preferred candidates and the final votes of the congregation's members.

Benedict would usually confirm the choice proposed by the congregation, but he would be particularly cautious when two candidates were considered equally "worthy." He would try to identify which of the two was most suitable for that particular office. Obviously, the larger and older a see, the more carefully he would reflect. Nuncios (i.e., representatives of the Holy See to the nearly 180 nations and international organizations with which the Holy See maintains diplomatic relations) were naturally proposed by the Secretariat of State.

One of the first orders of business was to appoint his own successor to the Congregation for the Doctrine of the Faith. Right away, contrasting stories circulated through the news that were sometimes—unsurprisingly—far-fetched. Naturally, the names of some Italian bishops immediately emerged, men considered sympathetic to Ratzinger's theology and on friendly terms with him: Tarcisio Bertone, Bruno Forte, and Angelo Scola, for example. But each of them was already at a disadvantage: Bertone because the number two at the congregation was already a brother Salesian, Angelo Amato; Scola because he had been Patriarch of Venice for only three years; Forte because he had just been appointed to the jurisdiction of Chieti-Vasto ten months earlier. Scola and Forte were also theologians of repute, and Ratzinger preferred not to nominate anyone who would instantly be compared with himself as a theologian.

In any case, since the secretary of the congregation was already an Italian, Benedict decided to look beyond the European continent. His eyes went across the Atlantic to the United States, mostly because he wanted to send a clear message that the Holy See was taking the clerical sexual abuse crisis with the utmost seriousness. So, on 13 May 2005, a press release announced that he had chosen the Archbishop of San Francisco, William Joseph Levada. Many were surprised, but in fact Ratzinger knew his *curriculum vitae* quite well. He had worked as an official at the Congregation for the Doctrine of the Faith from 1976 to

1982, and between 1986 and 1993 he was the only bishop from the United States to work on the editorial committee for the Catechism of the Catholic Church. He became a member of the congregation in 2000, and onward from 2003 he had been presiding over the doctrinal committee at the United States Conference of Catholic Bishops.

An utmost respect for others

Benedict also concerned himself with other appointments in the Roman Curia, mostly to mold the more important offices to his own theological and liturgical vision rather than to carry out a comprehensive reform of the entire Roman Curia (since he didn't think his pontificate was going to last long anyway). He thought it quite important not to make changes that would 'penalize' anyone. Despite interpretations to the contrary, it was not the intention of Benedict to 'demote' Archbishop Domenico Sorrentino, Secretary of the Congregation for Divine Worship and the Discipline of the Sacraments, to the prestigious Diocese of Assisi-Nocera Umbra-Gualdo Tadino, or to undermine Cardinal Crescenzio Sepe by sending him to the Archdiocese of Naples after a few problems were found at the Congregation for the Evangelization of Peoples when under Sepe's leadership. It was simply an opportune time to make a change by appointing Indian Cardinal Ivan Dias to the post.

Furthermore, the appointment of Michael Louis Fitzgerald, President of the Pontifical Council for Interreligious Dialogue, to the strategic post of Apostolic Nuncio in Egypt and Delegate to the League of Arab Nations on 15 February 2006 (with the objective of fostering a dialogue with the Islamic Al-Azhar University, often referred to as the "Vatican of Islam"), was essentially connected to the Holy Father's desire to trim curial bureaucracy, the first step of which took place on March of 2006 with the merger of the Pontifical Council for Interreligious Dialogue with the Pontifical Council for Culture. The purpose of the merger was to "foster a more intense dialogue between the world of culture and the world of religion." But the events of the following September in the wake of Benedict's "Regensburg Address"—when certain assertions of Benedict's speech were completely taken out of context and used as fuel for violence in parts of the Islamic world—provoked the pope to reconsider the idea and ultimately reestablish the preexisting dicasterial arrangement in 2007.

Following a tradition he developed when Prefect of the Congregation for the Doctrine of the Faith, Benedict had an informal meeting in the spring of 2009 with Cardinals Ruini, Scola, Schönborn, and Bagnasco to discuss issues in the Church and in the world more generally. Contrary to reports in the press, there was not the slightest suggestion at that meeting that Cardinal Bertone would remain in his position as Secretary of State. The pope himself stated unequivocally that the topic never came up. But the conversation at that meeting did touch upon the topic of the ever-weakening state of the Christian faith in European countries. It was Angelo Scola who floated the idea of establishing a dicastery to work in tandem with the Congregation for the Evangelization of Peoples that would concern itself with those who had already been evangelized but no longer practiced the faith.

This was the beginning of the Pontifical Council for Promoting the New Evangelization. After much reflection, Pope Benedict settled on Archbishop Rino Fisichella to lead the new dicastery, a man whom he had known for a long time as a collaborator with the Congregation for the Doctrine of the Faith. Ratzinger had actually considered making him his vicar for the Diocese of Rome in 2008 to succeed Cardinal Camillo Ruini. But Bertone expressed some hesitation at that time because of his close affiliation with Ruini. This led to choosing Cardinal Agostino Vallini, who indeed had more pastoral experience as a diocesan bishop.

The point here is this, Benedict did not intend to strengthen the curia and the Church by nominating only those who were completely in line with his own theological vision. To the contrary, he explicitly stated that "there should be room in the College of Cardinals for those with temperaments and opinions different than mine, provided they remain faithful to the teaching of the Catholic Church." And, it must be noted that 67 of the 115 voting cardinals at the conclave in 2013 were nominated by Pope Benedict.

Moreover, many of those who would be considered more "liberal"—to use a loose but commonly understood term—were promoted to important roles precisely during the pontificate of Pope Benedict XVI. Examples include: Mario Grech (Bishop of Gozo, 2005), Cláudio

Hummes (Prefect of the Congregation for Clergy, 2006), Odilo Pedro Scherer (Archbishop of São Paulo, 2007), Reinhard Marx (Archbishop of Munich and Freising, 2007), Joseph William Tobin (Secretary of the Congregation for Institutes of Consecrated Life and Societies of Apostolic Life, 2010), João Braz de Aviz (Prefect of the Congregation for Institutes of Consecrated Life and Societies of Apostolic Life, 2011), Jean-Claude Hollerich (Archbishop of Luxembourg, 2011), Luis Antonio Tagle (Archbishop of Manila, 2011), and Matteo Maria Zuppi (Auxiliary Bishop of Rome, 2012).

At the outset of his pontificate, Pope Ratzinger was naturally asked if he would continue some of the same customs that John Paul II had established, such as inviting people to attend his daily Mass in the private chapel, having guests over for breakfast and other meals, hosting the parish priests of Rome to dinner before making visits to their parishes, and so on. His answer was that Wojtyła not only had a different style and personality, but that he also began his pontificate at a younger age. Ratzinger therefore thought it better to avoid opening a door that would then have to be closed gradually over time, and limited himself to what he could sustain long-term.

Working lunches were exhausting for Ratzinger, as was clearly evident from the few he had while pope. They were organized only on the rarest of occasions. One such occasion was after the return from an apostolic visit abroad, when he would have a "feedback" lunch with his principal collaborators on such visits. These generally included the Assessor for General Affairs at the Secretariat of State, who was until 2009 first Gabriele Giordano Caccia and then Peter Bryan Wells; the director of the newspaper *L'Osservatore Romano,* Giovanni Maria Vian; the press secretary, Fr. Federico Lombardi; the chief logistics officer, Alberto Gasbarri (Benedict affectionally called him *Reisemarchall*, or "the trip marshal").

Benedict considered these lunch meetings a "critique of operations" and he expected everyone to offer honest evaluations of what went well and what did not go well, and to make suggestions for improvements in the future. I learned a lot from these meetings because I could see that there was a wealth of experience among the attendees that would lead to significant improvements for future journeys. And there was always a humorous anecdote or two that would give us a good chuckle.

Choosing a "number two"

Without a doubt, the most discussed and questionable appointment made by Pope Benedict was his Secretary of State, Tarcisio Bertone, not only because of his particular personality and curriculum vitae, but also because of the way he exercised his position. It seems appropriate, then, to look at this question in more depth in order to clarify the reasons for which Benedict appointed him, the context in which he did so, and the objectives of the appointment.

A good starting point would be to turn to a confession that Benedict made on 14 September 2006 to priests and permanent deacons during his apostolic journey to München, Altötting, and Regensburg: "So many things should be done, yet I see that I am not capable of doing them. This is true, I imagine, for many pastors, and it is also true for the Pope, who ought to do so many things! My strength is simply not enough. In this way, I learn to do what I can and leave the rest to God and to my assistants.... And then trust is needed: he will give me the assistants I need, and they will do what I am unable to do."

And so, before accepting the resignation of Cardinal Angelo Sodano, who had reached the mandatory retirement age of seventy-five, Pope Benedict reflected carefully on who should be his successor and narrowed the key qualifications down to two: First, he must have both pastoral experience and diplomatic know-how; second, he must be endowed with the human qualities that would allow him to share daily responsibilities in complete harmony with the pope. So, over a year into the pontificate, on 22 June 2006, Bertone's nomination became public. Even though rumors made their way into the press that it would be so, the appointment came as a surprise nonetheless.

In reality, his curriculum vitae did make him an attractive candidate for the job. During his years in Rome, he headed the Faculty of Canon Law at the Pontifical Salesian University, teaching both ecclesiastical law and international law, giving him a solid background to handle Vatican diplomacy. Moreover, he had taught courses on the rights of minors, legislation, catechesis, and the pastoral care of youth, all of which are core themes in the day-to-day work of Vatican diplomacy. As Secretary of the Congregation for the Doctrine of the Faith, he conducted heavy correspondence with nuncios throughout the world, and was constantly in touch with them by phone. He regularly met with each of them during meetings at the congregation.

Furthermore, Pope Benedict already had a solid working relationship with Cardinal Bertone from their collaboration at the Congregation for the Doctrine of the Faith. He had been a key consultor at the congregation since 1984, and his input was highly valued (in 1988, for example, he was part of the group of experts advising Ratzinger on how to proceed in negotiations toward a reconciliation between Marcel Lefebvre, the founder of the priestly Fraternity of Saint Pius X, who had been suspended by Paul VI in 1976 for his disobedience in performing an ordination without a papal mandate) and had been appointed archbishop secretary of the congregation on 13 June 1995, with the support of the head of the disciplinary section, Gianfranco Girotti.

When Cardinal Dionigi Tettamanzi was transferred to Milan by John Paul II, the Diocese of Genoa became vacant. Around the congregation, people were saying that Bertone had "opened the window to hear the call," meaning that he was considered a worthy candidate for the see. Ratzinger himself wryly remarked, "A cardinalature see has opened up. Let there be candidates!" thus indicating that Bertone's name must have been on the shortlist. So it was that Bertone was appointed Archbishop of Genoa on 10 December 2002 and created cardinal on 21 October 2003. It was actually an exceptional case since up until that point all of the superiors at the Congregation for the Doctrine of the Faith who had been promoted to the College of Cardinals remained in positions within the Roman Curia.

Moreover, given that the pope himself was German and that there were numerous prefects who were not Italian, Benedict thought it would be a good idea to appoint an Italian. (Angelo Scola, whose name also arose, was considered by Pope Benedict to be a better candidate for the presidency of the Italian Bishops' Conference.) I should also note that, right after the conclave, Bertone began to visit the papal apartments with some frequency as he was comfortable with the working relationship they had developed at the congregation. He was free to come up from the Courtyard of Sixtus V *via* the elevator whenever he had thoughts to share regarding curial affairs, and he made it clear that the pope could rely on him in all things.

I also remember that, beginning in May of 2005, certain authorities such as Cardinal Schönborn and Bishop Boccardo had been saying that Bertone was going around telling people that he was pretty sure he would be appointed Secretary of State. At the same time, his appointment was not a first: the French cardinal, Jean-Marie Villot, who was Secretary of State from 1969 to 1979 (appointed by Paul VI and serving through the first year of John Paul II's reign), had been an auxiliary bishop in Paris and Archbishop of Lyon before coming to the Vatican.

It was not an entirely smooth and undisputed transition. Sodano did not think it was a good idea to replace him with a cardinal who had no previous career in diplomatic service, and he told Benedict as much. Just before summer, when he realized that the decision was a done deal, he asked to stay in office until Benedict returned from his apostolic visit to Bavaria, which was scheduled from 9–14 September 2006. At the same time, Bertone trusted that the appointment would be made official as soon as possible.

The pope began to lose sleep due to the tension surrounding this situation, so he proposed an interim arrangement: the announcement would be made on June 22nd and the assignment would not officially begin until September 15th in order to ease the concerns of both Sodano and Bertone. However, grumbling mounted when Sodano delayed his departure from the secretary's apartments on the first *loggia,* forcing Bertone to live in the Tower of Saint John for awhile. Finally, on top of that, given that Bertone wanted to have extensive remodeling done to the apartments, we had to deal with the loud construction noise emanating from the first *loggia* that disturbed papal audiences on the second.

Caught between the IOR and Catholic health care

In hindsight, one of Bertone's biggest mistakes from the very beginning was to spend too much time abroad on trips that took him away from the essential task of presiding over the Secretariat of State, the purpose of which is to handle the day-to-day ministry of the Supreme Pontiff and to carry out the Holy See's diplomatic activities with foreign governments.

This was the reason behind a common complaint we received from officials in the Italian section of the Secretariat of State who decried the fact that they were spending more time preparing Bertone's speeches than the pope's. Whereas Sodano had stayed at the helm constantly and worked long hours nailed to his desk, Bertone was frequently absent and left a pile of important decisions unattended. The machine simply wasn't working. After a while, Benedict himself noticed this and asked Cardinal Bertone to cut down on obligations that took him away from the office. I recall the pope saying to me with a melancholic smile: "When Bertone was Archbishop of Vercelli and Genoa, he was often in Rome. Now that he is Secretary of State, he's hardly ever in town."

Truth be told, I am not revealing anything new here, since the Vatileaks affair revealed documents recording a host of complaints within ecclesiastic circles that were sent directly to Pope Ratzinger. On 5 February 2009, Paolo Sardi wrote that "work has been stopped for a month. The Cardinal Secretary of State is constantly on the move. In addition to his travels in Italy, he was recently in Mexico, he is now in Spain, and he'll soon be in Poland." Dino Boffo wrote on 6 January 2010, in a letter referring to a forged document on his account attributed to Giovanni Maria Vian (director of *L'Osservatore Romano*), that at least Vian "could perhaps count on accurately interpreting the mind of his superior." Dionigi Tettamanzi, after having received directions that Bertone claimed came from the pope regarding the Catholic University of Milan, wrote on 28 March 2011 that he was "seriously perplexed by the last letter received and the directions it contained attributed directly to the pope." And there was an anonymous letter written during the summer of 2011 that contained veiled threats against Cardinal Bertone, accusing him of not knowing how to make decisions and choosing collaborators only on the basis of his personal relationship with each of them.

Moreover, a mound of debacles was growing at the time, and Pope Benedict was not always informed enough to make the best decisions. For example, when Sodano was in office, every report sent to the pope included the Secretary of State's opinion on the matter as well as those of his two main assistants such that the pope might obtain a more complete picture of the situation and an idea of how to proceed. When Bertone was in office, such a detailed explanation of his opinion was lacking. He simply offered what amounted to a "yes" or "no," which he then needed to expand on during the *udienza di tabella* on Monday.

Two particularly thorny issues were the operations of the Istituto per le opere di religione (IOR) and the proposal for a centralized Catholic health system, both of which Bertone was deeply involved in, and, especially with regard to the latter, probably showed himself to be too ambitious. The condition of hospitals in some way linked to the Holy See was too precarious to allow for a restructuring of their balance sheets and a reorganization of their operations. There was a careful analysis of the health care institutions that would be involved in the process, but in the end it was too complicated and the initiative was dropped.

When in September of 2009 a new president was needed for the IOR, it was Bertone who suggested the name of Ettore Gotti Tedeschi, who in months prior had been an advisor for the financial affairs of the Governatorato of Vatican City State, and he had made a contribution to the Encyclical *Caritas in Veritate* on the social teaching of the Church. But over time, relations between the Board of Superintendence and Gotti Tedeschi soured, leading to a vote of no confidence on 24 May 2012 and the subsequent removal of the president for "failure to fulfill the primary functions of his office."

Benedict initially had no knowledge of what was going on, as some journalists have claimed. The Secretary of State informed him of the entire affair in an *udienza di tabella* and the pope expressed his explicit approval for the decision. Perhaps a misunderstanding had arisen from something I said during an interview with the *Messaggero*, where I referred to the pope's surprise at the no-confidence vote against Gotti Tedeschi, but I was actually referring to the rapid and somewhat unexpected development of divergent opinions among the IOR's board members. Subsequent statements by Gotti Tedeschi, rather than calming the waters, only made things more tense, so Benedict preferred to avoid any further contact with him. Thus, reports that a meeting had taken place between Gotti Tedeschi and Benedict XVI as a "gesture of reconciliation" are simply untrue.

In the following years, Bertone was also criticized for taking too much power into his own hands, symbolized by his appointment as *camerlengo* of the Holy Roman Church in 2007 (an important interregnum position when the Church transitions to a new pope), as well as his nomination to the presidency of the commission of cardinals overseeing the work of the IOR (which, among other things, nominates the highest-ranking members of the institute).

In an attempt to respond to complaints coming from every corner, I remember that I had once spoken to Cardinal Raffaele Farina, who had been Bertone's life-long friend, and was especially close to him during their time together at the Pontifical Salesian University. I asked Cardinal Farina to join forces with his brother Salesians Angelo Amato and Enrico dal Covolo to convince Cardinal Bertone that he needed to be more cautious. Farina responded: "Bertone does whatever he wants. Not even we can make him listen to us because he has lost all sense of balance."

In the end, I think Bertone himself finally came to his senses and grasped the entire situation, as revealed in the speech he gave in Syracuse on 1 September 2013, the day before Pope Francis officially appointed his successor, Pietro Parolin: "I certainly have my defects. If I had to reconsider my behavior at certain moments, I would have acted differently. However, this does not mean that I did not strive to serve the Church."

Blind-sided by betrayal

In that difficult period of 2011–2012, the darkest page of our pontifical family's story was written—namely, the leak of confidential documents from the papal apartments. Looking back on that situation, I still feel like the father who doesn't know that his own son is stealing jewels from his own wife, and, even after the true nature of the crime comes to light, he cannot harbor even the slightest suspicion toward his son. Even now, as I think back on the people involved in that scandal, the notion is lodged somewhere in my mind that they thought they were acting in good faith. But the truth is the sheer amount of bad acts they set in motion is undoubtedly something approaching the diabolical.

It all started on 25 January 2012, when the television program *Gli intoccabili* ["The Untouchables"] on channel *La7* revealed letters written by Archbishop Carlo Maria Viganò regarding his transfer from the Vatican to the nunciature in the United States of America. At that time, it seemed like nothing more than the exposure of an internal spat over promotions and removals from high curial positions. But things became more complicated when the daily newspaper *Il Fatto* published a text that Colombian Cardinal Darío Castillón Hoyos had sent to the Secretariat of State on 30 December 2011 to inform authorities of alleged indiscretions attributed by German entrepreneurs to the Archbishop of Palermo, Cardinal Paolo Romero, during a trip he had taken to China in November.

According to those anonymous sources, Romeo conveyed four pieces of information to his Chinese interlocutors: (1) Pope Benedict consulted him and Cardinal Scola on the most important matters confronting the Church; (2) The pope's relationship with the Secretary of State was extremely conflictual, and Benedict even hated Bertone; (3) the pope was secretly already thinking about his successor and had already chosen Cardinal Scola as the ideal candidate; (4) and the pope would die within the next twelve months, probably due to a plot against his life. A rapid consultation led to a simple declaration from Father Federico Lombardi: "It is so far-fetched that I won't even take it in consideration."

At the direction of Pope Benedict, I met with both Castrillón and Romeo, and I came away with the distinct impression that Cardinal Castrillón had given credence to people who were anything but credible and instead motivated by dark interests. Romeo made it clear that he had obviously informed the Secretariat of State that he was making a private trip to China. He had previously been a nuncio and he knew well how to conduct himself abroad. The conclusion drawn from these bizarre claims was that Cardinal Romeo was involved only because, at that time, he had been the highest-ranking ecclesiastical authority to visit China, and none of us had any doubt that the statements attributed to him were nothing but pure sensationalism.

The true turning point came when the so-called *corvo* ("crow," or "whistle-blower") explained that he was involved with a group of employees who wanted the truth to be known about shady and scandalous things going on in the Vatican. Listening to his electronically distorted voice, I didn't recognize any inflection or speech patterns as familiar, so I thought it must have been someone I didn't know, or perhaps someone just making the whole thing up. But it was undoubtedly a foreshadowing of more revelations to come, as the recorded message warned.

The moment the affair broke out, the pontifical Gendarmeria began an investigation. On February 3rd, the commander of the Gendarmeria, Domenico Giani, sent a memo to the Promoter of Justice, Nicola Picardi, and within three days the first charge was formalized against the unknown perpetrators. But a further leak of documents prompted Benedict to set up a commission of cardinals on April 24th who, "by virtue of the pontifical mandate granted to them at every level" (as explicitly stated), may confidentially question anyone they judge to be in possession of knowledge regarding the case.

The commission was composed of three well-respected cardinals, all of whom were beyond the voting age of eighty and therefore were able to work "without a conflict of interest": Julián Herranz, an expert in canon law; Jozef Tomko, thoroughly familiar with the Roman Curia; and Salvatore De Giorgi, an outsider to Vatican circles. Franciscan Father Luigi Martignani of the Secretariat of State served as secretary. Cardinal Bertone suggested that the commission report to him, but Benedict decided that the commission should surpass the Secretariat of State and report directly to the pope himself.

The final shoe dropped the following May 19th when Gianluigi Nuzzi's book *Sua Santità* was released. Flipping through it, I realized that some of the documents cited—and even photographed—by him had passed through my office alone and no one else's. I had shown these documents directly to the pope, who had marked them with his papal seal and given me directions on how to proceed, and I kept them on a shelf located above my right shoulder at my desk.

I immediately made a mental picture for myself of how we conducted our work in the secretarial office located next to the pope's study, and it was clear to me that absolutely no one entered that space apart from the adjunct secretary Monsignor Xuereb and the butler, Gabriele. I then decided to confront the mystery head-on. With the permission of Benedict XVI, I called a meeting on the morning of the 21st with Xuereb and Gabriele, as well as with the four Memores and Sister Birgit. I asked each of them individually if he or she were the one who had divulged the documents, and each firmly denied it. At that point I became quite stern, and, turning to Paolo, I accused him of theft, confident in my assessment, given that he had a desk with a computer to electronically manage and file documents in his room.

I made the induction from our working procedure. When the mail bag arrived from the Secretariat of State in the morning, I sorted through its contents and handed the pope whatever documents he had to look at personally. He would read them, make some notes, and sometimes ask for clarification, and at the end he would give everything back to me with his responses. These documents and letters were then kept in a special place in my office while I accompanied Benedict down to the second *loggia* for audiences. Then, before lunch, a courier from the Secretariat of State would come back for the bag containing the material that had already been worked on.

Paolo would usually come with us to the second *loggia,* but then he would often go back up to the apartments to finish his work. Since he had a key to the Sixtus V elevator, he was able to use it whenever he wanted and nobody would bat an eye. Since Monsignor Xuereb was usually also out at that time, Paolo was practically left alone. Thinking back on it, I remembered that, after lunch, Paolo would constantly go back to his office and then leave around 3:00 p.m. (he usually arrived in the morning at 7:00 a.m. for Mass), giving the impression that he would have to catch up on work later so that he would have time to attend to his "personal business."

Hence, I had no qualms about placing the blame on him, showing him that at least two of the letters published in Nuzzi's book—regarding donations from a journalist and a banker who wished to support the pope's charitable works—had only passed through Gabriele's hands, insofar as they had been brought directly to me and they had never left the office. Moreover, I had asked Paolo personally to make photocopies of the letters and to draft thank-you letters to them. But Paolo was thoroughly prepared to deny this completely, even to the point of pretending that he was offended, asking me how I could even harbor such suspicions.

After lunch, I went into the chapel. I didn't expect to find him there, but there he was. I went right up to him and asked him to tell me the truth about what happened. He then finally started to tell the truth, admitting that he had met Nuzzi and given him some documents. I was completely shocked. Afterward, I learned that Gabriele had immediately gone to Archbishop Harvey to tell him what had happened, perhaps in the hope that Harvey would back him up, but Gabriele's revelation left the archbishop utterly speechless.

When I think back on it, what really disturbs me even to this day is the way Paolo reacted when I told him that he would have to be temporarily suspended from his duties until more light was shed on the situation. He firmly believed that he was only a scapegoat, and he coldly affirmed that he was at peace and in good conscience with his actions since he had discussed his motives with his spiritual director, Father Giovanni Luzi.

Although the details are muddled due to the seal of confession between Gabriele and Luzi, it became clear during the judicial proceedings that Father Luzi did receive some documents from Gabriele, but he claims that he burned them as soon as he realized that they had been obtained illegally and dishonestly. Above all, it emerged that Father Luzi had given Gabriele a "censorable command" [*censurabile indicazione*], as the Vatican judges euphemistically put it, to "wait things out, and deny any wrongdoing unless the pope himself asks him directly."

A morass of human weakness

In the meantime, the ongoing investigation by the Gendarmeria pointed the finger at Gabriele, especially with the help of a camera that had been placed near the entrance of Gabriele's home not far from the Porta Sant'Anna with the intention of filming any attempt to smuggle compromising material. They took a break from the search on May 22nd and discussed how to proceed. They decided to continue the search on the 23rd both at the Vatican and at Castel Gandolfo, where they had found a pile of material—both originals and photocopies—much of which was taken from the internet and involved speculations about Masonry and secret intelligence. This ultimately led to Paolo's arrest.

Confirmation of these charges was a hard blow to Pope Benedict, who had come to consider Paolo a son, just as all of us in the pontifical household considered him not only a co-worker, but a brother. The pope opened his heart and expressed the depth of his sentiments at the general audience on May 30th: "The incidents of these days concerning the Curia and my co-workers have filled my heart with sorrow but have never obscured the firm certainty that, despite the human weakness, difficulties and trials, the Church is guided by the Holy Spirit and the Lord will never withhold his help to sustain her on her journey. However, rumors, exaggerated by some of the media, totally gratuitously and that have gone far beyond the facts, paint an image of the Holy See that does not correspond to reality. For this reason, I wish to renew my trust in—and my encouragement to—my closest collaborators and all of those who, in a spirit of fidelity, sacrifice, and anonymity, help me in fulfilling my daily ministry."

In the days that followed, since I was Paolo's direct superior, I offered my own resignation to Pope Benedict, asking him to give me an assignment outside of the pontifical household. He simply responded that it was out of the question. He reaffirmed his support toward the beginning of June, when the daily newspaper *La Repubblica* printed two documents—rendered illegible—but with my signature visible in the bottom corner. The anonymous source that divulged these documents claimed that the documents were blurred in order to avoid offense to the Holy Father, who had already been hurt by his closest collaborators. They wrote: "We reserve the right to publish the texts in their entirety if anyone persists in hiding the truth from us."

The succeeding weeks proved that such a threat didn't amount to anything, especially since the only document they were able to verify—a letter dated 19 February 2009—was simply a note to the Secretariat of State assigning specific tasks. I was therefore convinced that the reason for blurring the contents of the letters was simply to persuade readers that they contained secrets, when in fact they contained nothing but the banal details of a working agenda.

The most absurd claim emerging from this affair was connected with the campaign to "expel the true culprits of the crime: Monsignor Gänswein and Cardinal Bertone." That is, the accusation was that countless confidential documents from my personal archive had been made public, which were "reserved exclusively for the Cardinal Secretary of State, Tarcisio Bertone." But since Bertone was in charge of the secretariat, he clearly had no need of me to know the contents of documents that had been processed by the Secretariat of State in the first place! And in the event that they hadn't, the pope would surely have shown them to Bertone at their weekly *udienza di tabella.*

A meeting took place at Castel Gandolfo on 26 July 2012, at which the commission of cardinals gave an oral report of their provisional findings from their investigation. In short, evidence emerged that there had been other individuals involved in the scandal who, due to various personal interests, had contact with Paolo and had supported his decision to divulge the documents, thus giving him greater confidence and dispelling any doubts from his mind about the legitimacy of his actions. None of these people, however, directly acted to abet Paolo in the plot.

In particular, there had been frequent contact between Paolo and Ingrid Stampa, partially because they lived in the same apartment complex. Perhaps, even if not realizing it, Ingrid had a psychological influence on Gabriele, and the psychiatrist, Roberto Tatarelli, found that Gabriele was a "fragile personality with paranoid tendencies, covering up a deep personal insecurity and an unresolved need to enjoy the esteem and affection of others," and that "on several occasions, he referred to plots and conspiracies either in favor of or against certain people, be they laity or—more frequently—clerics."

On 6 October 2012, the Vatican Tribunal sentenced Paolo Gabriele to three years in prison. The sentence was subsequently reduced to a year and a half. He was officially charged with "having carried out—through an abuse of the trust he enjoyed with colleagues working in the same office space—the removal of items which, by virtue of the relationship he had with those some colleagues, were available to him precisely due to the presumed bond of trust."

Even though Benedict was deeply disappointed by this case—especially since Paolo was always free to speak to him and clarify any misunderstandings—the decision to reduce his sentence was taken even before Paolo formally requested it *via* a letter sent to the pope at the beginning of September in which he acknowledged his guilt and begged the pope's forgiveness for having betrayed his trust. Benedict responded personally to the request, sending him a book of Psalms with his Apostolic blessing affixed to the first page of the volume.

Benedict XVI decided to wait a while before making a more public display of pardon. He did so on the following December 22nd, when I accompanied him to the jail cell in the Gendarmeria where Paolo was being detained. I stood at a distance to let them have some time alone. I have no idea what words were exchanged, but I did have the distinct impression that Paolo finally realized the extent of the damage he had caused, and that he was truly sorry for it.

A few days before the pardon was made official on December 17th, the report of the commission of cardinals was handed over to Pope Benedict. They had listened to the testimony of around twenty people, including all the members of the pontifical family. The conclusions of the report were satisfactory enough, since, in the end, there were no signs of any intent to sabotage the Holy Father, Cardinal Bertone, or me. Rather, there was the sad reality that some Vatican employees had developed the idea of fighting against something not well defined, and who consequently exploited opportunities and were themselves exploited. Essentially, however, as stated in a memo released after the final meeting between the members of the commission and Benedict XVI, the investigation found that "among the human weaknesses and imperfections that one would find in any institution, there is also clearly a sense of generosity, uprightness, and dedication on the part of most who serve the Holy See to assist the Roman Pontiff in the mission Christ has entrusted to him."

On 23 March 2013, during the first meeting between the pope emeritus and his successor, Pope Francis, the former handed over to the latter all the documentation related to the investigation in the unforgettable image of a "white box." To facilitate Francis's study of the documents, I had prepared a detailed table of contents and index. The first page consisted of a lengthy letter written by Benedict in which he gave his own assessment of the facts and the situation. The box also included the final report of the three cardinals, transcripts of the interviews with witnesses, cassette recordings of the same interviews, in addition to memos and reports presented by some of those who had given testimony.

In his observations, Benedict never used the term "Vatileaks," nor did he make any explicit proposals or suggestions. He preferred to allow the new pontiff to use his own judgment and to make his own decisions freely. Pope Francis himself affirmed this in an interview with Gian Marco Chiocci on 30 October 2020: "During the meeting, he handed over to me a big, white box. He said, 'Everything is contained within: the acts, a summary of the more difficult situations, the actions I've already taken, how I intervened in certain cases, whom I've dismissed, and so on.... [N]ow it's up to you.' So there: I've done nothing more than accept Pope Benedict's testimony, and I've carried on his work."

The mystery of Emanuela

It was only natural for the story of the tragic kidnapping of Emanuela Orlandi to surface again amid the chaos of the Vatileaks affair. In fact, the story cyclically reemerges in the press every few years or whenever new revelations—some accurate, some not—are brought forth surrounding the case. On 22 February 2012, during a broadcast of the television program *Chi l'ha visto?* [Who has seen him/her?] certain passages from a note Father Lombardi had sent to me were revealed when he was acting as press secretary. From the way the media covered it, one would think that the Vatican leadership had all of a sudden turned its attention once more exclusively to the thirty-year-old case (Emanuela disappeared on 22 June 1983).

In reality, the background was more prosaic. It was related to a meeting I had with Pietro Orlandi, who wanted to give me a copy of his book, *Mia sorella Emanuela* ("My Sister Emenuela"), and to update me on some developments in the case. He also told me that he and all those who had signed a petition begging for more information about the investigation planned to attend the Angelus in Saint Peter's Square on December 18th. He asked if the pope might extend a special greeting to them.

I only had a limited knowledge of the facts surrounding the case, so I asked Father Lombardi to bring me up to speed and to take a look at Pietro's book. Meanwhile, Monsignor Giampiero Gloder in the Secretariat of State was tasked with looking into the issue more deeply. Gloder's response, which was subsequently published in Nuzzi's book, was that it would not be appropriate for the pope to publicly mention the case. His thinking on the issue was reasonable: "Orlandi's brother maintains firmly that, at various levels, the Vatican is observing a code of silence on the case and is therefore hiding something. Even a mere allusion to the case on the part of Pope Benedict would give weight to Mr. Orlandi's hypothesis, suggesting that the pope 'is not sure' of how well the case has been handled."

In a report by Father Lombardi prepared between December 2011 and the beginning of January 2012 (and presumably given to Pietro Orlandi by Paolo Gabriele, for they knew one another), it was emphasized with a tone of sympathy that "one has the impression that the tragedy this family has suffered is not just the loss of their daughter, but also the prolonged torture of messages, claims of responsibility, and contradictory information that keeps them constantly in doubt and breathes life into the issue even today, always with some presumably new evidence." This led to a reexamination of the various aspects of the tragic case and possible responses to some issues raised in the book.

These were subsequently developed into a lengthy note published by the Vatican press office on 14 April 2012: "[T]here have been some initiatives, covered by the press, to raise doubts about whether institutions or persons affiliated with the Vatican have really done everything possible to cooperate in the search for the truth about what happened," yet "thanks to some particularly credible witnesses and a re-reading of all the available documentation, it has been possible to substantially ascertain the criteria and the motives for which Vatican authorities have proceeded to confront this situation."

Personally, I assured Pietro Orlandi of my solidarity and my willingness to help if I could, just as he recounted in an interview with Federica Sciarelli on *Rai* television. But Father Lombardi's declaration naturally represents the most authoritative reconstruction upon which to base an opinion on the matter: "[T]he central issue is that, unfortunately, there is no concrete entity within the Vatican that can offer a resolution of the case to anyone searching for an ultimate answer. At that time, the Vatican authorities, on the basis of messages it had received making reference to Ali Agca—precisely at the same time when an investigation into the assassination attempt on John Paul II's life was underway—concurred in their prevailing opinion that the kidnapping was the means by which an obscure criminal organization might send messages or exert pressure on the decision to incarcerate and interrogate the man charged with an attack on the pope's life. No one could think of any other motive for the abduction. But the claim that someone connected to the Vatican had knowledge of secrets connected with the kidnapping, without putting forth any names, does not correspond in any way to any trustworthy or well-founded information; in fact, it sometimes seems like an alibi in the face of the discomfort and frustration of not being able to ascertain the truth."

I was also assured that, through the years, everything possible had been done to help the Orlandi family, and I duly handed on this information to Pope Benedict. Even the Commander of the Gendarmeria, Domenico Giani, reviewed the documentation from that time and concluded that nothing had been hidden from the Italian authorities regarding the case, and that in the meantime there were no further developed hypotheses that could been pursued through investigations within the Vatican.

The various and contrasting hypotheses advanced—from the connection of the attack on John Paul II to the claim that the kidnapping was an attempt to abduct and trade a prisoner for Ali Agca; from the claim that it was part of a war between Eastern and Western intelligence to the suspicion that it was the work a the criminal gang, *Banda della Magliana;* from questions concerning the IOR when it was under Marcinkus's leadership to the presumed funding of the Polish Solidarity movement—have each had positive and negative elements, but there has never been anything even close to definitive proof of what happened. There is another question to add to the mix: whether Pope John Paul II's deep concern with the case—evident in the impassioned appeal he made on behalf of the Orlandi family during the Angelus on 3 July 1983—led the unscrupulous criminals to do something worse to their hostage, a girl barely fifteen years old, and a citizen of Vatican City-State (and may we also not forget another victim of the same age, Mirella Gregori, who went missing around the same time).

For my part, I should calmly point out that the outrageous claims posted by journalist Pino Nicotri on *www.blizquotidiano.it* on 13 January 2015, are nothing but pure inventions: "A few months ago, the magistrates discovered through confidential channels that 'during the trial, the Secretariate of State and the Vatican Gendarmeria were simply terrified by the idea that Paolo Gabriele had photocopied a dossier carefully prepared by Gänswein.' But the dossier does not appear among the photocopied documents given to Nuzzi nor those found in the Vatican apartment of the ex-butler, indicating that it was never photocopied. So, the magistrates were asked why there would be so much fear that a photocopy of it was among the documents that were divulged? The inevitable hypothesis is that the dossier contains the entire truth about what happened and who had done it." A much simpler—and more accurate—explanation is that I had never written anything that had anything to do with the Orlandi case, such that this ghost dossier never appeared for the simple reason that it never existed!

Equally unfounded was a polemic surrounding a claim made by ex-magistrate Giancarlo Capaldo in December of 2012 about two meetings I had with Domenico Giani and his vice, Costanzo Alessandrini. The heads of the Gendarmeria were summoned by him to confront the problem of the tomb of Renatino De Pedis, leader of the Roman gang *Banda della Magliana,* in the crypt of the Church of Saint Apollinare. It had been hypothesized that Emanuela Orlandi was buried in the same grave, so Giani wanted to be sure that representatives of the Holy See were present for the opening of the coffin in order to verify its contents, thus avoiding any trace of suspicion.

The Vatican's offer to participate in the exhumation—approved by Cardinal Bertone and brought to my own attention—was then apparently so badly misinterpreted that the ex-magistrate claimed that "on that occasion, I asked about the possibility of rediscovering the body of Emanuela Orlandi or at least of figuring out what happened to her. They showed that they were willing, and said, 'we will let you know.'" As has been pointed out on several occasions, this hasty reconstruction of events was completely contrary to the facts, so much so that even more recently then-procurator of the Republic of Rome, Giuseppe Pignatore, clarified that, at the time, "Doctor Capaldo did not say anything to me as he indeed should have, judging from his alleged conversations with Vatican 'emissaries,'" but instead only "mentioned this to me after he had retired (23 March 2017)."

6
A Well-Rounded Magisterium

A Christocentric pontificate

Obviously, it is impossible to summarize the magisterium of Benedict XVI in a few pages. It was as dense in quality as it was voluminous in quantity. But I would nonetheless like to highlight a few essential points of his pontificate, which have already proven to be his greatest legacy and gift to the Church. The decisive core of this inheritance is the Christocentric witness he bears as a believer, in everything he said and did.

The Word of God is Christ himself, who is and must be at the center of the Church and her life. Considered in this light, a Christian is a person who believes in Jesus Christ and lives in a personal friendship with him. Precisely for this reason, a pope cannot run ahead of the Lord and attempt to show the way himself, for Jesus has already defined the way. Just like any other Christian—in fact, more so than any other Christian—the pope must follow Christ, placing Christ before himself and his own personal interests and goals.

Within this constant context of the Savior and of Christocentric preaching, we can see and appreciate more readily the reason for which Benedict withdrew himself from the exhausting daily grind of papal duties to dedicate time and energy to writing three volumes on Jesus of Nazareth. Just as Peter, in the name of all the apostles, witnessed to the Lord at Caesarea Philippi with the words, "You are the Messiah, the Son of the living God," so Benedict, as a successor of Peter, wanted to utter his own profession of faith in Christ in the Caesarea Philippi of today in order to convince his brothers and sisters of the truth and beauty of the Christian faith, and to lead them into a personal relationship with the Lord.

Pope Benedict's witness to Jesus Christ renders visible the meaning and necessity of the Petrine ministry in the Church, showing that it is, when viewed through the light of faith, a gift of the Holy Spirit to the entire ecclesial community.

Pope Ratzinger was firmly convinced that he had to write a trilogy on the life of Christ as a synthesis of his own theological vision, centered on his certitude that the salvific message of Jesus was not simply a doctrine, but a concrete encounter with the person of Jesus, with the God who really became man and continues to be present to the human race in every age. Ultimately, he wanted to publish the book under his own name so that it might be evaluated on the basis of his own theological competence and not on the basis of authoritative, magisterial teaching.

What impressed me the most was that, when he sat down at his desk every Tuesday to work on the book, he would pick up right where he had left off, as if the interval had been no more than ten minutes. I told him in jest that he was like a sewing machine that could be turned off on the spot and turned back on again to pick up the stitching wherever it had left off, no matter how long the break. But in fact, the only reason the book was turned into a trilogy was to ensure that at least some of it would appear before he would start to lose his strength and be unable to complete it.

As Ratzinger himself wrote in the foreword to the first volume, his reflection on the connection between the Jesus of faith and the Jesus of history represented "a long, interior journey" in his "personal search for the Lord's face." Thinking back on the project, I can't help but connect it to the words he shared on 1 September 2006 during a personal pilgrimage to the shrine at Manopello to see the Holy Face, that "to 'see God' it is necessary to know Christ and to let oneself be molded by his Spirit who guides believers 'into all truth' (cf. Jn 16: 13). Those who meet Jesus, who let themselves be attracted by him and are prepared to follow him even to the point of sacrificing their lives, personally experience, as he did on the Cross, that only the 'grain of wheat' that falls into the earth and dies will bear 'much fruit' (Jn 12: 24). This is the path of Christ, the way of total love that overcomes death."

In a meditation he shared on 2 May 2010 during a pastoral visit to Turin to behold the Holy Shroud, he said, "from the darkness of the death of the Son of God, the light of a new hope gleamed: the light of the Resurrection. And it seems to me that, looking at this sacred cloth through the eyes of faith, one may perceive something of this light.... This is the power of the Shroud: from the face of this 'Man of sorrows,' who carries with him the passion of man of every time and every place, our passions too, our sufferings, our difficulties and our sins—from this face a solemn majesty shines, a paradoxical lordship."

In the second volume, Benedict turns to the Lord's resurrection as the most decisive turning point for Christianity: "The question of whether Jesus *only existed* in the past or *continues to exist* in the present hinges entirely upon the resurrection. The 'yes' or 'no' we give to this question doesn't pertain to a single event that occurred among others, but to the very person of Jesus as such.... The Christian faith rises or falls on the truth of the witness that Christ has been raised from the dead." Moreover, if Benedict, commenting on the Eucharist, had already affirmed that "with the Eucharist, the Church herself is instituted," here he goes even deeper by making it clear that "the account of the resurrection becomes *per se* ecclesiology: the encounter with the risen Lord is the mission that gives the nascent Church its very form."

Together with the resurrection, the topic of the virginal conception of Jesus is perhaps the most scandalous affirmation of the Christian faith in the modern world. Therefore, in the third volume on the infancy of Jesus, Pope Ratzinger makes a firm declaration: "Obviously, we cannot attribute anything to God that is dissonate or unreasonable with the nature of his creation. Yet we are not dealing with something unreasonable or contradictory here, but something absolutely positive: the creative power of God which embraces all being. Therefore, these two points—the virginal birth and the historical resurrection of Jesus from the dead—are the bedrocks against which the faith is measured. If God does not have power over matter as well, then he is no longer God. But he does possess this power, and the conception and resurrection of Jesus Christ inaugurated a new creation. So, insofar as he is the Creator, he is also our Redeemer. For this reason, the conception and birth of Jesus from the Virgin Mary are fundamental elements of our faith and a bright beacon of hope."

These affirmations are the basis of his deep admiration and devotion to Our Lady, who, at the moment she received the announcement of the angel, became the Mother of God and of the Church by expressing her "yes" to God with "an obedience that was free, humble, but also magnanimous, in which she enacts a decision that elevates human freedom to its highest level." For Pope Ratzinger, "we encounter the essence of the Church in the Immaculate Virgin in a way that is undeformed," and from her "we must learn to become 'ecclesial souls,' as the Church fathers put it, so that we too, as Saint Paul writes, might present ourselves 'immaculate' or 'unblemished' in the Lord's sight, just as he had willed from the beginning."

An evangelical Petrine service

The one driving and unwavering concern of Benedict XVI was that the Church keep at the center of her life a reality that she alone is capable of preserving in its fullness: the Word of God. The Word doesn't simply exist in a distant past that we look back upon nostalgically. It is, rather, a Word that speaks "to" and "in" our present age and grounds our daily, personal lives.

Pope Ratzinger dedicated himself to the Word of God with the knowledge that, as he said in his homily at the opening Mass of his pontificate, he would not be proposing any specific "program" of governance, at least not in the sense that that word is usually understood. Rather, taking his primary duty to be that of binding the entire Church to the Word of God and guaranteeing her obedience to it, he was conscious of the fact that his first duty lie precisely in living that obedience himself in an exemplary way.

His love for Sacred Scripture and his mission of guiding others to know the Gospel through his proclamation and preaching prompted him to build his Petrine ministry on evangelization through and through. This is why, at his last audience as Bishop of Rome, Benedict could say with complete honesty that his Petrine ministry had always been carried out in the firm conviction that "the Word of truth, the Word of the Gospel, is the Church's strength and her life."

Ratzinger understood his pontificate in the sense expressed by Saint Ignatius of Antioch in his Letter to the Romans, written around 110 A.D., where he says that the Church of Rome lives as one who "presides in love." This is based on the conviction that to preside in the faith and in doctrine must necessarily entail a "presiding in love," since a faith without love would not be a faith in the biblical God, and the Church's doctrine reaches the hearts of men only if it leads to love.

This explains why one of the most brilliant aspects of Benedict's teaching is that truth and love are not only *not* contradictory, but in fact are in need of one another and mutually nourish each another. Truth without love risks unraveling into brute force, and love without truth into banality. Benedict, therefore, strove to emphasize the integral and inseverable unity of the truth of the faith, the love of God for man, and the love of man for God and for his brothers and sisters, placing his entire pontificate at the service of proclaiming this truth.

In fact, the first synod of bishops he convoked as pope was dedicated to the theme, "The Word of God in the Life and Mission of the Church" (October 2008), with the explicit objective of pointing out "certain fundamental approaches to a rediscovery of God's word in the life of the Church as a wellspring of constant renewal." In the Post-Synodal Apostolic Exhortation *Verbum Domini,* which was intended to synthesize the fruits of the synodal discussions, Benedict afforded special attention to the duty of all Christians to proclaim the word of God in the world in which they live and work.

A few aspects of this mission deserve particular attention. First of all, the awareness that both the starting point and the goal of the Church's mission is the mystery of God the Father: his word involves all the baptized, not simply as recipients of the word but as proclaimers of the Word, and the credibility of the Good News depends on the witness of Christians. Secondly, a particular duty of Christians in the world is reconciliation, justice, and peace among peoples, based on an active and creative charity aimed at relieving the suffering—both spiritual and material—of those in difficulty.

Thus, the word of God has an indispensable role in fostering relationships between cultures, even when they are secularized and non-believing, insofar as the Bible is universally recognized as a "great code" of anthropological and philosophical values that have had a positive influence on all humanity. This gives rise to the task of inculturation, which consists in strengthening different traditions with a greater knowledge of Scripture. It also underlies the task of interreligious dialogue, insofar as getting to know one another and working together with men and women of good will—especially those of different religious traditions—is an essential part of the proclamation of the Word of God, provided one avoids the temptation to syncretism and relativism and upholds an authentic spirit of universal religious freedom.

Another particular objective emerged from the synod: "Our own time, then, must be increasingly marked by a new hearing of God's word and a new evangelization. Recovering the centrality of the divine word in the Christian life leads us … to pursue the *missio ad gentes* and vigorously to embark upon the new evangelization." Therefore, in June of 2010, Benedict established a new pontifical council "whose specific duty it is to promote a renewed evangelization in those countries that have already had an initial proclamation of the faith, and in which there are churches of ancient origin, but which are living through an increased secularization of society and a sort of 'eclipse of a sense of God,' constituting a great challenge to find the adequate means of reproposing the perennial truth of the Gospel of Christ." As the pontiff affirmed at the first plenary assembly of the dicastery, "The Gospel is the ever-new proclamation of the salvation worked by Christ which makes humanity participate in the mystery of God and in his life of love and opens it to a future of strong, sure hope. Highlighting that at this moment in history, the Church is called to carry out a *new* evangelization, means intensifying her missionary action so that it fully corresponds to the Lord's mandate."

But perhaps Benedict made an even more significant and relevant assertion at the synodal gathering in October of 2012, this time dedicated to the theme of the "New Evangelization and the Transmission of the Christian Faith." He synthesized the relationship between the new evangelization, traditional evangelization, and mission *ad gentes* as "three aspects of the single reality of evangelization that complete and enrich each other."

God always stands at the origin of any initiative to evangelize: "The Church does not begin with our own doing, but with the 'doing' and 'speaking' of God. If God does not act, our attempts are nothing but our own attempts, and they are insufficient; only God can ultimately give witness that it is He who speaks and has spoken. Pentecost is the very condition for the birth of the Church: only because God has acted first can the apostles act with Him and with his presence, and thus present to others how much He has done. God has spoken, and this 'has spoken' suggests a perfect tense, but it has bearing on the present: God's 'having done' not only affects the past, because God's past, though a true past, always enlivens both the present and future."

The ministry of the proclamation

As professor and cardinal prefect, Ratzinger already had a clear concept of the specific nature of his ministry, always aimed at the service of the faith and of the truth. He alluded to this understanding of his ministry as pope when he said during the inaugural Mass of his pontificate on 7 May 2005 at the Basilica of Saint John Lateran: "… [T]he Chair is the symbol of the *potestas docendi,* the power to teach that is an essential part of the mandate of binding and loosing which the Lord conferred on Peter, and after him, on the Twelve." In fact, as he stated in a letter to the Study Center in Bydgoszcz in March of 2016, "I never wanted to develop my own theology; I simply wanted to serve the faith of the Church and contribute to a greater understanding of it in our time."

Hence, it was a happy coincidence that, precisely at the time he was elected pope, work on the *Compendium to the Catechism of the Catholic Church*—which was launched by John Paul II in February of 2003—was brought to completion. The compendium—ten years in the making—was a response to the need to present the essential elements of Catholic faith and morals in a synthetic, simple way accessible to all. At the presentation of the compendium on 28 June 2005, Benedict XVI called it "a renewed proclamation of the Gospel for today," arranged in the form of a dialogue in order to "propose once again a dialogue between Master and disciple by means of a series of questions that involve the reader directly, inviting him to persevere in the search for new aspects of the truth of the faith."

Benedict XVI also gave highest priority to cultivating a dialogue between the Christian faith and art as the "world of the beautiful," but also in order to shed light on the beauty of the faith itself. This is why he drew particular attention to the beautiful iconographic art that appears among the pages of the compendium, something he himself had requested, since "images and words are mutually enlightening. Works of art always 'speak,' at least implicitly, of the divine, of the infinite beauty of God, reflected in the Icon *par excellence*: Christ the Lord, the Image of the invisible God. Sacred images, with their beauty, are also a Gospel proclamation and express the splendor of the Catholic truth, illustrating the supreme harmony between the good and the beautiful, between the *via veritatis* and the *via pulchritudinis.* While they witness to the age-old and fruitful tradition of Christian art, they urge one and all, believers and non-believers alike, to discover and contemplate the inexhaustible fascination of the mystery of Redemption, giving an ever-new impulse to the lively process of its inculturation in time."

Perhaps the clearest thing in Benedict XVI's mind and heart was that the Christian faith, if it is truly to be human, must always be engaged in a dialogue with human reason. He was deeply convinced that faith and reason depend on each other and only when they are in a mutual dialogue can they overcome the pathologies of reason and any illness of faith: without faith, reason risks becoming unilateral and one-dimensional; without reason, faith risks hiding its connection with truth and becomes fundamentalist.

Convinced more than ever that the question of God is of vital significance for all other questions pertaining to the future of humanity, Pope Benedict strove to make a significant contribution to keeping the question of God alive in every aspect of modern society. The dialogue between faith and reason was essential for him since God himself is *Logos,* and all of creation witnesses to this "reason." *Logos* is not limited to mathematical or logical reasoning; it also has a "heart" and is essentially love. This led Benedict to the following conclusion: "Truth is beautiful, truth and beauty go hand-in-hand. Beauty is the seal of truth."

At the same time, Pope Ratzinger never lost sight of the simple faith of everyday people in everyday circumstances. In fact, it would be closer to the truth to say that he was convinced that, ultimately, the truth of the faith is manifested better in the hearts of the humblest, and it can only be cultivated with the eyes of faith, as he himself said in his *Urbi et Orbi* message on Christmas in 2010: "If the truth were a mere mathematical formula, in some sense it would impose itself by its own power. But if Truth is Love, it calls for faith, for the 'yes' of our hearts."

All of this explains, quite simply, the final initiative of his pontificate: the Year of Faith, which he opened on 11 October 2012, on the fiftieth anniversary of the opening of the Second Vatican Council, but which he handed over to his successor, Francis, in that it was scheduled to close on 24 November 2013, the Solemnity of Christ the King. In the *Motu Proprio* Letter *Porta Fidei,* Benedict recalls that, since the beginning of his pontificate, he had "spoken of the need to rediscover the journey of faith so as to shed ever clearer light on the joy and renewed enthusiasm of the encounter with Christ." But he acknowledges with sincere honesty that "it often happens that Christians are more concerned for the social, cultural, and political consequences of their commitment, continuing to think of the faith as a self-evident presupposition for life in society," but, "in reality, not only can this presupposition no longer be taken for granted, it is often openly denied. Whereas in the past it was possible to recognize a unitary cultural matrix, broadly accepted in its appeal to the content of the faith and the values inspired by it, today this no longer seems to be the case in large swathes of society because of a profound crisis of faith that has affected many people."

Therefore, Benedict explained that he "would like to sketch a path intended to help us understand more profoundly not only the content of the faith, but also the act by which we choose to entrust ourselves fully to God, in complete freedom. In fact, there exists a profound unity between the act by which we believe and the content to which we give our assent…. Knowledge of the content of faith is essential for giving one's own assent, that is to say for adhering fully with intellect and will to what the Church proposes. Knowledge of faith opens a door into the fullness of the saving mystery revealed by God. The giving of assent implies that, when we believe, we freely accept the whole mystery of faith, because the guarantor of its truth is God who reveals himself and allows us to know his mystery of love."

Consequently, faith, "precisely because it is a free act, also demands social responsibility for what one believes. The Church on the day of Pentecost demonstrates with utter clarity this public dimension of believing and proclaiming one's faith fearlessly to every person. It is the gift of the Holy Spirit that makes us fit for mission and strengthens our witness, making it frank and courageous. The profession of faith is an act both personal and communitarian.... Confessing with the lips indicates in turn that faith implies public testimony and commitment. A Christian may never think of belief as a private act. Faith is choosing to stand with the Lord so as to live with him. This 'standing with him' points towards an understanding of the reasons for believing."

Love is always first and foremost

As the catechism teaches in paragraph 1813, the Catholic tradition has always defined the theological virtues—i.e., the virtues that ground, animate, and characterize moral action in the Christian sense and are infused by God into the souls of the faithful to make them capable of acting as his children and of meriting eternal life—as faith, hope, and charity, and in that order. As Benedict XVI was pondering the appropriate theme for his first encyclical, his thoughts turned to Saint Paul's First Letter to the Corinthians (13:13), where the "Apostle to the Gentiles" emphasizes that "faith, hope, love remain, these three; but the greatest of these is love."

He therefore decided to begin with the greatest of virtues in *Deus Caritas Est,* an encyclical that was encouraged by his friend Cardinal Paul Josef Cordes, who at the time was President of the Pontifical Council *Cor Unum,* and who had already begun to draft a document on charity. This served as the basis for the second part of the encyclical, whereas the first part was the fruit of Ratzinger's own prayerful reflection. In any case, I should make it clear that it was not the pope's intention to write a trilogy of encyclicals on the virtues, but rather to handle a series of themes that he thought were central to the mission of proclaiming the Gospel in the world today.

Dated 25 December 2005, the encyclical was released to the public on 25 January 2006. Around that time, Benedict explained that the word "love" had lost its vigor because it had been exploited and abused to the point that we are almost afraid to use it at all today. Yet the word itself is primordial. We can never simply abandon it. We must rather repossess it, repurify it, and restore it to its original splendor so that it may shed light on our lives and show us the way to salvation. It was this realization that led Benedict to choose love as the theme for his first encyclical.

He was well aware that, at first glance, the text might appear too difficult or theoretical. He therefore decided to offer a guide to reading it which was published in the weekly magazine *La Famiglia Cristiana:* "I wanted to respond to two very concrete questions in the Christian life. The first is, 'Can we really love God? Or rather: can love be forced? Isn't it simply a feeling we either have or don't have?' The response to the first question is: Yes, we can really love God since he has not kept himself at an unreachable distance from us, but has entered into our very lives. The second question is: 'Can we truly love our neighbor if he is really a stranger or perhaps even an enemy?' Yes, we can, if we are friends of God, and therefore it is clearer to us that he has loved us and continues to love us, even though we often turn our eyes away from him and don't pay much attention to him. Finally, there is another question: 'With all its commandments and prohibitions, doesn't the Church sour the joy of *eros,* of being loved; an *eros* that drives us to love others and to want to become one with them?' In the encyclical, I have tried to show that the deepest promise of *eros* can mature only when we try to check our drive for instant happiness. Rather, let us try to find the patience to discover the 'other' in the depths of his or her being, in the totality of his or her body and soul, in a way that his or her happiness becomes more important than my own. Then we will not only want to take, but to give, and it is precisely in this liberation from the 'I'—from ourselves—that we find ourselves and are filled with joy."

He continues: "The second part of the encyclical speaks about charity as the Church's communal service of love for all those who are suffering in body or mind and are in need of the gift of love. Here, I am primarily concerned with two questions. The first is, 'Can't the Church leave this service to other philanthropic organizations that form in lots of different ways?' The response is, 'No, the Church cannot do that. She must practice love of neighbor also as a community; otherwise, she proclaims the God of love in an incomplete and insufficient way.' The second question is: 'Shouldn't we be striving for a society, an order of justice, in which no one is in need, and therefore charity becomes superfluous?' The response is: 'Yes, the purpose of a political order is to create a just ordering of society in which each is given his due and no one suffers miserably.' In this sense, justice is the true end of politics, just as peace is, which cannot exist without justice. By her very nature, the Church does not play a political role in the 'first person,' but rather respects the autonomy of the state and its ordering, although she is passionately engaged in the battle for justice. But this is only the first part of the response to the question. The second half—which I think is at the heart of the encyclical—is that justice can never render love superfluous. The world is waiting for a witness to Christian love inspired by faith. In a world so clouded by darkness, the light of God burns with this love."

The sign of hope

Less than two years later (30 November 2007), the second encyclical appeared, taking as its inspiration a passage from Saint Paul's Letter to the Romans (8:24): "For in hope we are saved" (*spe salvi facti sumus*). The theme of hope was indeed most dear to Ratzinger's theological work, for he had edited a book in 1977 entitled, *Eschatology: Death and Eternal Life,* the only volume he managed to complete in a series entitled *A Primer to Catholic Doctrine* before being appointed to the archepiscopal see of Munich and Freising. I would like to say personally that this is the encyclical I would want to have with me if I were shipwrecked on a deserted island. Every time I reread it and reflect on it, I discover new details that respond to the most basic existential questions of every man and woman alive today.

Benedict gets to the heart of the question right away, explaining that the redemption wrought by Jesus Christ "is offered to us in the sense that we have been given hope, trustworthy hope, by virtue of which we can face our present: the present, even if it is arduous, can be lived and accepted if it leads towards a goal, if we can be sure of this goal, and if this goal is great enough to justify the effort of the journey." But this gives rise to a driving question: "What sort of hope could ever justify the statement that, on the basis of that hope and simply because it exists, we are redeemed? And what sort of certainty is involved here?"

Pope Ratzinger immediately delves into a question that modern society is afraid to confront (precisely because it is afraid of proposing any question for which it cannot find an adequate response)—namely, the question of the life and death of man himself. His reflection begins with the dialogue between the parents and the priest at the beginning of the Rite of Baptism: “What do you ask of the Church?” “Faith.” “And what does faith give?” “Eternal life.” Then Benedict poses an excruciating question: “Do we really want this—to live eternally? Perhaps many people reject the faith today simply because they do not find the prospect of eternal life attractive. What they desire is not eternal life at all, but this present life, for which faith in eternal life seems something of an impediment. To continue living for ever—endlessly—appears more like a curse than a gift. Death, admittedly, one would wish to postpone for as long as possible. But to live always, without end—this, all things considered, can only be monotonous and ultimately unbearable.”

In my opinion, this is precisely the question that stands at the center of Pope Benedict’s entire magisterium: “So, what do we really want? Our paradoxical attitude gives rise to a deeper question: What in fact is ‘life’? And what does ‘eternity’ really mean?” His answer to this question can reasonably be taken as the *summa* of his theology: “The term ‘eternal life’ is intended to give a name to this known ‘unknown.’ Inevitably it is an inadequate term that creates confusion. ‘Eternal,’ in fact, suggests to us the idea of something interminable, and this frightens us; ‘life’ makes us think of the life that we know and love and do not want to lose, even though very often it brings more toil than satisfaction, so that while on the one hand we desire it, on the other hand we do not want it. To imagine ourselves outside the temporality that imprisons us and, in some way, to sense that eternity is not an unending succession of days in the calendar, but something more like the supreme moment of satisfaction, in which totality embraces us and we embrace totality—this we can only attempt.”

What follows is Benedict’s definitive and comforting conclusion: “We need the greater and lesser hopes that keep us going day by day. But these are not enough without the great hope, which must surpass everything else. This great hope can only be God, who encompasses the whole of reality and who can bestow upon us what we, by ourselves, cannot attain. The fact that it comes to us as a gift is actually part of hope. God is the foundation of hope: not any god, but the God who has a human face and who has loved us to the end, each one of us and humanity in its entirety.”

Fully conscious of the importance of both dimensions of human life—the material and the spiritual—Benedict XVI dedicated his third encyclical to a theme that has garnered increasing importance over time—namely, integral human development in charity and in truth. The initial purpose of *Caritas in Veritate* was to commemorate the fortieth anniversary of Paul VI's *Populorum Progressio,* published in 1967. But a series of problems, among which was the global financial crisis that crippled the world, placed severe restrictions on the time he and his collaborators could dedicate to the encyclical. In the end, it was signed on 29 June 2009 and presented on the following July 7th.

Various economic experts were consulted to deepen the encyclical's analysis, including professors Stefano Zamagni and Ettore Gotti Tedeschi, as well as the chief executive of the Bank of Italy, Mario Draghi. In any case, the connection with Paul VI's encyclical was clear enough thanks to three perspectives that were recapitulated in *Caritas in Veritate.* Above all, there is the idea that "the world suffers from a lack of thinking," and therefore the idea that "there is no true humanism if it is not open to the Absolute," and finally that "the core reason for underdevelopment is a lack of solidarity."

Love in truth—*caritas in veritate*—explains Benedict, is the "principle around which the Church's social doctrine turns, a principle that takes on practical form in the criteria that govern moral action. I would like to consider two of these in particular, of special relevance to the commitment to development in an increasingly globalized society: justice and the common good." And it is "a great challenge for the Church in a world that is becoming progressively and pervasively globalized. The risk for our time is that the *de facto* interdependence of people and nations is not matched by ethical interaction of consciences and minds that would give rise to truly human development. Only in charity, illumined by the light of reason and faith, is it possible to pursue development goals that possess a more humane and humanizing value."

The global crisis, writes Pope Ratzinger, "obliges us to re-plan our journey, to set ourselves new rules and to discover new forms of commitment, to build on positive experiences and to reject negative ones." Only then does the crisis become "an opportunity for discernment in which to shape a new vision for the future. In this spirit, with confidence rather than resignation, it is appropriate to address the difficulties of the present time."

But the primary appeal of this encyclical is for men and women of today to experience the incredible experience of receiving the gift of love: "Gratuitousness is present in our lives in many different forms, which often go unrecognized because of a purely consumerist and utilitarian view of life." At the same time, Benedict wanted to "demonstrate, in thinking and behavior, not only that traditional principles of social ethics like transparency, honesty, and responsibility cannot be ignored or attenuated, but also that in commercial relationships the principle of gratuitousness and the logic of gift as an expression of fraternity can and must find their place within normal economic activity."

According to the heart of God

Benedict XVI undertook several initiatives to support the lives of consecrated men and women, especially those of priests. The most poignant expression of his solidarity with and solicitude for priests was his inauguration of a Year for Priests, aimed at rediscovering priestly identity by meditating on the meaning of the ministerial life and priestly formation. He placed the Curé of Ars, Saint Jean-Marie Baptiste Vianney, at the center of this reflection, since the Church was commemorating the 150th anniversary of his death.

For Pope Ratzinger, this humble pastor of a tiny French parish with only a few hundred souls in Ars—a place where he spent forty-four tireless years of ministry at the altar and in the confessional, and because of this became the patron of parish priests—represents a model of "falling in love with Christ." The secret of his pastoral effectiveness was "the love he fostered for the Mystery of the Eucharist as a proclaimed, celebrated, and lived reality, which transformed into a love for Christ's flock, for all Christians, and for everyone searching for God." In the various reflections Benedict offered during the year, one citation from the saint continuously reemerges: "A good pastor, a pastor after the heart of God, is the greatest treasure that the good and gracious God can give to a parish, and is one of the most precious gifts of divine mercy."

Benedict thus decided to inaugurate the Year of Priests on the Solemnity of the Most Sacred Heart of Jesus on 19 June 2009, as that is the feast day traditionally dedicated to prayer for the sanctification of the clergy, with the year ending on the same feast in 2010. The motto chosen for the year was "the fidelity of Christ, the fidelity of the priest," precisely to show that the gift of divine grace precedes any human response to a pastoral need, and that missionary proclamation and divine worship are never separable in the life of a priest, just as it is vain to separate the sacramental identity of a priest from his mission to preach the Gospel.

In fact, Benedict came to an ever-deepening realization that the modern world had great difficulty in seeing and understanding the sacred. The one, all-encompassing category had become "utility," such that "the Catholic conception of priesthood risked losing its essential nature, even within the Church's total vision." Referring back to an earlier text on the ministry and life of priests, Benedict explained with determination that "not infrequently, both in theology and in the concreate pastoral practice and formation of priests, there are two different and often contrasting conceptions of the priesthood. On the one hand, there is the social-functional conception, which defines the essence of priesthood to be service to the community and the performance of a specific function; on the other hand, there is the sacramental-ontological conception of the priesthood, which naturally does not deny the character of priesthood as service, but it sees it as anchored in the 'being' of the ministry and maintains that this 'being' is determined by a gift given by the Lord through the mediation of the Church, which will call a 'sacrament.'"

The precise intent of this initiative, therefore, was to emphasize that "the priest is a servant of Christ, in the sense that his existence, configured to Christ ontologically, acquires an essentially relational character: he is *in* Christ, *for* Christ and *with* Christ, at the service of humankind. Because he belongs to Christ, the priest is radically at the service of all people: he is the minister of their salvation, their happiness, and their authentic liberation, developing, in this gradual assumption of Christ's will, in prayer, in 'being heart to heart' with him. Therefore, this is the indispensable condition for every proclamation, which entails participation in the sacramental offering of the Eucharist and docile obedience to the Church."

Benedict was firm and clear on this point: "The priest is not a mere office-holder, like those which every society needs in order to carry out certain functions. Instead, he does something which no human being can do of his own power: in Christ's name he speaks the words which absolve us of our sins and, in this way, he changes, starting with God, our entire life. Over the offerings of bread and wine he speaks Christ's words of thanksgiving, which are words of transubstantiation—words which make Christ himself present, the Risen One, his Body and Blood—words which thus transform the elements of the world, which open the world to God and unite it to him. The priesthood, then, is not simply 'office' but sacrament: God makes use of us poor men in order to be, through us, present to all men and women, and to act on their behalf."

This is why Benedict also emphasized the importance of clerical clothing and the obligation to wear it, as was made clear in a revised edition he approved of the *Directory for the Ministry and the Life of Priests* published in 2013 (61): "Moreover, in its form, color, and dignity, the cassock is most opportune, because it clearly distinguishes priests from laymen and makes people understand the sacred nature of their ministry, reminding the priest himself that forever and at each moment he is a priest ordained to serve, teach, guide, and sanctify souls mainly through the celebration of the sacraments and the preaching of the Word of God. Wearing ecclesiastical attire is also a safeguard for poverty and chastity."

The priesthood is not a "job"

Pope Ratzinger offered particularly pointed reflections on the priesthood in a dialogue with priests in Saint Peter's Square on 10 June 2010, and in a homily at Mass on the following day. He started with some deeply considered observations on the theological formation of clerics: "In our time, we must know Sacred Scripture well, in order to combat the attacks of the sects. We must really be friends of the Word. We must also know the currents of our time to respond reasonably in order to give—as Saint Peter says—'reason for our faith.'" This was the impetus for his promulgation of the *motu proprio* entitled *Ministrorum Institutio,* with which he transferred the responsibility for seminaries from the Congregation for Catholic Education to the Congregation for the Clergy, which now assumed the responsibility for "the promotion and governance of all that concerns the training, life, and ministry of priests and deacons: from the pastoral care of vocations and the selection of candidates for Holy Orders, including their human, spiritual, doctrinal, and pastoral training in seminaries and in special centers for permanent deacons, to their continuing formation."

He also turned his attention to reaffirming the value of priestly celibacy: "In a certain sense, this continuous criticism against celibacy may surprise us in a time when it is becoming increasingly fashionable not to get married. But this not-getting married is something totally, fundamentally different from celibacy. The avoidance of marriage is based on a will to live only for oneself, of not accepting any definitive tie, to have the life of every moment in full autonomy, to decide at any time what to do, what to take from life; and therefore a 'no' to the bond, a 'no' to definitiveness, to have life for oneself alone. While celibacy is just the opposite: it is a definitive 'yes.' It is to let oneself be taken in the hand of God, to give oneself into the hands of the Lord, into his 'I.' And therefore, it is an act of loyalty and trust." He also offered a reflection on the lack of priestly vocations: "The temptation to take things into our own hands is great, the temptation to transform the priesthood—the Sacrament of Christ, to be chosen by him—into a normal profession, a 'job' with specific working hours, and for the rest one belongs only to oneself. If we do so, we make it just like any other vocation; we make it accessible and easy. But this is a temptation that does not solve the problem. Three points: first, each of us should strive to live his priesthood in such a way as to be convincing; secondly, we must invite, as I said before, people to join in prayer, to have this humility, this trust to speak to God forcefully, decisively; thirdly, we must have the courage to talk with young people about whether God is calling them, because often a human word is required to open one to hear the divine call."

He did not hesitate to speak sternly about the tragedy of clerical sexual abuse, which at that time had been surfacing as a painful problem in several parts of the world and had provoked bitter criticism of the Church: "It was to be expected that this new radiance of the priesthood would not be pleasing to the 'enemy'; he would have rather preferred to see it disappear, so that God would ultimately be driven out of the world. And so it happened that, in this very year of joy for the sacrament of the priesthood, the sins of priests came to light—particularly the abuse of the little ones, in which the priesthood, whose task is to manifest God's concern for our good, turns into its very opposite. We too insistently beg forgiveness from God and from the persons involved, while promising to do everything possible to ensure that such abuse will never occur again; and that in admitting men to priestly ministry and in their formation, we will do everything we can to weigh the authenticity of their vocation and make every effort to accompany priests along their journey, so that the Lord will protect them and watch over them in troubled situations and amid life's dangers."

Benedict also gratefully acknowledged and expressed his deep appreciation for the invaluable support offered by the community of the faithful for priests and their daily ministry. He particularly highlighted the spiritual motherhood of religious and lay women who offered prayers, works of penance, daily communion, and Eucharistic adoration for the sanctification of priests. This was particularly evident in a special letter issued by the Congregation for the Clergy in 2008 on the occasion of the World Day of Prayer for the Sanctification of the Clergy: "Finally, there is another form of spiritual motherhood that, throughout the history of the Church, has silently accompanied the holy order of priests: that is, the concrete entrustment of our ministry to a specific face, a consecrated soul, called by Christ, and therefore chosen to offer herself, her suffering, and the little inconveniences of life to intercede for priests, by living in the sweet presence of Christ. It is our particular prayer that such motherhood, a living reminder of the loving face of Mary, may continue in the Church, because only God can inspire and sustain it." At a general audience on 24 November 2010 dedicated to the great figure of Saint Catherine of Siena, Pope Benedict noted that "today, too, the Church receives great benefit from the exercise of spiritual motherhood by so many women, lay and consecrated, who nourish souls with thoughts of God, who strengthen the people's faith and direct Christian life towards ever loftier peaks."

Dialogue at the service of peace

Firmly committed to the teaching of the Second Vatican Council, Benedict XVI placed particular emphasis on the Church's ongoing commitment to ecumenism, interreligious dialogue, and religious freedom. Even though, after so many dedicated years, the visible unity of all Christians had not been reached (in fact, that goal had seemingly become less and less perceivable and attainable), Pope Benedict remained firmly convinced of the necessity to persist in the dialogue of love. For this reason, he dedicated much time and energy to meeting with representatives of other churches and ecclesial communities, and opportunities were constantly arranged, promoted, and pursued, all of which were already successful realizations of the ecumenical task.

He was very clear that "among Christians, fraternity is not just a vague sentiment, nor is it a sign of indifference to truth.... It is grounded in the supernatural reality of the one Baptism which makes us all members of the one Body of Christ. Together we confess that Jesus Christ is God and Lord; together we acknowledge him as the one mediator between God and man, and we emphasize that together we are members of his Body." Benedict also affirmed that "thanks precisely to this spiritual ecumenism—holiness of life, conversion of heart, private and public prayer—the common search for unity has in recent decades recorded considerable development. This has been diversified in multiple initiatives: from mutual knowledge to brotherly contact between the members of different Churches and Ecclesial Communities, from ever more friendly conversations to collaboration in various fields, from theological dialogue to the search for concrete forms of communion and collaboration."

Ratzinger was most diligent in his promotion of interreligious dialogue, since "for the Church, dialogue between the followers of the different religions represents an important means of cooperating with all religious communities for the common good," and "the Church herself rejects nothing of what is true and holy in the various religions." Speaking as a former Prefect of the Congregation for the Doctrine of the Faith, Ratzinger unequivocally stated that "the path to take is not the way of relativism or religious syncretism. The Church, in fact, proclaims, and is in duty bound to proclaim without fail, Christ who is 'the way, the truth and the life,' in whom man must seek the fullness of religious life and by whom God has reconciled all things to himself." "God reconciled all things to himself, people find the fullness of the religious life. Yet this in no way excludes dialogue and the common pursuit of truth in different areas of life, since, as Saint Thomas Aquinas would say, 'every truth, whoever utters it, comes from the Holy Spirit.'"

A privileged moment in Benedict's task of promoting interreligious dialogue occurred in Assisi in October of 2011, when he invited representatives of Christian churches, other religions, and notable agnostics, to send a clear message about the irrevocable commitment of all people of goodwill to promoting peace in the world, thus giving public witness to the inseverable bond between religion and peace and the complete rejection of violence. The occasion was the twenty-fifth anniversary of the World Day of Prayer for Peace, launched by John Paul II in 1986 to manifest religion's role in the promotion of unity and peace and the rejection of division and conflict. Benedict ardently wished that by commemorating this occasion, the world might recapture the memory of that experience insofar as it "gives reason to hope for a future in which all believers will see themselves, and will actually be, agents of justice and peace." Looking back on Benedict XVI's pontificate, we see that the destination of his last apostolic voyage—Lebanon, the cornerstone of the Middle East—was yet another key indication in his enduring concern for peace, as he brought hope to the many men, women, and children suffering from terrorism, and made an impassioned appeal for peace in this battered region.

The pontiff was no less interested in promoting intercultural dialogue, which he believed was of primary importance in strengthening the relationship between culture and religion, as he affirmed in December of 2008 in a letter for the occasion of a study day on "Culture and Religions in Dialogue": "In today's context, in which our contemporaries ask themselves ever more often the essential questions on the meaning of life and its value, it appears more important than ever to reflect on the ancient roots from which abundant sap has flowed in the course of centuries. The theme of intercultural and interreligious dialogue, therefore, is emerging as a priority for the European Union and transversally concerns the sectors of culture and communication, of education and science, of migration and of minorities, reaching as far as the sectors of youth and of work. Once diversity has been accepted as a positive factor, it is necessary to ensure that people not only accept the existence of other cultures but also desire to be enriched by them."

Free to live one's faith

Pope Ratzinger, in addition to numerous behind-the-scenes initiatives to promote religions liberty, made several unequivocal and courageous public speeches, clearly asserting, "Religious freedom is not the exclusive patrimony of believers, but of the whole family of the earth's peoples. It is an essential element of a constitutional state; it cannot be denied without at the same time encroaching on all fundamental rights and freedoms, since it is their synthesis and keystone." Similarly, in January of 2011, he deplored the fact that "Christians are the religious group which suffers most from persecution on account of its faith. Many Christians experience daily affronts and often live in fear because of their pursuit of truth, their faith in Jesus Christ and their heartfelt plea for respect for religious freedom. This situation is unacceptable, since it represents an insult to God and to human dignity; furthermore, it is a threat to security and peace, and an obstacle to the achievement of authentic and integral human development,"

We also cannot forget the weighty letter to Catholics in the People's Republic of China, written in the third year of his pontificate, in which he expressed his sense of "the urgent need, as my deep and compelling duty and as an expression of my paternal love, to confirm the faith of Chinese Catholics and favor their unity with the means proper to the Church." Benedict clearly states that "the solution to existing problems cannot be pursued via an ongoing conflict with the legitimate civil authorities; at the same time, though, compliance with those authorities is not acceptable when they interfere unduly in matters regarding the faith and discipline of the Church," and he specifically asked the Chinese governmental authorities "to guarantee to those same Catholic citizens the full exercise of their faith, with respect for authentic religious freedom." Sadly, this letter did not receive the attention it deserved when first published, but it still stands as a beautiful witness to Benedict's pastoral character, that even while he considered his primary *munus* to be "Bishop of Rome," he never lost sight of the universality of the Church and the need of feeding and caring for the entire flock.

Among the Church's many initiatives to promote peace, Ratzinger kept his sights on an abiding care for creation, incorporating integral ecology into his teaching: "Since faith in the Creator is an essential part of the Christian creed, the Church cannot and must not limit herself to passing on to the faithful the message of salvation alone. She has a responsibility towards creation, and must also publicly assert this responsibility. In so doing, she must not only defend earth, water, and air as gifts of creation belonging to all. She must also protect man from self-destruction. What is needed is something like a human ecology, correctly understood." At the root of such a human ecology is the awareness "that integral human development is closely linked to the obligations that flow from man's relationship with the natural environment. The environment must be seen as God's gift to all people, and the use we make of it entails a shared responsibility for all humanity, especially the poor and future generations."

At the same time, Benedict XVI clearly conceived an integral human ecology as necessarily entailing a hierarchy of values: "A correct understanding of the relationship between man and the environment will not end by absolutizing nature or by considering it more important than the human person. If the Church's magisterium expresses grave misgivings about notions of the environment inspired by ecocentrism and biocentrism, it is because such notions eliminate the difference of identity and worth between the human person and other living things. In the name of a supposedly egalitarian vision of the 'dignity' of all living creatures, such notions end up abolishing the distinctiveness and superior role of human beings. They also open the way to a new pantheism tinged with neo-paganism, which would see the source of man's salvation in nature alone, understood in purely naturalistic terms. The Church, for her part, is concerned that the question be approached in a balanced way, with respect for the 'grammar' which the Creator has inscribed in his handiwork by giving man the role of a steward and administrator with responsibility over creation, a role which man must certainly not abuse, but also one which he may not abdicate."

Between politics and culture

Throughout his pontificate, Benedict XVI was constantly meeting with political and cultural leaders from nations and international organizations from the world over. This led him to dedicate much of his thinking to the political and juridical order, an arena of the most fundamental questions facing society today, as well as the relationship between faith and reason, laws and rights, and justice and religious liberty.

One of the most significant speeches he gave in this regard was to the General Assembly of the United Nations in New York on 18 April 2008, in which he commended the UN's efforts to safeguard human rights, especially as they developed in the wake of World War II with the Universal Declaration published in 1948. Referring to the founding principles of the United Nations—the desire for peace, the commitment to justice, the respect for the dignity of the human person, the coordination of efforts to relieve human suffering—he noted that these express "the just aspirations of the human spirit, and constitute the ideals which should underpin international relations." He emphasized that a respect for human rights and efforts to ensure them "serve to evaluate the relationship between justice and injustice, development and poverty, security and conflict. The promotion of human rights remains the most effective strategy for eliminating inequalities between countries and social groups, and for increasing security."

Pope Benedict assured his own personal involvement in these commitments, affirming that "the United Nations remains a privileged setting in which the Church is committed to contributing her experience 'of humanity,' developed over the centuries among peoples of every race and culture, and placing it at the disposal of all members of the international community." He further stated that "this experience and activity, directed towards attaining freedom for every believer, seeks also to increase the protection given to the rights of the person. Those rights are grounded and shaped by the transcendent nature of the person, which permits men and women to pursue their journey of faith and their search for God in this world. Recognition of this dimension must be strengthened if we are to sustain humanity's hope for a better world and if we are to create the conditions for peace, development, cooperation, and guarantee of rights for future generations."

A few months later, in a speech to representatives from the world of culture at the Collège des Bernardins in Paris on 12 September 2008—an audience generally considered secularist or indifferent toward religion—

Benedict described the contribution made by the Christian faith to the development of European civilization, particularly in its power to purify reason and strengthen civil society in the wake of the barbarian invasions that resulted in a collapse of the old world order and the securities it provided. The pope turned particularly to the example of the Order of Saint Benedict, which was keenly dedicated to promoting the search for God by utilizing ancient wisdom and the natural sciences: copying manuscripts, teaching grammar, building libraries, managing schools—all of these were central activities to the Western monastic tradition. In addition to promoting the cultivation of literacy, they also promoted a culture of work, without which the development of Europe, its *ethos,* and its influence on the world would have been unthinkable.

But Ratzinger went even deeper, explaining that there was a specific objective to their mission—namely, *quaerere Deum* (seeking God). "Amid the confusion of the times, in which nothing seemed permanent, they wanted to do the essential—to make an effort to find what was perennially valid and lasting, life itself. They were searching for God. They wanted to go from the inessential to the essential, to the only truly important and reliable thing there is." Their challenge was this: "[T]o seek God and to let oneself be found by him, that is today no less necessary than in former times. A purely positivistic culture which tried to drive the question concerning God into the subjective realm, as being unscientific, would be the capitulation of reason, the renunciation of its highest possibilities, and hence a disaster for humanity, with very grave consequences. What gave Europe's culture its foundation—the search for God and the readiness to listen to him—remains today the basis of any genuine culture."

During his apostolic journey to the United Kingdom in 2010, Pope Benedict XVI delivered a speech on September 17th to representatives of British society in the halls of the oldest parliamentary body among democratic Western nations. His words still find resonance among those with a deep appreciation for the democratic liberal tradition, even though he spoke unambiguously about his concern for the preservation of an authentic religious liberty in the West, which was still vulnerable to subtle forms of manipulation: "[T]he world of reason and the world of faith—the world of secular rationality and the world of religious belief—need one another and should not be afraid to enter into a profound and ongoing dialogue, for the good of our civilization. Religion, in other words, is not a problem for legislators to solve, but a vital contributor to the national conversation."

Benedict therefore took the opportunity to clear up a grave misunderstanding in today's culture about the role of Christianity and the Catholic Church in public debate. It is often thought that by intervening in public discussions about the common good, the Catholic Church appeals to some privileged "principle of authority" about the decisions that need to be made in the realms of law and politics. But the view Benedict proposes neither allows the faithful to stay out of the fray, nor to bracket their use of reason, entrenching themselves within the walls of religious precepts and commands. In his strong conviction that the divine, as *logos,* can be encountered in the rational search for truth, Benedict XVI did not hesitate to recall the fact that the ultimate sources of law are to be found in reason and nature, not in a baseless command, whatever it may be.

Finally, in a speech he gave at the Reichstag Building in Berlin on 22 September 2011 during his apostolic journey to Germany, Benedict XVI hit the root of the question when he touched upon the topic of the foundation of the juridical order and the limits of legal positivism, which had become the dominant twentieth-century legal theory across Europe. Explaining how it is that we can come to know what is just, he said that "in history, systems of law have almost always been based on religion: decisions regarding what was to be lawful among men were taken with reference to the divinity. Unlike other great religions, Christianity has never proposed a revealed law to the State and to society, that is to say a juridical order derived from revelation. Instead, it has pointed to nature and reason as the true sources of law—and to the harmony of objective and subjective reason, which naturally presupposes that both spheres are rooted in the creative reason of God."

This passage reiterates the originality inherent in Christianity that influences political thinking: "Politics must be a striving for justice, and hence it has to establish the fundamental preconditions for peace. Naturally, a politician will seek success, without which he would have no opportunity for effective political action at all. Yet success is subordinated to the criterion of justice, to the will to do what is right, and to the understanding of what is right.... To serve right and to fight against the dominion of wrong is and remains the fundamental task of the politician. At a moment in history when man has acquired previously inconceivable power, this task takes on a particular urgency."

Quoting the pope out of context

In his book *The Vatican Diaries,* American journalist John Thavis makes a particularly striking remark: "So, when Pope Benedict strolled back for his flying press conference above the Sahara Desert, the coach class buzzed with excitement. This is what our companies were paying the big bucks for—access to the man in white. This is where our expertise as *Vaticanisti* would pay off, in prodding the pontiff on tough issues and interpreting his unrehearsed answers.... In years past, backpedaling on a pope's verbal miscues was easy because, quite simply, journalists couldn't file their stories until the plane landed several hours later. But the Alitalia 777 was equipped with phones, and the genie was already out of the bottle."[7]

Thavis gives us a snapshot of one of those delicate moments in the relationship between Pope Ratzinger and the press, as the *Vaticanisti* would snoop for any piece of news that would really stir things up in a quick tweet or blog post, something that might explode into a polarizing argument, and grip the public's attention for days if not weeks. This could be accomplished by extrapolating a single quote out of its layered context or giving no background at all to the larger argument, thus provoking quick, spontaneous reactions that are typical of our short-term, around-the-clock news cycle. The obvious result was that anyone who felt he had the authority—be it in good or bad faith—to impulsively express a criticism, often had to retract it later once the larger picture became clear.

A prime example of this occurred during the journey to Cameroon and Angola in March of 2009, when, during the flight from Rome

7 John Thavis, *The Vatican Diaries: A Behind-the-Scenes Look at the Power, Personalities and Politics at the Heart of the Catholic Church* (Viking, 2013), pp. 37–38.

to Yaoundé, a French reporter posed the following question: "Your Holiness, among the many ills that beset Africa, one of the most pressing is the spread of AIDS. The position of the Catholic Church on the way to fight it is often considered unrealistic and ineffective. Will you address this theme during the journey?" Benedict courageously tackled the question at once, arguing that "the most efficient, most truly present player in the fight against AIDS is the Catholic Church herself." He went on: "I would say that this problem of AIDS cannot be overcome merely with money, necessary though it is … the problem cannot be overcome by the distribution of prophylactics: on the contrary, they increase it."

Unsurprisingly, the headlines read as follows: "Pope in Africa: Prophylactics are useless" (*Corriere della Sera*); "A 'No' to prophylactics in the fight against AIDS" (*La Repubblica*); "Benedict XVI challenges the effectiveness of prophylactics" (*Le Monde*); "The Pope says that prophylactics are not the way to fight the spread of HIV" (*New York Times*), and so on. There was no space, of course, to elaborate on the twofold solution he proposed: "[F]irstly, bringing out the human dimension of sexuality, that is to say a spiritual and human renewal that would bring with it a new way of behaving towards others, and secondly, true friendship offered above all to those who are suffering, a willingness to make sacrifices and to practice self-denial, to be alongside the suffering." In fact, the pope had based his reasoning on solid scientific and sociological research, as a respectable British journal, *The Lancet,* had pointed out in an article published in January of 2000: "There are three ways that a substantial increase in condom use could nevertheless fail to reduce disease transmission: First, condom promotion appeals more strongly to risk-averse individuals who contribute little to epidemic transmission. Second, increased condom use will increase the number of transmissions that result from condom failure. Third, there is a risk-compensation mechanism: increased condom use could reflect decisions of individuals to switch from inherently safer strategies of partner selection or fewer partners to the riskier strategy of developing or maintaining higher rates of partner change plus reliance on condoms."[8]

8 John Richens, John Imrie, and Andrew Copas, "Condoms and Seat Belts: The Parallels and the Lessons," *The Lancet* 355 (2000): 400–403.

Controversies and misunderstandings

There are several other examples of knee-jerk reactions to statements made by Benedict XVI—reactions characterized by opinions that had to be modified or abandoned once the pope's arguments were considered more carefully and in proper context. Perhaps the most memorable of these occurred on 12 September 2006, when Pope Benedict visited the *Aula Magna* of the University of Regensburg, where he had taught dogmatic theology and the history of dogma from 1969 to 1977, and served as vice president of the university. He was overjoyed at the invitation to give a *lectio magistralis* on the topic of "Faith, Reason, and the University: Memories and Reflections" on 12 September 2006. I remember how diligently he prepared for the event and considered it a truly academic lecture with the intent of clarifying how necessary it was for Europe to rediscover its Christian roots.

The drama revolved around a citation the pope had made in his lecture: "Show me just what Mohammed brought that was new, and there you will find things only evil and inhuman, such as his command to spread by the sword the faith he preached." The passage is, in fact, a quote from Emperor Manuel II in the fourteenth-century correspondence he had with an educated Persian on the subject of Christianity and Islam. Regrettably, it was taken out of context and framed it as a personal affirmation of Benedict XVI himself, thus raising unnecessary political turmoil. There were protests in some Islamic countries, some resulting in the death of innocent people. To help quell the violence, two clarifications were made by the Holy See, one by press secretary Fr. Lombardi, and the other by the Secretary of State, Cardinal Bertone. In any case, no one who had read the text in advance suggested the pope change it, simply because the context in which it had been placed was clear enough.

Once the storm had passed and the waters had calmed, many Islamic scholars read the text in its entirety and even affirmed the pope's line of reasoning. A few months were needed for things to settle down, but once they did a letter signed by 138 Muslim scholars and 43 leaders of nations was sent to Benedict emphasizing the importance of a sincere and mutually respectful dialogue, and, as a sign that there were no long-term injuries to mutual goodwill, King Abdullah of Saudi Arabia made a historic visit to the Vatican on 6 November 2007, the first ever by a Saudi monarch, someone who is also recognized as the supreme religious guardian of the two sacred mosques in Mecca and Medina.

Another academic venue—this time, the Sapienza University in Rome—misunderstood Benedict to the extent authorities cancelled a proposed *lectio magistralis* before the pope could even deliver it. The visit was scheduled for 17 January 2008. In fact, preparations for the visit had been underway for a long time; the official invitation from the Rector, Renato Guarini, was received by the Vatican on 17 March 2006, and the visit was scheduled to coincide with the completion of the renovation of the university's stunning baroque chapel.

The controversy broke out when it was announced to the academic senate on 23 October 20017 that the pope would deliver a *lectio magistralis.* Even though the rector clarified on the following November 13th that the pope would only give a speech, and the *lectio magistralis* would be delivered by Professor Mario Caravale on the topic of the death penalty, a group of teachers from the physics department asked that the event be cancelled, the motive being that Ratzinger, in a speech he had given on 15 March 1990, had cited the following affirmation by Feyerabend: "At the time of Galileo, the Church remained much more faithful to reason than Galileo himself. The trial against Galileo was reasonable and just."

In several ways, it was practically a repeat of what had happened in Regensburg, for as university chaplain Fr. Vincenzo D'Addamo explained, at the conference where Ratzinger gave this speech dedicated to the topic of "The Church and Modernity," the scholar "did not share the opinion of the author he cited. Rather, he wanted to explain the implications of the changes in the cultural paradigm at various stages in the modern period for the Church, and he wanted to consider the Church's image at those various historical moments, both within and outside of ecclesiastical circles. This was the context in which the speaker quoted Feyerabend and his controversial judgment on 'modernity' and 'reasonableness,' and on the Church's actions toward Galileo."

In any case, Benedict preferred not to attend the event in person and sent his written text, which was then read in the *aula magna* by the pro-Rector for social activities, Piero Marietti. I would also take a moment here to respond peacefully to Carlo Cosmelli, one of the physicists who signed the letter, and who provocatively asked if the pope would have delivered the same speech if he had come in person: "Yes, I would not have changed a single iota!" But Benedict was indeed disappointed—more for the fact that he missed being welcomed at such a historical cultural center that had been founded by one of his predecessors, Pope Boniface VIII (who established it as the *Studium Urbis* on 20 April 1303), than for the intellectual narrow-mindedness of the scholars who, in fact, demanded the *cancellation* of a speech that was effectively merely a cancellation of academic freedom.

A misunderstood reconciliation

Yet another example of a regrettable misunderstanding regards the controversy surrounding the removal of the excommunication of four bishops who had been consecrated by Archbishop Marcel Lefèbvre without a pontifical mandate. The pope made this gesture of goodwill precisely to overcome an impasse in negotiations between the Holy See and the Priestly Fraternity of Saint Pius X.

As Prefect of the Congregation for the Doctrine of the Faith, Cardinal Ratzinger had been engaged in a lengthy dialogue with Archbishop Lefèbvre. The two of them had, in fact, signed a working agreement on 5 May 1988, but on the following day the French cleric changed his mind and proceeded with the episcopal ordination of four men—Bernard Fellay, Bernard Tissier de Mallerais, Richard Williamson, and Alfonso de Galarreta—thus causing all to fall into excommunication *latae sententae* reserved to the Apostolic See (this is the punishment incurred automatically after one transgresses an ecclesiastical law, without any need to pronounce the excommunication explicitly).

After further talks, Monsignor Bernard Fellay, superior general of the fraternity, sent a letter on 15 December 2008 to Cardinal Darío Castrillón Hoyos, President of the Pontifical Commission *Ecclesia Dei.* In the letter, Monsignor Fellay stated that "we continue firmly resolute in our desire to remain Catholics and to put all our strength at the service of the Church of our Lord Jesus Christ, which is the Roman Catholic Church. We accept her teachings in a filial spirit. We firmly believe in the primacy of Peter and in his prerogatives, and for this reason the current situation causes us much suffering." Subsequently, in a gesture of goodwill, Benedict XVI decided to reconsider the canonical situation of the four excommunicated bishops and remitted the penalty of excommunication *latae sententiae.*

To fully understand what happened, however, it is necessary to consider the timeline as reconstructed by Cardinal Castrillón: "On 14 January 2009, I received the decree approved by the Holy Father and signed by Cardinal Re. I handed the letter over to Monsignor Fellay at my house on January 17th, asking him to inform the other three bishops of the fraternity. So, at that time only they knew that, on January 21st, they would be freed from the excommunication, and they were asked to keep it a secret until the 24th when the decree would be officially published."

But on January 20th, the German weekly magazine *Der Spiegel* published a declaration that Monsignor Williamson gave to a Swedish journalist on 1 November 2008 (which was then included in a broadcast by Sveriges Television on the evening of January 21st), in which the bishop denied that Jews were killed in gas chambers during the Holocaust. The controversy spread like wildfire, and there were certainly communication errors at the Vatican that coincided with the declaration. Specifically, the declaration gave an imprecise explanation of the remission of the excommunication, which only had an ecclesial value and did not bear on other aspects of the matter. More importantly, it did not clearly state that Benedict and I were not aware of Fellay's statement regarding the Jews (indeed, there was such a long delay before it was broadcast, it was as if the television station were waiting for the right moment).

Moreover, Castrillón had communicated to Benedict and Bertone that Williamson was very sick with cancer and that he would die within a short time, for which reason he sped up the process in order to grant the remission of the excommunication as quickly as possible. The news ended up being false and raised other flags at the Vatican. But even within the fraternity, the presence of a holocaust-denying bishop could not have been considered something to be wished. So it was that on 24 October 2012, the bishop was formally "declared expelled from the Fraternity by a decision from the Superior General and of his Counsel."

With his usual graciousness, Benedict decided to try to mend the misunderstanding, and he bore the responsibility on his own shoulders. There was a meeting at which we had a long discussion, and some of us maintained that whoever had not given the situation the attention it deserved should ultimately accept rebuke over the matter. But Benedict did not want anyone to conclude that he was hiding something from his collaborators, so he went to his study and wrote a personal letter in his own name that was then published on 10 March 2009, containing the admission that "the quiet gesture of extending a hand gave rise to a huge uproar, and thus became exactly the opposite of a gesture of reconciliation, is a fact which we must accept."

At the same time, Pope Benedict wished to express his sadness that "even Catholics who, after all, might have had a better knowledge of the situation, thought they had to attack me with open hostility," and, citing a passage from Saint Paul—"Do not use your freedom as an opportunity for the flesh, but through love be servants of one another" (Gal 5:15)—he offered this confession: "I am always tempted to see these words as another of the rhetorical excesses which we occasionally find in Saint Paul. To some extent that may also be the case. But sad to say, this 'biting and devouring' also exists in the Church today, as an expression of a poorly understood freedom."

7
The Landmark Renunciation That Marked an Age

The reasons for the decision

Paraphrasing the famous verse from Dante, "Galeotto was the book and he who wrote it" (*Inferno* V, 136), one might say instead, "Galeotto was the World Cup and he who announced it." Let me explain myself. On 30 October 2007, FIFA designated Brazil the sponsors of the World Cup of Soccer to be held in 2014. When on 21 August 2011 in Madrid, at the end of the 26th World Youth Day, Benedict noted the fact that the location of the next occurrence of the event would be in Rio de Janeiro, he specified that he thought it fitting to schedule the 27th World Youth Day earlier—meaning it would take place in 2013 instead of according to the triennial cycle—so as to avoid the coincidence of these two well-attended events.

One might accept or deny the pope's conviction but—and I say this carefully to clear the air of any equivocation—it was precisely the question of his personal participation in that World Youth Day that triggered reflection on his part, which little by little intensified with respect to the continuation of his pontificate. The joy he witnessed in the eyes of so many young men and women present on the clearing of Madrid's Cuatros Vientos Airport for the prayer vigil and holy Mass had indeed indelibly settled his certainty that a meeting of the youth without the physical presence of the pontiff would have been like being there but without arms.

The vision of that great number of people burned in his eyes and mind (calculated to be around two million), singing and inciting him even while standing under a terrible storm. At a certain point his white *zuchetto* flew off his head and the downpour soaked him so much that his red shoes bled through to his feet. Yet when a cardinal urged me to ask him to leave and take shelter, he answered me firmly, "I'm staying!" And then out loud he said smiling to the young people gathered: "In the rain the Lord sends you an abundance of blessings!"

In Madrid, Pope Ratzinger made his own thoughts explicitly clear in the final greeting, in which he referred to the next meeting in Rio, and he invoked the Lord asking that he might make smooth "the way of all young people in the world that they may meet again with the pope in the beautiful Brazilian city." I am therefore quite convinced that were the date confirmed, as it should have been, for 2014, Benedict would not have allowed himself to dwell on his physical and mental weariness in the course of 2012, but would have steadily advanced throughout the year 2013.

It may be insightful to document certain statements he made at the beginning of 2012. During the consistory of 18 February, Benedict asks in his speech for prayers, "that I may continually offer to the People of God the witness of sound doctrine and guide holy Church with a firm and humble hand." These words in no way seem to be hiding any premonition of abdication. On 16 April, the day of his eighty-fifth birthday, he greeted his Bavarian compatriots and expressed legitimate concern over his advanced age. "I find myself facing the last leg of the way of the course of my life, and I do not know what awaits me." From the meeting with Fidel Castro on 28 March, who was practically the same age but decidedly more run-down (he died in fact in 2016 at the age of ninety) we have reports of the pope's candid remark: "I'm old, but I can still do my job."

Unfortunately, during his apostolic visits to Mexico and Cuba—between 23 and 29 March 2012—he was made suddenly aware of just how much his strength was consistently diminishing, imposing on him a serious reflection regarding his immediate future. The pastoral visit had indeed gone very well, but because of the exuberance of the people during the many public meetings (even apart from all the various private events), the trip was clearly very taxing for a man now eighty-five years old, especially considering the noteworthy time change and the discomforts of travel by car and airplane.

Furthermore, in Mexico the pope tripped on a rug while in the bathroom shaving and fell on his shoulder, hitting his head on the shower door upon raising himself. He did not lose consciousness or experience any acute problems, but a few stitches were needed for the wound. The medication did not stop the bleeding, such that Monsignor Guido Marini was compelled not to remove the pope's *zuchetto* at the moment in the liturgy that required it because it covered the stained gauze underneath (This happened during the Mass celebrated at the "Parque del Bicentenario" of León). Many thought the master of ceremonies was distracted!

Returning to the Vatican, Doctor Polisca was firm in his counsel against any additional transatlantic travel, and suggested he only undertake excursions that were much less demanding. Benedict took this proscription seriously, broadening his own meditation with respect to other aspects of his pontifical ministry as well. He also spoke often with his personal doctor to better understand the possible trajectory of his health issues.

As I learned later, he had already hinted to Cardinal Bertone in an audience on 30 April 2012 of his idea to abdicate the Petrine ministry, but there were no immediate developments. On that occasion the Secretary of State left the meeting and asked me, vaguely: "The pope said something strange to me regarding his weariness and fear of not being able to continue. Has he spoken to you of this as well?" I answered that I knew nothing and yet I was not particularly struck by these words. In the meantime the so-called Vatileaks broke in the news and our thoughts were overwhelmed by the concerns relating to this affair, and at the same time those questions stemming from the controversies surrounding the Institute for the Works of Religion, on top of the news of the pedophile scandals among the clergy.

Between 30 May and 3 June, we were in Milan for the 7th World Meeting of Families and here too the atmosphere was quite festive, which pressed Benedict deeper into his reflection on the need for the pope's physical presence among the faithful. I must, however, contradict an alleged account of Jesuit Silvano Fausti with respect to the meeting on 2 June in the archbishopric of Milan between the pope and Cardinal Carlo Maria Martini, who was gravely ill with Parkinson's and died the following 31 August. According to Fausti, Martini mentioned problems in the Vatican Curia and suggested that Benedict remove himself: "Now is the time, you know, for at this point one is able to do anything." I remember that day well. The cardinal was seated in a wheelchair and in a terrible state, practically unable to speak—from his throat emerged only indistinguishable sounds. It was essentially an encounter that lasted a few minutes between just the two, but there was no real dialogue, as the pope himself told me. Unfortunately, there was no possibility to confront the veracity of this story given Fausti's death on 24 June 2015, and the interview containing these views was rendered only on 15 July 2015 online.[9]

During that time I began to notice an unusual tension in Benedict. Particularly after celebrating Mass in the chapel, I noticed him very concentrated on prayer during his time of thanksgiving. On the kneeler he dropped his head in his hands and almost seemed to collapse in on himself, a posture that was foreign to his normal style. He normally held a more composed and rigid posture. I attributed these marks of disquiet to the difficulties of the moment, and when we left for Castel Gandolfo on 3 July, I had thought as well that this was related to the mental effort exerted as he completed the third part of his book on Jesus, which covered the period of his infancy and childhood.

In the second half of August, I began to see him more peaceful, but at the close of the month an alarm bell sounded in me, for Cardinal Bertone, at the end of his audience, once again hinted to me the fact that the pope had spoken with greater concreteness about his feelings of strain and fatigue. The Secretary of State did not elaborate further because even he did not know what to think. In his autobiography he describes that moment in this way: "It was quite hard to believe that he really would make such a decision and, with respect but emphasis, I presented him with a series of arguments that I thought were foundational for the good of the Church and for warding off general depression among the People of God before their good Shepherd."

Our definitive return to Rome was scheduled for 1 October, and the week prior the time came for him to tell me as well. I remember it perfectly. On September 25th after breakfast, he asked me to come by a bit earlier than our usual morning meeting—when we looked through mail and discussed the events of that day—and I expected he wanted to talk to me about something important. This had happened other times before,

9 Accessed at: www.glistatigenerali.com.

for example when there was some matter that required direct and specific attention. Yet as always, I was not overly anxious by such a request.

When I took a seat in front of him, I could see that his face was at once both serious and serene. Then without mincing words, he said to me: "I have reflected, I have prayed, and I have come to the conclusion that, on account of my diminishing strength, I must renounce the Petrine office." Impromptu, I reacted with my heart: "Holy Father, if your strength is no longer enough, you can lessen the responsibilities of work, the appointments during the course of the day can be rearranged, more delegation and less concentrating for you."

With mildness, he articulated the bare bones summary of his reasons, revealing to me just how long and with what scruple he had dwelled upon every aspect. I immediately understood that any attempt on my part to convince him otherwise would have been in vain. By now I knew Benedict deeply and I knew well that when he made a decision—particularly in that case, after intense prayer and meditation—he was determined to see it through.

The first point he brought to my attention was precisely relating to World Youth Day, and I tried to tell him that with big screens and internet connections his constant presence would be possible in real time, guessing that regardless nearly all the participants would be following *via* video footage in Rio as well, given the extensive grounds and massive number of people expected. But I was not able to overcome his sense of importance in knowing that the pope was physically among them, rather than his being placed in the Vatican and appearing only virtually.

Benedict then asked me to think about John Paul II, who himself died at almost eighty-five years of age, and he emphasized: "I have already been pope as long as he was pope in his illness and I do not want to end as he did. On the whole, what I have been able to do I have done, for the Church my abdication would be better, with an election of a younger and more vigorous pontiff. This is the right moment, the problems of recent months have subsided, I can pass the helm to another without too much difficulty."

In fact, one of his obvious concerns was avoiding any one of his collaborators rushing into pockets of power, well aware of how things had gone with Pope Wojtyła at the end of his pontificate, who was never able to maintain full control of the reigns of governance. At that time Ratzinger had been kept outside the sphere of play, but he had witnessed how in substance the main Vatican proponents had gained more and more influence, and at times even competed with each other for it—apart from his personal secretary, Don Stanislaus, and Secretary of State Sodano, there were the Substitute Leonardi Sandri and the Prefect for the Congregation of Bishops, Giovanni Battista Re, and in the Italian sphere the president of the Italian Bishops Conference, Camillo Ruini. In 2012, there was already chatter surrounding the power that Bertone and I would have begun to wield, and that is when Benedict intended to break it off at the source.

In secret, small steps

Benedict's original idea was to communicate his abdication at the end of his audience with the Roman Curia when he extended his Christmas greetings, which that year was scheduled for 21 December, and herein he would declare the last day of his pontificate to be 25 January 2013, the feast-day of the conversion of Saint Paul. When halfway through October he informed me of this, I replied: "Holy Father, permit me to tell you that if you were to do so no one would celebrate Christmas this year, neither in the Vatican nor anywhere else. It would be like a sheet of ice over a garden in bloom."

On 11 October 2012, in the fiftieth anniversary of the opening of Second Vatican Council, the Year of Faith was inaugurated, which would be concluded 24 November 2013. For the occasion, Pope Ratzinger had sent a draft of an encyclical written on the theme of faith, and in those days he was also editing the manuscript of his volume on the infancy of Jesus, in sight of its release in bookstores on 21 November. Therefore, discussing things with Cardinal Bertone, we came to the agreement that with respect to the abdication, though having undertaken all possible approaches, we were no longer able to move him to change his mind, whereas at least in what concerned the date of his announcement there was an understanding of the merits of moving it to the following year.

Benedict understood our reasons and in the end chose 11 February, a Vatican holiday commemorating the Lateran Pact between Italy and the Holy See, on which day there was already planned a so-called "white" consistory for the announcement of several canonizations. (A "red" consistory is instead intended for the creation of new cardinals.) In addition to this, it was also the memorial of the blessed Virgin Mary of Lourdes and on that day in the sanctuary at Altötting, a place very dear to him, the World Day of the Sick would be celebrated. Spiritually, then, the pope likewise expressed his feeling of closeness to those living "a difficult moment of trial through infirmity and suffering," as he wrote in the message given for that occasion, associating himself with their own hardships.

The liturgical timing was also favorable, for in two days it would be Ash Wednesday and on this recurring holy day he was able to celebrate his last public Mass, leading one to grasp once again the heart of his message: what matters most in ecclesial life is conversion to Jesus Christ and orienting oneself toward Christ's Easter of Resurrection, without which Christianity would be rendered meaningless. Hence, from 15–23 February Lenten spiritual exercises would be conducted for the Roman Curia, which allowed everyone a "buffer" or "moment to digest" both within and on the outside. Cardinal Gianfranco Ravasi was to preach, and it was decided that he should be informed in time for this such that he would be able to prepare meditations appropriate for the circumstances.

In the last week prior to the abdication, Benedict informed members of the pontifical household. On 5 February, he met with the second secretary, Monsignor Xuereb, who in an interview remembered the encounter in this way: "Pope Benedict invited me to make myself comfortable in his study and he declared to me the enormous decision of his abdication. For me in that moment it was almost spontaneous, my desire was to ask him, 'But why not think about it for a bit?' But then I caught myself since I was convinced that he had prayed about it at length." On the same day at a separate time he told Sister Birgit, whereas he spoke to the Memores on 7 February. It was for everyone certainly an emotionally packed moment.

Among the few others to be made aware—apart, obviously, from his brother, Georg—were Monsignor Guido Marini, Master of Pontifical Liturgical Ceremonies, and Father Federico Lombardi, Director of the

Holy See Press Office. Both received this news from Cardinal Bertone in order to set preparations in motion for the a consistory, and to be ready to deal with the anticipated onslaught of journalists.

Naturally, Cardinal Sodano, Dean of the College of Cardinals, was also informed. The pontiff met with him in person on 8 February and gave him the news. Contrary to what some journalists have hypothesized, the text read by the dean in the *Sala Clementina*—read as a response to the declaration of abdication—was not coordinated with Benedict's own speech (and much less was it written directly by the pope). It was not Sodano's habit to submit his speeches for review in advance, a practice that was on the whole similar to that of Ratzinger with John Paul II when the former was dean of the college.

Benedict had begun to pen his draft of the text to be read at the consistory at the end of January. His decision to do so in Latin was clear, for this has always been the language of all official documents of the Catholic Church. The formulation of his abdication was finalized by the pope on 7 February. I personally carried this paper to Cardinal Bertone's apartment, where we read it together with Monsignor Giampiero Gloder, coordinator of editing the pontifical texts in the Secretariat of State. Slight orthographic corrections were suggested and certain juridical precisions made, and a definitive text was ready for Sunday, 10 February, when the other translations of the text commenced—including in the Italian, French, English, German, Spanish, Portuguese, and Polish.

The extreme secrecy with which the text was put together involved very few people. As is obvious, a certain linguistical competency often gifts the ability to read a foreign language and understand its nuances. There is not always a likewise, perfect rendering of that language, particularly when there is not constant practice. Therefore, in attempting to give a harmonious flow from Latin construction, no one noticed that there were some words not in agreement with the Latin. For example, the accusative *commissum* linked to the dative *ministerio* instead of *commisso* in the sentence, "declaro me *ministerio* Episcopi Romae, Successoris Sancti Petri, mihi per manus cardinalium die 19 aprilis MMV *commissum*" ("I declare that I renounce the ministry of Bishop of Rome, Successor of Saint Peter, entrusted to me by the cardinals on 19 April 2005").

Through hasty typing, the first version issued by the press office added two more errors, and the press office quickly made fixes to the Vatican website in the early afternoon of 11 February—namely, *pro Ecclesia vita* was changed back to *pro Ecclesia vitae* ("for the life of the Church") and the time *20:00 hors* replaced *29:00 hors.* Yet these mistakes were not on the paper that Benedict held in his hands, and later a video review revealed that both were indeed correctly given orally.

In reality, a letter of abdication signed by Benedict already existed, which had changed from those drawn up by Paul VI and John Paul II. (It is worth noting a declaration of then-Cardinal Ratzinger, in April of 2002 in the *Münchner Kirchenzeitung,* the weekly diocesan newsletter of Munich and Frisinga: "If Pope Wojtyła had seen himself absolutely unable to carry on, then he would surely abdicate.") In 2006, Benedict signed a declaration wherein he expressed beforehand the desire to abdicate in the event his physical or mental state rendered him unfit to be pope, consenting that at such a time this written request would be divulged and the Apostolic See would be free to set in motion a pontifical succession.

To give evidence of the legitimacy of this course of action there was a letter from an old friend and doctor, who brought attention to his health problems and the risk of a repeated attack, for which reason he suggested it would be a gesture of responsibility to provide some explicit indication in this regard. In this case, too, Benedict prepared a personal written note, asking Cardinal Julián Herranz—president emeritus for the Pontifical Council for Legislative Texts—to verify its contents and adjust its juridical form and substance. Herranz kept a copy of this himself and was later asked to return it in 2013, and it has been filed in the archives of the Secretariat of State.

One precise determination Benedict made was to plan an interval of separation between the day of his announcement and the date of the end of the pontificate. He deemed it essential that the cardinals be able to have time to pause and prepare, psychologically corresponding in some way to what had prior been the period of the pope's long dying and the nine days of mourning following his death and funeral, during which time certain specific celebrations in the Vatican basilica were planned. Furthermore, there needed to be the possibility of disclosing the *motu proprio Normas nonnullas,* on certain modifications to the rules in the Apostolic Constitution *Universi dominici gregis,* regarding the election of the Roman Pontiff, after the appropriate verification by the Pontifical Council for Legislative Texts and the Secretary of State—all of this would have been impossible to accomplish beforehand because it would have had to pass before too many eyes.

The surprising announcement

When my morning alarm sounded on 11 February 2013, after an uneasy night given the tension, I realized I was about to live an event that would be remembered throughout history. But from the first sighting of Benedict XVI in the chapel preparing for Mass, I could see that he instead was incredibly calm. Of course, now and again on his face appeared a brief suspension, like a flash, as he seemed to halt in front of what was about to be written in stone. But I knew well, once he became determined all of his being remained in perfect peace.

The serenity with which he endured that demanding day, and which I can assure you he maintained until his death, allows me today to speak of for the first time—*sommessamente*[10] as is said in the language of the Curia—the conviction that Benedict, too, had mystical-ascetical tendencies, spiritually akin to those of John Paul II. All his decisions were due to a direct relationship with God, by whom he felt himself inspired and incessantly guided.

He himself had made me "read between the lines" on multiple occasions and perhaps it is enough just to pay more attention and grant more credence to his words. For example, in *Introduction to Christianity* (written as a theology professor in 1960) he explains: "[T]hat which cannot be seen, that which absolutely has no way of entering our line of sight—this is not unreal, but in fact it is *the* authentic reality. It is that which renders possible and sustains all other realities." In *God and the World* (written as a cardinal prefect in 2001), in his answers to Peter Seewald's inquiries, one reads: "You speak with God personally, has

10 Translator's Note: This means "in a soft voice," and in curial language it bears the connotation of letting someone in on a secret.

communication with Him become something natural? Like making a telephone call?" To which Ratzinger responds: "In certain respects this comparison holds. I know He is ever present. And He in turn knows who I am and what I am. All the more reason I advise the need to invoke Him, communicate with Him, speak to Him. With Him I can challenge myself with the smallest and most interior questions as well as those that are serious and profound. It is in some way natural for me to always have the possibility of addressing him constantly throughout the day." In *Light of the World* (written as pope in 2010), again responding to Seewald's questions: "Is there now a 'better connection' to heaven, or something like a grace of office?" Ratzinger responds: "Yes, one often feels that. In the sense of: Now I have been able to do something that did not come from me at all. Now I entrust myself to the Lord and notice, yes, there is help there, something being done that is not my own doing. In that sense there is absolutely an experience of the grace of office."

Even if he never spoke to me of explicit supernatural insights—such as visions or interior locutions (generally he was extremely careful in matters of private revelation)—in this specific case he constantly emanated a moral certainty, that in praying, reflecting, and suffering he came to the conviction that he may have to abdicate due to his lack of strength. Thinking about it today, I feel a sense of indirect *déjà-vu* in relation to the episode of May 1945, when during the war the young Joseph Ratzinger decided to return home and risked being deemed a deserter and shot on his feet. Perhaps in this defining experience that saved his life there is a hidden interpretative key to understanding the step he took at the end of his pontificate when—overcoming a thousand obstacles and many good reasons—simply and reserved in silence he decided for a second time to return home....

When I entered the room of the consistory directly behind Benedict, I saw fifty cardinals and some other bishops and monsignors waiting in lines along the walls. My immediate thought was how much I would have liked to freeze time in that moment, with the smiling and broadened faces of so many who considered that meeting one of the many ceremonies proper to the workings of the Holy See throughout the centuries. The underlying murmuring was quickly hushed and everyone became fixed on the pope in the natural curiosity of observing his bearing and how he walked. And of course, the pope's health has always been one of the main topics of gossip in the Vatican.

The meeting was set for 11:00 a.m., and it started exactly on time. According to practice, the consistory was convoked for the so-called "vote" pertaining to certain causes for canonization. In the procedure surrounding the promulgation of new saints, a further step is in fact required—that is, the pope has to confirm the positive opinion of the cardinals and bishops regarding the holiness of a person already deemed "blessed" and announce the date the ceremony will take place. Regardless of how quickly it unfolds, this formality is nonetheless conducted with solemnity, and the pope speaks *ex cathedra* with his decree of canonization. In doing so, he exercises his own infallibility according to its definition from Second Vatican Council.

The key figures of that morning were Antonio Primaldo and around eight hundred companion witnesses to the Christian faith, martyred at Otranto in August of 1480 during an Ottoman excursion along the coastline of Puglia; Laura di Santa Catarina da Siena Montoya y Upegui (1874–1949), founder of the Congregation of Missionary Sisters of the Blessed Immaculate Virgin Mary and Saint Catherine of Siena, and Maria Guadalupe García Zavala (1878–1963), co-founder of the Congregation of Servants of Saint Margaret Mary and the Poor. The date for the celebration on the *sagrato* of the Vatican basilica and this inscription in the *Albo* ("roster") of the saints was fixed for Sunday, 12 May 2013. After this announcement, Benedict would have been expected to rise, impart the proper blessing and be on his way.

Instead, as I privately announced to Guido Marini prior to the ceremony, I placed another piece of paper in front of the pope. It was a Latin text that the acoustics of that open space did not make easy to understand. Yet in the arc of less than three minutes there sounded certain words whose meaning was clear as can be, which caused mounting confusion among those present: "decisionem magni momenti" ("a decision of great importance"), "ingravascente aetate" ("due to advanced age," invoking the title of the *motu proprio* by which in 1970 Paul VI emanated various norms connected to the age of cardinals), "incapacitatem meam ad ministerium mihi commissum" ("my incapacity to properly undertake the ministry entrusted to me"), "declaro me renuntiare" ("I declare that I renounce"), "conclave ad eligendum novum Summum Pontificem" ("the conclave to elect the new Supreme Pontiff").

In the English translation, the entirety of the declaration is given thusly:

> Dear Brothers, I have convoked you to this Consistory, not only for the three canonizations, but also to communicate to you a decision of great importance for the life of the Church. After having repeatedly examined my conscience before God, I have come to the certainty that my strengths, due to an advanced age, are no longer suited to an adequate exercise of the Petrine ministry. I am well aware that this ministry, due to its essential spiritual nature, must be carried out not only with words and deeds, but no less with prayer and suffering. However, in today's world, subject to so many rapid changes and shaken by questions of deep relevance for the life of faith, in order to govern the barque of Saint Peter and proclaim the Gospel, both strength of mind and body are necessary, strength which in the last few months, has deteriorated in me to the extent that I have had to recognize my incapacity to adequately fulfill the ministry entrusted to me. For this reason, and well aware of the seriousness of this act, with full freedom I declare that I renounce the ministry of Bishop of Rome, Successor of Saint Peter, entrusted to me by the Cardinals on 19 April 2005, in such a way, that as from 28 February 2013, at 20:00 hours, the See of Rome, the See of Saint Peter, will be vacant and a Conclave to elect the new Supreme Pontiff will have to be convoked by those whose competence it is.
>
> Dear Brothers, I thank you most sincerely for all the love and work with which you have supported me in my ministry and I ask pardon for all my defects. And now, let us entrust the Holy Church to the care of Our Supreme Pastor, Our Lord Jesus Christ, and implore his holy Mother Mary, so that she may assist the Cardinal Fathers with her maternal solicitude,

> in electing a new Supreme Pontiff. With regard to myself, I wish to also devotedly serve the holy Church of God in the future through a life dedicated to prayer.

Benedict hereby acts precisely according to the prescriptions of the Code of Canon Law (can. 332, §2): "Should it happen that the Roman Pontiff resigns from his office, it is required for validity that the resignation be freely made and properly manifested, but it is not necessary that it be accepted by anyone." Clearly, in response to anyone still maintaining that this action has no formal validity, imposed on this slip of paper were the date and signature of the pope and his declaration was recorded by an apostolic protonotary who drafted the *rogito* of the consistory. This document is now preserved in the designated section of the archives for all of posterity.

With a voice at times broken in emotion, Cardinal Sodano read his response, wherein he alternated between passages both dramatic and lyrical in tone. In my view he succeeded in communicating the feelings brewing in the *sala*, a mixture of gratitude and concern, and likewise expressing an awareness that the firm decision of the pope was not up for discussion: "Like lightning across a quiet sky did his message resound in this room. We have listened with a sense of being lost, almost in disbelief.... In the name of this apostolic inner circle,[11] the College of Cardinals, in the name of your dear associates, allow me to tell you that we remain closer to you than ever, as we have ever been in these luminous eight years of your pontificate.... That day wherein you gave your 'yes' and initiated your bright pontificate in the furrow of the continuity of your 265 predecessors on the Seat of Peter, in the course of two thousand years of history since the Apostle Peter, the humble Galilean fisherman, up to the great popes of the last century, from Saint Pius X to Blessed John Paul II.... During this month we will still have plenty of opportunities to hear your paternal voice. And your mission will continue yet. You have told us that you will always remain close to us by your witness and prayers. The stars in the sky will certainly still continue to shine before us as will the star of your pontificate."

11 Translator's Note: the Italian original is *cenacolo.*

A few minutes later, at 11:46, Giovanna Chirri, a Vaticanista with the Italian journalism agency Ansa, working from the press office during the event through an internal television feed, was the first to launch the news that flew around the world: "The Pope is leaving the pontificate beginning 2/28." From that moment I was bombarded by an enormous amount of phone calls, messages, and emails, to which I had no possibility of answering. Every now and again I would look at something that came to me from persons of authority—including cardinals and bishops not present in the *sala* during the consistory—and I noticed that many expressed disbelief and sought confirmation, as if they were simply unable to believe such a situation were even possible.

The hour of lunch immediately followed, during which silence reigned. Afterward, we took a brief walk along the terrace, the afternoon pause and the 4:00 p.m. rosary in the Lourdes grotto in the Vatican gardens. The work it took to organize my correspondence kept me occupied until dinner, while the pope examined documents in his study and reflected on the speeches to be given during engagements in the coming days. After dinner, the television station *Tg1* unsurprisingly dedicated a good amount of time to this news, but not even then did Benedict utter any remarks. I think the only person with whom he spoke that day was his brother during their usual evening phone call, but for all I know he had no further interactions, either by phone or in person.

The ancient roots of the notion

Even before becoming pope, actually just as he was made archbishop in Germany, Ratzinger was quite aware of what strain guiding the Church presents and he implicitly showed himself grateful to Paul VI for the *motu proprio* by which it was established that every bishop at the age of seventy-five was compelled to submit his resignation, and that at eighty even cardinals had to abandon all offices, including participation in the conclave.

In his homily of 10 August 1978, given in Munich's cathedral in Bavaria during the requiem Mass for Pope Montini (who died four days earlier at nearly eighty-one years of age and after fifteen years of his pontificate), Ratzinger remarked: "Paul VI allowed himself to ever be led where humanly, alone, he did not wish to go. Ever more, his pontificate meant for him to have to be dressed by another and be nailed to the cross. We can imagine how heavy must be the weight of the thought that one no longer belongs to himself. To no longer have a private moment. To be in chains until the end with one's own body that wears out, to a task that requires day after day the full and robust engagement of all man's power."

A couple of years later, in dialogue with philosopher Ulrich Hommes on how a Christian ought react when he personally feels unable to do anything, he above all clarified that "this moment comes for us all, not necessarily in the moment of death, rather in many situations in the course of life," and thus affirmed that "the sense of life must be stronger than that which we can produce, must be something that even now I begin to think about. We must be aware that no man can accomplish everything; faith is renouncing something, but it is precisely this renouncement that leads us to change and opens to us the way forward."

During his years as prefect in the Vatican, among the things that stirred his passion was the Petrine primacy and its "martyrological framework." Revisiting the writings of English Cardinal Reginald Pole of the mid-1500s, Ratzinger emphasized that "the See of the Vicar of Christ is that upon which Peter in Rome sits as he wept at the cross of Christ. In all the time of the exercise of this pontificate he has never come down from it—rather, raised with Christ according to the spirit, his hands and feet were likewise at such points fixed by nails, which did not then go where his will led him. There likewise remained nailed, too, his thoughts and feelings."

Interviewed by Peter Seewald for the book *God and the World* in 2001, when John Paul II was already evidently ill, the cardinal reflected: "When the danger is great one must not run away. For that reason, now is certainly not the time to resign. Precisely at a time like this one must stand fast and endure the difficult situation. This is my view. One can resign at a peaceful moment or when one simply cannot go on. But one must not run away from danger and say that someone else should do it." And on 7 May 2005 at Saint John Lateran during the homily at the Mass of his installation in the Chair of the Bishop of Rome, he was unafraid to say: "The one who holds the office of the Petrine ministry must be aware that he is a frail and weak human being—just as his own powers are frail and weak—and is constantly in need of purification and conversion. But he can also be aware that the power to strengthen his brethren in the faith and keep them united in the confession of the Crucified and Risen Christ comes from the Lord."

He has always been well aware that man's strength does not derive from personal capacity, but from divine grace. In many of his homilies he acknowledges human weakness that finds sustenance in the Lord's own strength. His response in July 2010 does not surprise me at all, again given to Seewald for his book, *Light of the World.* The question concerned whether he had ever considered stepping down. "When the danger is great one cannot evade it. This is exactly why this is surely not the moment to step down. It is moments like these when one needs to press on and overcome hard situations. This is my thought. In times of calm one may step down, or when it is no longer possible. But one cannot run at the moment of danger, saying, 'Someone else can take it on.' When the pope comes to a clear realization that he is no longer physically and mentally able to undertake the duties entrusted to him, then he has the right and in some circumstances the responsibility to step down." Of course, his abdication must be placed in a different context than that of Celestine V on 13 December 1294, the hermit pope to which many have referred in this circumstance. Yet it is undeniable that Benedict has many times juxtaposed his own life with that of this monk, "who in cowardice made the great refusal" (*Inferno* III, 60) as Dante would have reproached in his *Divine Comedy.* Celestine is nevertheless proclaimed a saint in the Church, and the Roman martyrology remembers him thusly: "[H]e practiced a hermetical life in Abruzzo, renowned for his reputation of holiness and miracles, at eighty years of age he was elected Roman Pontiff and took the name Celestine V, yet that same year he abdicated his office and opted to retire in solitude."

Television screens repeatedly played the images of 28 April 2009 when Pope Ratzinger passed through the basilica at Collemaggio in Aquila to venerate the tomb of Pope Celestine during his visit to the region of Abruzzo wrecked by earthquakes. Everyone was struck by the fact that Benedict placed his papal pallium on the urn, but this was absolutely in no way representative of a symbolic gesture by which he wanted to hint at his idea of abdication. It was, rather, a courteous way of honoring his saintly predecessor and acknowledging his courageous decision, while also valorizing with that display a part of his vestments that he actually no longer had it in his heart to wear.

The truth is, Benedict only used that pallium at the impetus of the master of ceremonies, Piero Marini, which came into being prior to the death of John Paul II off of a model used in the early Christian centuries and relating to the latter's own theological-liturgical conviction. Intersected on the left with its elongated and asymmetrical form, like the character Ч, this pallium ended up being decidedly uncomfortable and often fell off Benedict's shoulders, whereas the pontiff's preference leaned more toward a symmetrical and oval form with the tail-end hanging at the center of his chest, like the letter Y.

And so much so that when the diocesan bishop, Giuseppe Molinari, proposed that he make an act of homage to Celestine V, Benedict willingly accepted and departed Rome with the precise intention of offering that awkward pallium, which he explicitly asked the new liturgical master, Guido Marini, to bring with him, though not expecting any liturgical celebrations or having requested its use. And I remember well how with Monsignor Guido I smiled at the way in which the pontiff used such finesse to resolve an uncomfortable situation. Yet Benedict in no way commented on this episode since he was at the time deeply shaken by the images of the damage caused by the earthquake of 6 April and furthermore, being German, he felt dismay for the massacre that was committed in the village of Onna in June of 1944 by Nazi soldiers.

On 4 July 2010, he embarked on a pastoral visit to Sulmona on the occasion of the eight-hundred-year anniversary of the birth of Celestine V. On account of the nearly impassable path, he was unable to make it all the way up to the hermitage of Saint Onofrio where in 1294 cardinals came to tell the monk Pietro Angelerio of his election as pontiff. Yet Pope Benedict accepted the bishop's invitation to go and pay homage to the relics kept in the crypt of the cathedral.

Here, too, there was a link to distant memory—his brother Georg's battalion (Georg was forced to enlist in 1942 in the German army and was wounded in the retreat) was stationed in those parts, along the so-called Gustav Line. In 2008, Monsignor Georg brought himself to once again see those places and he was welcomed by the local community, and he found a way to make peace with himself and his past. Returning to the Vatican, Georg recounted his experience of this to his brother Joseph, and so when the latter received the invitation from Bishop Spina, Georg's younger brother accepted right away and with enthusiasm.

Lastly, the coincidence between the last days of Benedict as pontiff and the canonical posting on the tomb of Celestine V is quite remarkable—his body was taken away on 21 February 2013 from Collemaggio on the occasion of the 700th anniversary of his canonization. When the relics were returned to the basilica, the seventh-century vestments that clothed the saint were replaced with others, of modern manufacturing but inspired by the style of medieval popes, but he was now also worthily clad in the pallium left him by Benedict.

The missed ominous signs

In the days following his renunciation, mass media scrambled to find references to what had happened, in particular in the realm of literature and film. The most frequently mentioned was, unsurprisingly, the film *Habemus Papam,* made by Nanni Moretti not two years prior, with Michel Piccoli's dramatic line: "I beg the Lord's pardon for that which I am about to do.... I realize that I am unable to fulfill the role you have entrusted to me."

But in this case the plot was imagined by the director in the immediate aftermath of a conclave, with a crisis of panic occurring in a newly elected pope, who then had recourse to rapid and ineffective analytic psychotherapy. This was substantially a manifestation of weakness in the face of an unexpected nomination. It was the contrary for Benedict, who never had recourse to psychoanalysis or psychopharmaceuticals, and was clearly courageous in grasping his diminishing physical and spiritual energy after eight years of governing from the Seat of Peter, being now in his eighty-sixth year.

Someone else uncovered an anthology of fantasy stories printed in the magazine *Urania,* published by Mondadori in March of 1978, entitled *Il dilemma di Benedetto XVI* (the story of the man also known as Herbie Brennan). Yet here the recourse to a psychiatrist to solve the underlying issue of the predicament did not have to do with the permanence (or lack thereof) of the pontiff in his guidance of the Church, but his mental sanity. The objective was to understand whether the mystical vision that compelled him to take military action against the ferocious, imaginary dictator, Victor Ling, was concrete or imaginary, the villain being considered an antichrist figure akin to Nero and Hitler. The evolution of the story followed a trajectory completely foreign to that of Pope Ratzinger.

Looking at the facts *a posteriori,* many commentators have instead realized they overlooked an important Vatican event occurring the previous November, when the mini-consistory took place with the creation of six new electoral cardinals, soon after which in February there were another eighteen created. At the time, Vaticanistas explained that this pertained to the predominance of Europeans (thirteen, and seven of them Italian) in the appointments of early 2012, which was the provided motive behind the subsequent remedy to this with the insertion of five non-Europeans.

Perhaps the presence of Archbishop James Michael Harvey among them was not adequately perceived, the only one among those nominated who held a curial role. It is true that the ecclesiastical post as head of the pontifical household—throughout history called Master of the *Camera* of the Pontifical Court, Majordomo of the Sacred Palace and Prefect of the Pontifical Household—nearly always becomes a member of the College of Cardinals, and of the ninety-seven total men succeeding this post in the last four centuries ninety-two of them have been elevated in this way. But this generally only happens at the end of their terms, not as they are actively engaged.

This was indeed Benedict's own personal idea, something he hinted at with me for the first time at the end of September 2012, explaining that he thought the place of prefect of the pontifical household, which Harvey would leave upon his reception of the rank of cardinal, as most suited to me. My first sense was that he thought that after his abdication I would be able to fulfill a function of *trait d'union* with his successor. When some weeks later he returned to this notion, I thanked him but answered that I would only do so in obedience, given this seemed to me an assignment certainly of great prestige but too formal for my qualities. I reminded him that at the moment of his election I had promised him fidelity *in vita et in morte* and that I therefore desired to remain employed with him, something he greatly appreciated and willingly accepted.

In reality, he had once before this expressed an interest in naming me Secretary of the Congregation for the Causes of the Saints to replace the Archbishop Michele Di Roberto (retired due to age in the fall of 2010), and consequently elevate me to the episcopacy. The pope even spoke of this with Cardinal Prefect Angelo Amato, who expressed his full agreement. But when he announced this to me I admitted it would be a great honor, yet I felt it more important to continue to be faithful in my responsibility toward him and remain his private secretary. And so the second time Benedict was resolute in telling me that he asked this fidelity of me in obedience and I then answered in the affirmative.

There was in fact no habit of making a pope's private secretary a bishop simultaneous to his serving as such. Even if a precedent had been set during the previous pontificate with the nomination of Monsignor Stanislaus, the closest confidant to John Paul II (to whom was given the previously unknown office of adjunct prefect of the papal household). Yet in this circumstance Pope Wojtyła placed him side by side with the Master of Ceremonies Piero Marini in the episcopal consecrations, something that Pope Ratzinger did not do with the new master, Guido Marini (of the same name but not related to his predecessor).

Confidentially, Benedict had me understand that among his reasons—and at the time this practically converged with the grace conferred on Paolo Gabriele—he was of the mind to publicly document *ad abundantum* that he in no way shared the accusations that were directed at me by various people of a presumed negligence on my part in the Vatileaks affair. It was his way of reaffirming his full trust in me.

In any event, there was no "special treatment or favor" in my regard, given this was a usual request that indeed followed the rules, and involved the Secretary of State as well, and in the end the nomination was announced on 7 December 2012. From among the titular churches proposed to me I chose Urbisaglia, today a small village in the Macerata Province, but during the Roman Empire it was a thriving central post along Via Salaria Gallica. Due to its proximity to Rome I was able to actually visit and, as is ideal, "take possession" of this episcopal see (whereas the other two historical dioceses are places now lost in North Africa and the Middle East).

My ordination was presided over by Benedict on 6 January 2013, and certainly on a personal level this represented the most solemn liturgical ceremony in which I have ever taken part, something that moved me like none before and none since. In his homily, Pope Ratzinger made it clear that the bishop "must above all be a man concerned for God, for only then will he also be truly concerned about men." And he must have "the courage to stand firm in the truth [as] is unavoidably demanded of those whom the Lord sends like sheep among wolves." When the pontiff offered me his *pax* after the consecration, he whispered to me a simple but meaningful exhortation: "As a bishop may you remain always in faithfulness to the Lord."

Toward the middle of October, Benedict expressed having reflected on where to live after renouncing his ministry and had the idea of moving into Mater Ecclesia, the cloistered monastery on Vatican territory desired by John Paul II. He inquired about it and learned that the Visitandine monks had just departed, as was established three years prior, and the new community meant to occupy it had not yet moved in.

Hence, during a scheduled audience the pope informed the Substitute Angelo Becciu of the abdication and also revealed his own desire regarding future living quarters. With the archbishop, almost as if conspiring together, one evening in November without drawing attention to ourselves we went to visit the structure and realized that some reconfiguration of the space was needed. An architect was hired for the project and little by little work began. The amusing element in this was that voices began to circulate in the Vatican that attributed the initiative to Cardinal Bertone, who according to the *vox populi* was preparing a residence wherein he might retire. We let the gossip fly so as to dispel all possible suspicion.

Less easy to control among the "unrevealing forewarnings," there was in the arc of a few months the concession of various honorific titles by which Benedict wished to show his personal gratitude to his principal lay collaborators. On 29 September 2012, he granted the commendation with a plaque of the Order of Saint Gregory the Great to Commander Domenico Giani, and did the same on 27 November with Giuseppe

Bellapadrona, who managed the pontifical farm at Castel Gandolfo. On 18 January 2013 he did the same for his private doctor, Patrizio Polsca. Knighthood in the Order of Saint Gregory the Great was awarded on 15 November 2012 to Francesco Cavaliere and to Sandro Mariotti, both of the Pontifical Ante-chamber, and on 18 January 2013 to a photographer of *L'Osservatore Romano,* Francesco Sforza. But these proceedings were not particularly publicized so as not to arouse certain questions or put anyone in a state of alert.

Lastly, the concert with the orchestra of the Florence Musical May directed by Zubin Mehta represented a kind of portent that took place on 4 February in the Paul VI auditorium. It was sponsored and promoted by the Italian Embassy to the Holy See in honor of Benedict XVI and by the President of the Italian Republic, Giorgio Napolitano, on the occasion of the 84th anniversary of the Lateran Pact. In the program there were two pieces that indeed might have been interpreted as meaningful in light of what was about to happen: the symphony by Giuseppe Verdi, *The Force of Destiny,* and Ludwig von Beethoven's Symphony n. 3, *Eroica.*

Taking leave of the Palazzo

I do not believe Benedict expected any gesture on the part of the cardinals to convince him to change his mind, but I am certain that he would never have turned around and gone back. Even if someone had tried to conduct a survey, the futility of a public appeal would have been acknowledged and it would have only have caused pointless tension. Therefore, in those days leading up to the start of spiritual exercises of the Roman Curia, nothing beyond the meetings already scheduled in the agenda were carried out.

After the usual pause on Tuesday, 13 February, the Lenten season began and Pope Ratzinger used catechesis in his general audience and the homily for the Mass on Ash Wednesday to propose certain reflections of an autobiographical flavor, focused on the liturgy of that day. In the morning, in front of a large number of faithful gathered in the Paul VI auditorium, he spoke of Jesus's retreat into the desert, where he endured temptations from the devil: "[I]t is the place of silence and poverty, where man is deprived of material support and faces the fundamental existential questions; where he is driven to the essential and for this very reason can more easily encounter God.... Reflecting on the temptations to which Jesus was subjected in the wilderness invites each one of us to answer a fundamental question: What really counts in my life?... What is the essence of the three temptations to which Jesus is subjected? It is the proposal to exploit God, to use him for one's own interests, for one's own glory and for one's own success. And therefore, essentially to put oneself in God's place, removing him from one's own existence and making him seem superfluous. Each one of us must therefore ask him- or herself: what place does God have in my life? Is he the Lord or am I?"

Later that afternoon, his voice resounded firmly through Saint Peter's Basilica: "To 'return to God with all your heart' on this Lenten journey means embracing the cross, following Christ along the path which leads to Calvary, unto complete self-giving. It is a journey which teaches us each day to abandon our selfishness and self-absorption in order to make room for God, who opens and transforms our hearts.... Jesus makes it clear that it is the quality and the truthfulness of our relationship with God which reveals the authenticity of any religious practice. Consequently, he denounces religious hypocrisy, ways of acting meant to impress others and to garner applause and approval. The true disciple serves not himself or the 'public,' but his Lord, simply and generously.... Our witness, then, will always be more effective the less we seek our own glory and the more we realize that the reward of the just is God himself; being one with him here below on the journey of faith, and, at life's end, in the luminous peace of seeing him face to face for ever."

As is custom, the day after Ash Wednesday is dedicated to an encounter with the priests of the Diocese of Rome, something that had been added to the agenda months prior along with the assigned meditation entitled, "Reliving Vatican Council II: Memories, Hopes, and Witness." The theme was chosen by Roman parish priests who desired to hear an account of that event from a living person who was its last participant to remain active in the ministry.

Benedict prepared himself thoroughly, having at one sitting written the entire speech. He had the sequence of points he intended to make fixed in his mind. Many were left amazed at his lucidity, the manner in which he went on to speak for nearly an hour without holding a single paper in his hands with notes. But his prodigious memory and competency with respect to this topic facilitated his comprehensive analysis of all that happened during and after the Council. He shared his own convictions regarding the hermeneutics of the conciliar texts as well.

"So off we went to the Council not just with joy but with enthusiasm. There was an incredible sense of expectation. We were hoping that all would be renewed, that there would truly be a new Pentecost … to rediscover the union between the Church and the best forces of the world, so as to open up humanity's future, to open up true progress." These were the words with which he decided to proceed with a broad examination of the intentions of the Council Fathers. "The first, initial, simple—or apparently simple—intention was the reform of the liturgy … the second was ecclesiology; the third was the word of God, revelation; and finally ecumenism." The essential ideas, he explained, differed, "above all, the Paschal Mystery as the center of what it is to be Christian—and therefore of the Christian life, the Christian year, the Christian seasons, expressed in Eastertide and on Sunday which is always the day of the Resurrection." Then there were the various principles: "intelligibility … and also active participation. Unfortunately, these principles have also been misunderstood."

Here he expounded on a harsh criticism that had already surfaced on other occasions and, unsurprisingly, was the only piece to be printed in the press: "[T]here was the Council of the Fathers—the real Council—but there was also the Council of the media. It was almost a Council apart, and the world perceived the Council through the latter, through the media. Thus, the Council that reached the people with immediate effect was that of the media, not that of the Fathers. And while the Council of the Fathers was conducted within the faith—it was a Council of faith seeking *intellectus,* seeking to understand itself and seeking to understand the signs of God at the same time, seeking to respond to the challenge of God at that time and to find in the word of God a word for today and tomorrow…. [T]he Council of the journalists, naturally, was not conducted with the faith, but within the categories of today's media, namely apart from faith, with a different hermeneutic. It was a political hermeneutic: for the media, the Council was a political struggle between different trends in the Church. It was obvious that the media would take the side of those who seemed to them more closely allied with their world." Yet his conclusion was markedly optimistic: "[T]he real Council had difficulty establishing itself and taking shape; the virtual Council was stronger than the real Council. But the real force of the Council was present and, slowly but surely, established itself more and more and became the true force which is also the true reform, the true renewal of the Church."

The spiritual exercises conducted for the Roman Curia took place on 17–23 February, in the Redemptoris Mater Chapel. The pope, Don Alfred and I took part from the chapel of Saint Lawrence, on the right-hand side where there was a large kneeler for the pope and two smaller ones for his two secretaries. There were seats but without any surfaces upon which to write. The pope took no notes, rather listened to the contents of the meditations of Cardinal Gianfranco Ravasi (President of the Pontifical Council for Culture) with great interest and concentration.

During that week we never spoke during meals, and to maintain an environment of reflection we listened to classical music. In the room where we took lunch a stereo was installed and Benedict gave strict instructions each day as to which disk would be inserted—particularly, motets by Bach and concertos by Beethoven and Mozart; but never passions or Masses, which he preferred to reserve for other moments. Even his correspondence was reduced during this period and he reviewed only the most important letters and other documents that required his signature.

Ravasi succeeded in lifting spirits, advancing biblical icons of great spiritual import, but who also seemed in sync with the moment we were all currently living. His introduction was particularly memorable, with the passage from Exodus when Moses prays on the summit of a hill, while below in the valley the Israelites battle against Amalek. Turning directly to Benedict, he emphasized: "This image represents the principal function of the Church—namely, intercession. We will remain in the 'valley,' that valley where there is dust and neglect, where there is fear—terror even, and nightmares—but also, hope, where you have been these past eight years, with us. Yet, from now on we will know that there on the mount is your intercession for us." He ended with a parting on behalf of all of us: "Moses was 120 years of age when he died. Yet his eyes were never been blurred and the vigor of his mind never declined. This is indeed a great wish we have for you. And also because Jewish tradition surrounding this moment has so many enticing stories, and great affection for Moses and his waiting throughout the history of his existence."

Mindful of these words, in the Angelus of Sunday, February 24th, Pope Ratzinger shared a profound thought carved on his heart and gave meaning to a series of controversial observations that practically not until the end of his life would start to fade away: "The Lord is calling me 'to scale the mountain,' to devote myself even more to prayer and meditation. But this does not mean abandoning the Church; indeed, if God asks me this it is precisely so that I may continue to serve her with the same dedication and the same love with which I have tried to do so until now, but in a way more suited to my age and strength."

Along the same notion, during the general audience of January 27th in Saint Peter's Square, he described the course of his eight-year pontificate like this: "It has been a portion of the Church's journey which has had its moments of joy and light, but also moments which were not so easy; I have felt like Saint Peter with the Apostles in the boat on the Sea of Galilee: the Lord has given us so many days of sun and light winds, days when the catch was abundant; there were also moments when the waters were rough and the winds against us, as throughout the Church's history, and the Lord seemed to be sleeping. But I have always known that the Lord is in that boat, and I have always known that the barque of the Church is not mine but his. Nor does the Lord let it sink; it is he who guides it, surely also through those whom he has chosen, because he so wished. This has been, and is, a certainty which nothing can shake."

Returning again to the thoughts of 19 April 2005, the day of his election, he made other remarks, and regarding these massive amounts of ink have been poured out: "The real gravity of the decision was also due to the fact that from that moment on I was engaged always and forever by the Lord. Always—anyone who accepts the Petrine ministry no longer has any privacy. He belongs always and completely to everyone, to the whole Church. In a manner of speaking, the private dimension of his life is completely eliminated.... The 'always' is also a 'forever'—

there can no longer be a return to the private sphere. My decision to resign the active exercise of the ministry does not revoke this. I do not return to private life, to a life of travel, meetings, receptions, conferences, and so on. I am not abandoning the cross, but remaining in a new way at the side of the crucified Lord."

Here Benedict used 'poetic license' to mirror the state of his soul in that moment. Yet in retrospect, after a few years this "always and forever" acquired an undesirable ambiguity. Once while presenting a book he tried to expand on this expression, speaking of a "broadened pontificate" and I must acknowledge in this case that the remedy seems worse than the disease, as an old proverb goes. Nevertheless, his original intent was simply to express that he would no longer be a theologian or professor, and he would never go back to the life he truly desired.[12]

To avoid further equivocation, I will limit myself to reproducing the wise words of Joaquín Navarro-Valls, the iconic spokesperson for John Paul II and for the early days for Benedict as well, taken from his autobiography: "The pope as such never again really goes on vacation. For the institution he bears with himself never leaves him alone, being impressed forever within him and permanently inscribed in his interior from the moment of his mandate until the end of his life. To be pope is as if to have a tattoo permanently and indelibly impressed on one's soul."[13]

Exit from the scene

I lived the last day of his pontificate as if in a daze. In the morning, in the Clementine room, there was a meeting with Benedict and the cardinals present in Rome. It was his burning desire to be able to warmly address them all collectively, and the decision to extend his stay on the Chair of Peter carefully considered the allowance of enough time for them to organize their affairs in their dioceses before coming to Rome. Of the 207 members of the College of Cardinals, 90 of which were created in his

12 Translator's Note: The notion of a 'widened' pontificate is discussed again with added clarity in chapter nine.

13 Joaquin Navarro-Valls, *A passo d'uomo: Ricordi e riflessioni tra storia e attualitá* (Mondadori, 2009).

five consistories, 144 cardinals were present in their purple, among them 103 under the age of eighty who would proceed to the conclave (together with those who would later trickle in).

His words that day were of gratitude: "… [F]or me too it has been a joy to walk with you in these years, in the light of the presence of the Risen Lord.… [Y]our closeness and your advice have been of great help to me in my ministry." And referring to the theologian Romano Guardini, he offered a thought that came straight from his heart: "[T]he Church is a living body, enlivened by the Holy Spirit and which is really brought to life by God's power. She is in the world but not of the world; she is of God, of Christ, of the Spirit.… The Church is alive, she grows and is reawakened in souls who—like the Virgin Mary—welcome the Word of God and conceive it through the action of the Holy Spirit; they offer to God their own flesh. It is precisely in their poverty and humility that they become capable of begetting Christ in the world today. Through the Church, the Mystery of the Incarnation lives on forever. Christ continues to walk through the epochs and in all places. Let us stay united, dear Brothers, in this Mystery: in prayer, especially in the daily Eucharist, and in this way we shall serve the Church and the whole of humanity. This is our joy that no one can take from us."

Dean Angelo Sodano delivered a tribute on behalf of the college, saturated with his personal emotion: "Holy Father, with deepest love we have tried to accompany you on your way, reliving the experience the disciples had on the road to Emmaus, who after walking with Jesus along a good stretch of the road said to one another, 'Were not our hearts burning within us as he spoke to us?' (Lk 24:32). Yes, Holy Father, may you know that our hearts, too, burned within us as we walked with you these eight years. Today I would like to once more express to you the fullness of our gratitude." I believe he succeeded in expressing the feelings of the greater part of the cardinals, revealing the emotions that I too perceived later in various conversations and letters that came from many of them. One could feel in that encounter a sincerity in the pain, in the inability to fully understand, and in some sense also in embarrassment. Perhaps some of this has been overcome with the passing of time.

Yet I must say that a few days later, in the homily for the Mass *pro eligendo Romano Pontifice* there were statements that appeared to many to offset the warmer sentiments given just days before. Dwelling on the meaning of the pope's mission, Cardinal Sodano stated: "The basic attitude of every Shepherd is therefore to lay down one's life for his sheep. This also applies ot the Successor of Peter, Pastor of the Universal Church. As high and universal the pastoral office, so much the greater must be the charity of the Shepherd." I was present at that Mass and I realized in the looks I received from my brothers how much these words were perceived as a thinly veiled criticism. Yet Benedict did not watch the ceremony on the television nor make any note of it, since it was understood that he did not want to be in the mix of what was happening during the conclave.

After the Memores were already on their way to Castel Gandolfo, in the afternoon Monsignor Alfred and I ensured that everything in the pontifical apartment was in order. A bit before five o'clock in the evening we gave one last look to those rooms and then we descended using the *nobile* elevator. There was a farewell, which I must say caused me great pain and which I felt in the deepest parts of me, and at a certain point I could do nothing to stop the flow of tears.

On the ground floor there were two cardinal vicars for the Diocese of Rome and Vatican City, Agostino Vallini—who sensed my being upset and tried to comfort me—and Angelo Comastri, who told the pope of his weeping and received this calming answer in reply: "A pope comes and a pope goes, but importantly there is always Christ." There were also members of the Secretariat of State and other collaborators waiting to greet him in the courtyard of San Damaso, and the Swiss Guard lined up the honor guard. All around gathered so many of those employed by the Vatican, who with an intense applause showed their affection. And then quickly it was all over. The Twitter account, @Pontifex (inaugurated in December 2012), displayed his last message: "Thank you for your love and support. May you always experience the joy that comes from putting Christ at the centre of your lives."

We took a car to the helipad and took off as the bells of the Vatican basilica and other Roman churches rung their bells in the distance. There was absolute silence in the helicopter—we looked out upon the scene that fell away under our eyes, also because it was the first time we passed over the historic center of Rome (on previous occasions to get to

Ciampino Airport or Castel Gandolfo the pilot took a route more in the periphery of the city).

It was only months later that together with Benedict we saw the pictures shared on world television by a second helicopter that followed the entirety of the trip. Later this footage was made into a documentary edited by the CTV (*Centro Televisione Vaticano*). It was a very emotional experience to relive that flight around the dome of Saint Peter's Basilica that the pilot conducted without informing us, and during which the pope maintained his impenetrable bearing and made no comment.

We reached the residence at Castel Gandolfo a little after 5:30 and Benedict went out on the balcony to greet the faithful and pronounce his last words as reigning pope: "Dear Friends, I am happy to be with you, surrounded by the beauty of Creation and your kindness, which does me so much good.… [T]hank you, I would still—with my heart, with my love, with my prayers, with my reflection, and with all my inner strength—like to work for the common good and the good of the Church and of humanity. I feel greatly supported by your kindness. Let us go forward with the Lord for the good of the Church and the world."

These were moments of extreme tension and even here Benedict showed emotion. He spoke spontaneously in Italian and made several errors, which he later corrected as he always did in the official release issued by the press office. But on one of these errors—the inversion of "Sommo Pontefice" and "Pontefice Sommo"—there was an absurd amount of meticulous study, people affirming that, as already mentioned in the errors occurring in the Latin in the letter of abdication, there was in reality a way of sending a subliminal message relating to the authenticity and validity of one's renouncing the Petrine office. Yet it is enough to listen to the whole speech to grasp that he inverted other words, such as "mio giorno" with "giorno mio" right before he said them, and again at the end while imparting the blessing he left it with an ellipse: "Sia benedetto Dio onnipotente …" rather than "Ci benedica Dio onnipotente."[14]

He reentered the house and retired to his room to arrange his personal items and pray vespers alone. At 7:30 there was the usual evening

14 Translator's Note: "May God be blessed," rather than "May God bless us."

meal, and at 8:00 we heard the front entrance close. Immediately after, we watched the news on television and the station *Tg1*'s segments dedicated to the day. There were no comments as we watched, and at most only a few words were exchanged while we took a walk later. That evening silence was sovereign. And yet what was there to say at this point? At the very end of the day we strolled through various rooms on the first floor: the private library, the room of the consistory, the gallery and then the room of the Swiss Guards where there is a wonderful terrace with a view over Lake Albano. We closed the day with compline recited together in the chapel, and then Benedict once again retired to his room. After 2,873 days, thus concluded the pontificate of the 264th successor of Saint Peter.

8
The Relationship between Francis and Benedict

Where's the telephone?

On the morning of 1 March 2013, Benedict XVI gave the public a glimpse of his new status, wearing only a white cassock and white zucchetto. Besides the red shoes—which he obviously gave up—he also ceased to wear the 'pilgrim' *mantelletta* and the *fascia* emblazed with his coat of arms. Even though no norms have ever been written on the appropriate attire for a pope emeritus, it seemed natural for Benedict to give the latter two up, for the former symbolizes the pope's distinctive office of proclaiming the Gospel, and the latter his office of governance.

Benedict also removed the ring from his right finger (i.e., the so-called "fisherman's ring") and consigned it to Cardinal Bertone, who saw to the ceremonial defacement of it on 6 March 2013 by scratching an "x" through it. (This is an ancient custom to prevent forgery.) Benedict gave the "apostles' stole," a red vestment worn by the pope at particular ceremonies, to Monsignor Marini. For my part, I turned over to Don Alfred the dry seal stamp I used to imprint parchments signed by His Holiness with the words *Segreteria particolare di Sua Santità* ("private secretary of His Holiness").

From then on, Benedict generally wore a ring engraved with a flock of sheep that had been given to him by the cathedral canons after he was appointed Archbishop of Munich and Freising. He selected it from several he had kept at Castel Gandolfo, preferring it to the ring of cardinalature ring Pope Paul VI had given him in 1977, which he rarely wore. In fact, after he had been made a cardinal, he preferred to wear the ring that his brother and sister had given him at his episcopal consecration. During a pilgrimage in September of 2006, he decided to offer this ring to Our Lady of Altötting, and the ring is still visible on the right hand of Our Lady's statue today. In his final years, he also wore a ring that had been given to him by the emeritus bishop Gino Reali, born in the Diocese of Norcia, whose ring bore symbols of the Order of Saint Benedict: "I would like to give this to you as a symbol of our union," he wrote, and Benedict graciously accepted it.

As the new conclave approached, Benedict showed no particular interest in what was happening. He generally caught the news on television after dinner on stations *Tg1* and *Tg2*, and I would point out to him a few articles of interest appearing in the newspapers. He was determined to exert absolutely no influence on the election of the new pontiff, so he refrained from any outside contact *via* telephone or personal meetings.

For him, it was sufficient to make it absolutely clear that, no matter whom the cardinals chose and no matter how unprecedented the circumstances were, that man would be the 266th pope. He alluded to this on several occasions in the closing days of his pontificate: "Continue to pray for me, for the Church and for the future Pope. The Lord will guide us" (General Audience, 13 February 2013); "I ask you to remember me in prayer before God, and above all to pray for the Cardinals, who are called to so weighty a task, and for the new Successor of the Apostle Peter: may the Lord accompany him with the light and strength of his Spirit" (General Audience, 27 February 2013); "I shall continue to be close to you with my prayers, especially in these coming days, that you may be completely docile to the action of the Holy Spirit in the election of the new pope. May the Lord show you the one whom he wants. And among you, in the College of Cardinals, there is also the future pope" (Farewell Address to the Cardinals, 28 February 2013).

Ad abundantiam, he made a spontaneous remark after the above statement at his final meeting with the cardinals that was not included in the prepared text: "… to whom today I promise my unconditional reverence and obedience." He reaffirmed this sentiment—both in person and in written correspondence—even after the election of Francis by always referring to him as "Holy Father." Whenever celebrating Holy Mass (in Italian on weekdays and in Latin on Sundays), following the norms of the Roman Missal of Paul VI, he made explicit mention of Francis in the Eucharistic prayer as anyone who concelebrated or attended his Masses will tell you.

During this period, I went to work every morning at the prefecture and returned to Castel Gandolfo in the afternoon. But on March 13th, I decided to stay until the smoke emerged from the chimney of the Sistine Chapel that evening. As soon as I noticed it was white, I headed for the *Sala Regia* and got in line in the Sistine Chapel to express my act of obedience to the new pope. As soon as I got to the front of the line, Francis spoke to me before I could even get a word out, "I want to speak with Benedict. Can you help me?" Cellphone signals were blocked in the chapel, so I headed for an adjacent room where I knew there was a landline for the use of the employees.

As the pope proceeded to greet the cardinals and members of the retinue, I dialed the landline at the papal residence in Castel Gandolfo. No answer. So, I tried Don Alfred's cellphone. Again, no answer. As I learned later, everyone was fixed to the television and they had all silenced their ringers. No one was even expecting such an impromptu call from the new pope. At that point, I told Pope Francis that I couldn't get anyone on the line. He told me to keep trying so that he could talk with Benedict as soon as possible after being presented to the crowd in Saint Peter's Square.

Finally, I was able to connect with the pontifical Gendarmeria after vice-commander Mauro De Horatis answered the phone. He personally went to the papal apartment at Castel Gandolfo and told everyone there that a call would be arriving from the new pope as soon as he was free. As soon as Pope Francis came off the Benediction *loggia*, he approached me as I was standing by the telephone, and I dialed the landline once again. After Don Alfred responded, I passed the receiver to Francis, while Benedict used a cordless phone on the other end. I stepped away at that point to give them privacy, but Don Alfred was able to hear Pope Benedict on the other end of the line: "Thank you, Holy Father, for thinking of me. I'd like to take this opportunity to pledge my obedience to you right away. And I promise you my prayers!"

From the few comments Benedict made in the days following the election, it was clear to me that Ratzinger was not expecting the name of Jorge Mario Bergoglio to emerge as the front runner. Although I did recall that some cardinals present at the 2005 conclave had mentioned the Archbishop of Buenos Aires as a possible contender, it seemed to me that Benedict thought that the time had passed for his Argentinian brother cardinal by 2013. I think that Benedict had three cardinals in mind as the most likely to emerge from the conclave as his successor—names that we also widely circulated in the Italian media: the 71-year-old Italian Angelo Scola, Archbishop of Milan; the 68-year-old Canadian Marc Ouellet, Prefect of the Congregation for Bishops; and the 63-year-old Brazilian Odilo Pedro Scherer, Archbishop of São Paulo.

In any case, Benedict knew the Archbishop of Buenos Aires well enough, who curiously had been the subject of one of his final appointments before his resignation. Just twenty days earlier, on 23 February 2013, Benedict had appointed him as a member of the Pontifical Commission for Latin America, a role he was to fill until his eightieth birthday. In December of 2011, when Bergoglio turned seventy-five and submitted his mandatory letter of retirement, Pope Benedict extended his appointment for two years, which is basically the norm for cardinals. But Ratzinger and Bergoglio didn't have many occasions to meet personally as the latter didn't much enjoy coming to the Vatican.

There was a significant—albeit indirect—part of their relationship that was connected to the issue of succession at the Society of Jesus [i.e. the Jesuits]. In 2007, the Superior General, Father Peter Hans Kolvenbach, having expressed to Pope Benedict XVI his desire to resign as soon as he turned eighty in 2008, launched preparations for the election of his successor. Pope Benedict, *via* a letter sent to Cardinal Bertone, expressed concerns regarding the spiritual and ecclesial preparation of the younger Jesuits, particularly regarding the value and observance of the "fourth vow"—that is, "special obedience to the Roman Pontiff." So, the Secretary of State asked Fr. Kolvenbach to involve the Cardinal Archbishop of Buenos Aires—a Jesuit himself—in the preparatory work for the election by asking him his opinion of the state of the Society of Jesus and the possibility of utilizing an external review committee to review conditions in the Society on an occasional basis. Later, after Kolvenbach's successor, Fr. Adolfo Nicolás, had his first meeting with Pope Francis on 17 March 2013, he reported that he heard from Pope Francis's own mouth how much Pope Francis opposed to this idea, and brought Kolvenbach into the mix, asking him to report back to Benedict XVI even in Francis's own name, expressing the inappropriateness of this course of action. He thought it problematic and received the promise that it would never happen.

I must say that I was struck by Pope Francis's words on 15 March 2013 in the presence of the cardinals. He avoided formalities and spoke straight from his heart, just as he had on several other occasions when I was next to him in my role as Prefect of the Papal Household: "My thoughts turn with great affection and profound gratitude to my venerable predecessor, Benedict XVI, who enriched and invigorated the Church during the years of his Pontificate by his teaching, his goodness, his leadership, his faith, his humility and his meekness. All this remains as a spiritual patrimony for us all. The Petrine ministry, lived with total dedication, found in him a wise and humble exponent, his gaze always firmly on Christ, the risen Christ, present and alive in the Eucharist. We will always accompany him with fervent prayers, with constant remembrance, with undying and affectionate gratitude. We feel that Benedict XVI has kindled a flame deep within our hearts: a flame that will continue to burn because it will be fed by his prayers, which continue to sustain the Church on her spiritual and missionary path."

From the Papal Apartment back to Casa Santa Marta

In the first days of his pontificate, Pope Francis did not have a personal secretary because even in Buenos Aries he was used to handling his own appointment book, telephone calls, and mail. So, at his request, I personally gave him directly all the information regarding the reserved bank account of the private secretary of His Holiness, as well as the keys to the two safes in the papal apartments. Francis eventually took on Don Alfred as his personal secretary since Benedict himself had written a personal letter of recommendation to Pope Francis. All of this made the rite of transition quite simple.

On March 15th, I was among those who accompanied Pope Francis to the papal apartments on the third *loggia* of the apostolic palace. After the cardinal *camerlengo,* Tarcisio Bertone, had broken the seals, I gave His Holiness a brief tour of the rooms. I told him that it would not be difficult to make the move from Casa Santa Marta because everything was well arranged in the apartments and all they needed was a simple cleaning. At the moment, he didn't give any direct response, but he did say he had to think it over. I read that the Superior General of the Jesuits,

Fr. Adolfo Nicolás, had received an invitation from Pope Francis for a meeting in the afternoon of March 17th: "Come to Casa Santa Marta because tomorrow I have to make the move to the apostolic palace and there is more freedom here." From these words, it seemed Francis was planning to move to the apostolic palace, but he had never mentioned to me that he was planning to do so on March 18th.

After a couple of weeks, I asked again about his plans, and Francis basically said: "I normally sleep like a rock, but I could barely sleep after having seen the papal apartments. I was reflecting on the fact that I was completely unaccustomed to live in such ample rooms. Is there any way you could find a smaller arrangement in the Vatican?" I consulted with the Substitute, Archbishop Becciu, and we were both in agreement that any other solution—such as the rooms of the Archpriest of Saint Peter's Basilica, the apartments at the Holy Office, or in the old Santa Marta building—would not have been functional and would have created problems in logistics and security.

I also mentioned to His Holiness that the locals and pilgrims to Rome were nostalgic about seeing the lights on in the papal apartments at night, and they certainly would miss that if he were to decide to live elsewhere. But I had the impression that, having lived on the other side of the ocean far from Rome, all this didn't mean very much to him. Benedict was also surprised at Francis's unwillingness to move to the apostolic palace, but he wisely concluded that if Francis didn't want to live there, no one should oblige him to do so!

In the end, Pope Francis made the decision entirely on his own and decided to remain in the patriarchal apartment at Casa Santa Marta. He explained his reasons on 7 June 2013 during an audience with students from Jesuit schools in Italy and Albania: "For me it is a question of personality: that is what it is. I need to live with people, and were I to live alone, perhaps a little isolated, it wouldn't be good for me. I was asked this question by a teacher: 'But why don't you go and live there?' I replied: 'Please listen, professor, it is for psychological reasons.'"

Ignoring this explanation, some wanted to use Francis's decision about where to live as another wedge to drive between him and his predecessor, alleging that the new pope did not want the pomp and ostentation of the apostolic palace, but rather preferred to live in a simple hotel room. But I can easily dispel this interpretation since the personal spaces of the previous pontiffs—the study, living room, bedroom, and bathroom—are basically the same as what Francis now has in his apartment at Casa Santa Marta. Similarly, other conveniences—including the kitchen, dining room, chapel, and personal spaces for a private secretary and other collaborators—are equally available at Casa Santa Marta, even if they are in more public space resembling a hotel.

In fact, from my experience of entering the papal apartments in the apostolic palace for the first time in 2005, I can attest that John Paul II in no way lived like a prince. I should also make it clear that the improvements we had made to the papal apartments were in no way a financial burden to the Holy See, since—thank God—there were many generous, private donors—some of them not even Catholic and most of whom wanted to remain anonymous—who wanted to donate appliances and building materials for the project. Besides, in order to avoid having it fall into disrepair again through lack of use, the papal apartments must be cared for daily even now, so there was no question of wanting to spare costs. It was, just as Pope Francis had said, simply a matter of his own psychological well-being.

This habit of people taking one side or the other and placing the reigning and retired pontiffs at loggerheads was something that terribly upset Benedict, especially if it were coming from voices inside the Vatican. Paraphrasing a popular saying, many tried to "tug" on Benedict XVI's "cassock." It was not always easy to determine who was acting in good faith or with upright intentions and who was trying to foment confusion and rebellion in order to consolidate their positions of power or to garner new power. Almost all of the thousands who spend their lives in service to the Holy See do so in a spirit of complete devotion to the pope and to the Church. But, just as in any large bureaucracy, there are a few malicious 'black sheep' who try to disguise themselves as 'angels of light.'

Francis himself was asked directly about the issue of "two popes" during his in-flight press conference when returning from Armenia. He answered: "I heard—I don't know if this is true—I stress that I heard this and it may be gossip, but it sounds like him, that some people have gone there to lament about 'this new pope …' and he has sent them packing!

In the best Bavarian style, politely, but he sent them packing. Even if it isn't true, it is a good story because he is like that. He is a man of his word, an upright, a completely upright man!" I can confirm that Francis is exactly right about Benedict XVI on this point.

Except for a very few rare cases when it came to old friends who received personal invitations, every other visitor Benedict received was someone who had made a request ahead of time. The pope emeritus himself decided whether or not to grant the request, and in some cases, he even refused to see cardinals, bishops and politicians if he deemed it inappropriate to do so in this new situation. Only occasionally did it happen that he received a letter from an ecclesiastical authority and preferred to meet him personally rather than responding in writing. In any case, it was always crystal clear to everyone, even if it wasn't said aloud, that at the monastery, no one was to ask about how Pope Francis was doing in his ministry, let alone complain about something.

To give just one example, I must say that I was astonished when I read a response that writer Vittorio Messori gave to Stefano Lorenzetto in the *Corriere della Sera* of 2 March 2021. Lorenzetto asked Messori if he still met with the pope emeritus. He responded, "I wouldn't dare disturb him. One day, his secretary Georg Gänswein called me: 'His Holiness would gladly see you again, but you have to forget that you are journalist.' It's a shame because he himself had made comments on the situation of the Church that made the front page." More recently, a transcript appeared of some public statements the writer made on 23 May 2016 during a gathering at the Franciscan Center "Rosetum" in Milan. Referring to a meeting he had at 12:30 p.m. on 9 September 2015, Messori said, "His secretary telephoned me, saying, 'His Holiness would be happy to see you to talk about old times. Come visit whenever convenient. But please understand that His Holiness will receive you as a friend and not as a journalist. You'll be able to have a private meeting and there won't be anything public to report'.... [W]hen Ratzinger asked me my opinion on the situation in the Church, I talked about, with all sincerity, a climate of confusion (to use a euphemism) and a sense of unease about how it would all finish after these new precedents. In any case, I told him what I thought, and it's interesting that, after he listened to me, he opened his hands, raised his eyes to heaven, and said, 'I can only pray.'"

Now, I understand how it can sound good to say that one is requested by the pope emeritus, but the reality is that Benedict generously granted him an audience only after Messori had written to him asking for one. Furthermore, the words Messori attributes to me are not what I really said because neither in that situation nor in any other did I allow myself to impose something regarding the confidentiality of a meeting or of the topics discussed. Benedict admired Messori, who was the author of a noted book-length interview published in 1984 under the title *Rapporto sulla fede* (in English, *The Ratzinger Report*). But, at least during the time that I was Benedict's personal secretary, their contact was sporadic, for which it was decidedly improper, in my opinion, to refer to the pope as a "friend." This is a term Ratzinger reserved to very few people. Moreover, the gesture and response he attributed to Ratzinger are dubious, especially if interpreted in such a way as to suggest criticism of Pope Francis.

On the other hand, everyone can see that Francis's way of handling himself and the subtle theological emphasis with which he addresses problems in the Church are different from those of Benedict XVI. But even if someone tried to elicit a comment out of him, Benedict never offered opinions on Francis's strategy. In fact, it seems to me that proper scrutiny in this case would not focus on the issue of two pope's co-existing (as having a reigning pontiff and an emeritus never meant there were 'two popes'), rather on the emergence of two different fan clubs. And this says something important about two different visions of the Church. Moreover, these fan clubs—each of which bases its opinions on supposed statements, gestures, or even just general impressions of the attitudes of Francis and Benedict (many of which are completely fictitious or sensational)—have created tensions that are then passed down to those with little to no knowledge of ecclesial dynamics.

The first meeting between Francis and Benedict XVI took place in the library-study at Castel Gandolfo on 23 March 2013, so that the latter could consign to the new pope the documentation of the study carried out by the commission of cardinals. In addition to his written observations, Benedict voiced further details to Pope Francis and responded to some of the latter's questions. Over lunch—at which Monsignor Xuereb and I were present as well—the pontiff and the emeritus chatted lightly about this or that, spending hardly any time on "business." The atmosphere was friendly and cordial, and both of them—as each told me later—really enjoyed the opportunity to meet.

A few weeks later, when the pope emeritus returned to the Vatican from Castel Gandolfo *via* helicopter on May 2nd, he was in for a big surprise: waiting at the front door of the monastery was a smiling Pope Francis. This unexpected gesture of kindness really filled Benedict's heart with joy because it was a sign that he was fully welcomed within the 'walls of the fisherman' at such an unusual and historic time. Benedict himself expressed his gratitude on 28 June 2016 in a speech prepared for the 65th anniversary of his priestly ordination: "First of all, thank you, Holy Father! Your goodness, evident from the moment of your election, has continually impressed me, and greatly sustains my interior life. The Vatican Gardens, even for all their beauty, are not my true home: my true home is your goodness. There, I feel safe."

Francis came to visit us at the monastery on various occasions, mostly on special holidays: on Benedict's patronal feast day and birthday, Easter, and Christmas. In the earlier years of his pontificate, he also came to bid farewell before leaving for an apostolic visit. He always invited Benedict for consistories of new cardinals, and when Benedict could no longer attend due to problems with his legs, Francis decided that they would all come to him. Twice we hosted him at Mater Ecclesiae and once Benedict and I went to see him at Casa Santa Marta.

Pope Francis generally brought a bottle of wine and a jar of *dulce de leche,* a delicious cream made from Argentinian milk. The idea probably came to Francis after he asked me what the pope particularly liked to eat, and I responded, "sweets." There was nothing sweeter in an Argentinian's mind than *dulce de leche.* Benedict always reciprocated with a bottle of limoncello made by the Memores from the fruit picked in our backyard, as well as a box of Bavarian sweets such as *Lebkuchen,* a traditional cookie Germans like to eat at Christmas.

An encyclical and an interview

With the Apostolic Letter *Porta Fidei* dated 17 October 2011, Pope Benedict XVI announced his intention to open a "Year of Faith" from 11 October 2012 to 24 November 2013 to commemorate the 50th anniversary of the Second Vatican Council. At the time, he didn't foresee that he would resign, so Pope Ratzinger decided to pen an encyclical in conjunction with the Year of Faith, which, as is generally interpreted, would ideally complete the "trilogy" on the theological virtues.

Strain from work during the months that followed prevented him from dedicating as much time to the encyclical as he would have liked, so, as the date of his resignation approached, he noticed that the text was nowhere near finished, and he therefore decided to leave it to his successor. The definitive text, which had been worked on by the competent authorities in the meantime, was signed by Pope Francis on 29 June 2013 and published on the following July 5th. A few modifications had been made to the last version seen by Pope Benedict before his resignation, and a substantial final part in harmony with themes dear to the heart of Pope Francis was added, yet the substance of the encyclical was as Benedict had left it.

This is essentially what Pope Francis himself explained at the Angelus address on July 7th: "For the Year of Faith, Pope Benedict XVI began this Encyclical, to follow up those on love and hope. I took up this great work and I brought it to conclusion. I offer it with joy to all the People of God: in fact, especially today, we all need to go to the essence of the Christian Faith, to deepen it and to confront it with our current problems. But I think that this Encyclical, at least in several places, can also be helpful to those in search of God and of the meaning of life. I place it in the hands of Mary, the perfect icon of faith, that she may bring forth the fruit desired by the Lord."

Regarding an infamous interview, six months after Francis was elected, a lengthy exchange between the pope and Fr. Antonio Spadaro, director of *La Civiltà Cattolica,* was published. Contrary to some attempts to reconstruct the series of events surrounding that interview we know for certain what happened. (As Massimo Franco claims in a recent book, "A draft of the interview arrived at the monastery.... [A]t the end of the text were two black pages and a hand-written note from Jorge Mario Bergoglio.... [I]t had been inserted for Benedict to write comments and suggestions....") The fact is that Pope Francis handed me an envelope with a copy of the already published interview on 19 September 2013, asking me to have Benedict take a look at it and provide his comments, if he had the time.

The pope emeritus, in fact, took the request seriously. He read the thirty-page article and took careful notes. He then prepared a personal letter, dated 27 September 2013, and asked that I return it to Pope Francis. In the first lines, Benedict explains to Francis why he chose to underline certain passages: "Holy Father, I want to thank you sincerely for sending me the long interview published in *La Civiltà Cattolica.* It was a joy to read the text. I received a lot of spiritual nourishment from it and concur with what you said. You also asked that I give you some feedback. Truth be told, I am in agreement with everything you said, but I would like to add two particular points. The first point is in regard to problems tied to abortion and the use of contraception. The second concerns the problem of homosexuality."

Here is what Benedict said regarding the first point: "Regarding the three problems that you point out on page 463 and following—i.e., that you 'have not spoken much about these things,' and that 'one needs to speak about them in a certain context,' and that 'a pastoral mission should not be obsessed with transmitting a disordered bunch of doctrines.... [W]e have to find new balance...,' I absolutely agree with you and I myself have said these things many times in similar words. That is why I, too, didn't speak about these topics much during my pontificate. But I would like to add something to what you said. Having lived next to John Paul II for 23 years, I can testify to the passion with which he did many things to support the pro-life struggle. I understood well how the blessed pope saw the pro-life struggle, together with the struggle for human rights, as the essential nucleus of his mission. I also understood how, for John Paul II, this was not a kind of moralism, but rather a struggle for the presence of God in human life. I learned over time that John Paul II understood abortion and various forms of artificial procreation, as well as the manipulation and destruction of human lives, as essentially a 'no' to the Creator. It is true that, in some corners of the pro-life movement, there has been a lack of this wider vision and a certain one-dimensional aspect to their mission. So, a rebalancing is indeed necessary; but the public battle against this concrete and practical denial of the living God certainly remains a necessity."

Regarding the second point, Benedict made the following observations: "On page 463, you speak about the difficult problem of the pastoral care of homosexuals. Here, too, I am in complete agreement with what you say. When we were preparing the Catechism of the Catholic Church, we sought—often in long debates—a balance between respect for the human person, pastoral charity, and the doctrine of faith. I sense this balance in your own words, but here too, I would like to add one observation that arises from public propaganda on this point. The philosophy of gender in play here teaches us that it is the individual person who makes himself/herself a man or woman. To be a man or a woman is no longer a reality of nature that precedes us. The human being is a product of itself. The philosophy of Sartre made this clear in a way that was still unforeseeable at the time. In other words, it involves a radical denial of the Creator and a manipulation of 'being' itself, asserting that man and man alone is master of himself. This kind of propaganda has absolutely no interest in the good of homosexual persons, but rather desires to manipulate the very notion of 'being' and launch a radical denial of the Creator. I know that many homosexual persons do not agree at all with this manipulation, and they feel that the problem they are dealing with in their lives has been made a pretext for ideological warfare. Hence, there needs to be a strong and public resistance to this pressure. We must bring about this resistance without losing a balance in practice between pastoral charity and the truth of the faith."

Before closing the letter, the pope emeritus made two further clarifications: "Your Holiness, allow me to make a final brief note. On page 464, you say that questions of a lack of orthodoxy 'are better handled on the spot.' How much I desired this in my years as Prefect of the Congregation for the Doctrine of the Faith! Unfortunately, in my twenty-three years of experience there, I discovered that bishops and episcopal conferences normally have little desire to take these problems seriously and handle them on their own; rather, they prefer to 'drop the hot potato' into the hands of the congregation. Lastly, I would like to say how happy it made me to see you distinguish between 'optimism' and 'hope' on page 470. I have repeatedly made this same point myself, and I am very happy to hear Your Holiness make this same distinction." Pope Francis asked me to convey his thanks to Benedict, but I honestly do not know if and how Pope Francis accepted Benedict's observations.

On November 25th, a white, leather-bound copy of the document that Francis—following the usual custom—had written after the October

2012 Synod of Bishops dedicated to the theme, "The New Evangelization for the Transmission of the Christian Faith." The dedication page read: "I am happy to send to Your Holiness a copy of the Apostolic Exhortation *Evangelii Gaudium.* Please do not forget to pray for me. May the Lord bless you and Our Lady protect you. Fraternally … and also filially, Francis." Similarly, Francis sent copies of his later encyclicals and apostolic exhortations when they were published, and they were always accompanied by a greeting card, signed, "fraternally and filially." The pope emeritus always sent a thank-you note in return. In any case, unlike the claims made in an interview with Spadaro, there was no request for comments on these texts.

Be that as it may, some of Francis's assertions in *Evangelii Gaudium* sound foreign to Benedict's theological sensibilities: "I dream of a 'missionary option,' that is, a missionary impulse capable of transforming everything, so that the Church's customs, ways of doing things, times and schedules, language and structures can be suitably channeled for the evangelization of today's world rather than for her self-preservation" (n. 27); "Within the Church countless issues are being studied and reflected upon with great freedom. Differing currents of thought in philosophy, theology and pastoral practice, if open to being reconciled by the Spirit in respect and love, can enable the Church to grow, since all of them help to express more clearly the immense riches of God's word. For those who long for a monolithic body of doctrine guarded by all and leaving no room for nuance, this might appear as undesirable and leading to confusion" (n. 40); "There are times when the faithful, in listening to completely orthodox language, take away something alien to the authentic Gospel of Jesus Christ, because that language is alien to their own way of speaking to and understanding one another" (n. 41).

It must be said that Benedict was always disposed to give the "benefit of the doubt" to the first Latin-American pontiff in the history of the Church and to never judge his teaching with a "Roman-centric" vision: "Each of us has his own nature, personality, and way of acting, and the Lord works with everyone. If we think about the twelve apostles, they had all kinds of problems, but the Church grew nonetheless. The history of the Church is also filled with different kinds of popes, not all of whom have been saints, yet the Church continues to exist. In his responsibility as the successor of

Peter, Francis follows the path he thinks is the best for the Church today. One may agree with him or not, but we must give our trust to all popes, just as I and my predecessors had received that trust from others."

One only has to reread the magisterial texts of Pope Ratzinger's pontificate to recognize the radicality of his thinking about the Petrine ministry (which can be applied to some of the controversial positions taken by his successor). For example, on 7 May 2005, at the Mass of Possession of the Chair of the Bishop of Rome, Benedict XVI said, "The power of teaching in the Church involves a commitment to the service of obedience to the faith. The Pope is not an absolute monarch whose thoughts and desires are law. On the contrary: the Pope's ministry is a guarantee of obedience to Christ and to his Word. He must not proclaim his own ideas, but rather constantly bind himself and the Church to obedience to God's Word, in the face of every attempt to adapt it or water it down, and every form of opportunism.... The Pope knows that in his important decisions, he is bound to the great community of faith of all times, to the binding interpretations that have developed throughout the Church's pilgrimage. Thus, his power is not being above, but at the service of, the Word of God. It is incumbent upon him to ensure that this Word continues to be present in its greatness and to resound in its purity, so that it is not torn to pieces by continuous changes in usage."

Cardinal Sarah's bungled book

A media storm broke out all of a sudden on 12 January 2020 when Vatican-reporter Jean Marie Guénois, in an interview appearing in the French newspaper *Le Figaro,* wrote that Cardinal Robert Sarah, at that time Prefect of the Congregation for Divine Worship and the Discipline of the Sacraments, was about to release with Benedict XVI "a co-authored book in which the two prelates express the same vision of the Church and an identical aversion to polemics."

The theme, scope, and basic judgment of the book were clear from the first question asked in the interview: "How can you explain the fact that Pope Emeritus Benedict XVI has published a book with you defending priestly celibacy, begging Pope Francis not to change the practice of the Church?" Sarah responded: "This book is an appeal; an appeal of love to the Church, to the Pope, to priests and all Christians. We want this book to be read by as many people as possible. We are witnessing a surprising crisis in the Church."

Emphasizing that the book was co-authored with pope emeritus Benedict, Cardinal Sarah responded to a very delicate question that immediately opened the door to extreme reactions, both positive and negative depending on one's point of view (especially with regard to how Francis's pontificate was proceeding). When asked, "If Pope Benedict has taken a vow of silence, why is he breaking it now?" Sarah answered: "Pope Emeritus Benedict is not breaking his silence with this book. He is offering us his fruit. He has not written a 'loquacious' theology in this book—a theology that he hopes enchants the media—but rather a contemplative reading of Sacred Scripture. Don't think he's looking for polemics, or that this is a disputed academic question with no connection to reality. I believe that, in his prayer, his paternal heart feels great compassion for priests all over the world who feel unappreciated, discouraged, or abandoned. He also wants to reassure tens of millions of faithful Christians who feel lost and disoriented."

Commentators on this interview immediately made a connection to the "Amazonia" Synod, where the possibility of opening the priesthood to married men was brought up. Even though it had been the most contested proposal of the synod—with 41 of the 169 members voting against paragraph 111 in the final document, which had been handed over to Pope Francis on 26 October 2019—the following the recommendation was inserted nevertheless: "We propose that criteria and dispositions be established by the competent authority, within the framework of *Lumen Gentium* 26, to ordain as priests suitable and respected men of the community, able to have a legitimately constituted and stable family."

Critics of the proposal feared that the situation in the Amazonia—a region that seemed to be having major problems in maintaining a sufficient number of priests for serving communities that were thinly spread out over a vast territory—might be exploited. The final section of the document was subtitled, "New paths for ecclesial synodality." Hence, any openness to changing the traditional norm of priestly celibacy—which has in recent times been reaffirmed by both Popes Paul VI and

John Paul II—was considered to be a possible breach that (as with so many other innovations in ecclesiastical discipline) would, in a brief span of time, be transformed from an exception to the norm.

In fact, already toward the beginning of Benedict XVI's pontificate, the issue was thrust into the international spotlight, when Cardinal Cláudio Hummes—who had just been appointed Prefect of the Congregation for Clergy—had said in a 2006 interview with the daily newspaper *O Estado de São Paulo* that "the lack of priestly vocations might lead the Vatican to discuss the possibility of ordaining married men." Hummes, who at that time was Archbishop of São Paulo in Brazil, had been summoned by Pope Ratzinger to work at the Vatican because the pope wanted to widen the breadth of international representation in the Roman Curia.

To give greater clarity to the issue, the Vatican Press Office—in conjunction with Secretary of State Tarcisio Bertone—decided to issue a press release on December 4th, in which Cardinal Hummes stated more carefully that "the norm of celibacy for priests in the Latin Church is very ancient and is supported, both from a theological-spiritual and practical-pastoral point of view, by solid tradition and persuasive argumentation, as has been reaffirmed by recent popes.... [T]he issue is therefore not currently an open question among ecclesiastical authorities, as was recently reaffirmed by the Holy Father at his most recent meeting with dicasterial heads."

But apparently the question was still percolating in the mind of the Brazilian cardinal when Pope Francis appointed him to the pre-synodal council in 2018 responsible for laying the groundwork for the general assembly on Amazonia. In that capacity, Cardinal Hummes likely had a significant role in drafting the Post-Synodal Apostolic Exhortation *Querida Amazonia.* The document was scheduled for publication toward the end of 2019, but—as Cardinal Michael Czerny explained in an interview with *Vatican News*—it didn't receive Pope Francis's final approval until December 27th, pushing back the publication date to 12 February 2020 (it would bear the official date of February 2nd). The delay—which on the surface seemed of no great import—was incidentally not unconnected to the Sarah's book and the unfortunate controversy surrounding it, for it had already been decided during the previous

Autumn that the publisher, Fayard, would send copies to stores after Epiphany 2020 (the exact date of distribution was January 15th).

An advance copy of the book arrived in the mail at the monastery on January 12th. As soon as I opened the envelope, a chill ran through my veins. The name "Benoît XVI" was spread across the front cover in print no smaller than the name of Cardinal Sarah, and a photograph of each appeared side-by-side (in fact, the one of Benedict showed him in a *mantellina,* a vestment he had not put on since his resignation). I immediately brought the book to Benedict, who was equally shocked, knowing full well what polemics the book would cause. Flipping through its pages, it was also clear that the book did not make clear what contribution belonged to which author. To justify the co-authorship, the book gave this enigmatic description: "Written by Cardinal Robert Sarah, read and approved by Benedict XVI" (the book's conclusion also indicated this alleged co-authorship).

The expected media frenzy broke out instantly, rife with claims that, since the post-synodal exhortation had not yet been released, the two authors wanted to pressure Pope Francis to take the topic of priestly celibacy and the ordination of married men seriously. Benedict, therefore, considered it absolutely necessary to make a public clarification, which I redacted into a press release to distribute to news agencies: "I can confirm this morning that, at the request of the pope emeritus, I asked Cardinal Sarah to contact the editors of the book to request that the name of Benedict XVI be removed as a co-author of the book, and to remove his signature from the Introduction and Conclusion. The fact is that the pope emeritus knew that the cardinal was preparing a book, and had sent him a brief text on the priesthood, asking him to use it as he saw fit. But in no way did he approve any project for a co-authored book, and had neither seen nor approved its cover. This has simply been a misunderstanding, and should not in any way put in question the good faith of Cardinal Sarah."

The wording was carefully crafted to give the cardinal an honorable way out of this sticky situation, both because Benedict and he were personal friends, but also because he was still in office as Prefect of the Congregation for Divine Worship and the Discipline of the Sacraments, and the pope emeritus did not want to create trouble at a time when his position at the Vatican was already precarious. In response, the cardinal issued his own press release, in which he stated: "After several exchanges with the pope emeritus regarding the preparation of the book, I finally sent him a final copy of the manuscript on November 19th, including—as we had agreed—the cover, the Introduction, the co-authored conclusion, my text, and Benedict XVI's text." Personally, I double checked and can say with certainty that the cover was not among the contents that the cardinal had sent in advance. The cardinal's statement continued: "[T]he controversy aimed to defame me by suggesting that Benedict XVI had not been informed about the publication of *Des profondeurs des nos coeurs* is completely outrageous." This was a disappointing attempt to shift blame, since the issue hinged not on Benedict's knowledge of the publication, but rather the way in which the book was published.

In any case, *via* telephone, Sarah promised me that he would proceed according to pope emeritus' wishes and asked if he could have a personal meeting with him. The appointment was set for 5:15 p.m. at the monastery on January 17th, and Benedict wanted me to be present as well. The cardinal, almost in tears, expressed regret over the whole affair and then pulled from his briefcase a proposed press release that he wanted Benedict to sign. It read: "'The Catholic Priesthood' is probably the last thing I will write before I go to meet the Lord. I approve and accept everything contained in this book entitled *From the Depths of Our Hearts,* and I thank Cardinal Sarah for having published it as he did, including the cover. I beg everyone to cease perpetuating this absurd controversy and calumny that are defaming this man of God and dividing the Church on an essential question. I encourage all priests to read this book."

I immediately burst in, making it absolutely clear that the pope emeritus had never issued a press release before, and I pointed out that any public position taken by Benedict would only add fuel to the fire. To seek a solution, Benedict told the cardinal he would think about it and reformulate the text, asking him to return an hour later around 7:00 p.m. When Cardinal Sarah returned, the pope emeritus explained that he had made some substantial edits, especially in eliminating any reference to the cover, but he made it clear that his status as pope emeritus gave him no authority to approve issuing any statement without prior contact with the Secretariat of State and Pope Francis. The cardinal expressed his disappointment, but he was forced to accept the decision. As I accompanied him to the door of the monastery, he said to me, "Please, don't let that press release be thrown into the trash." I firmly responded, "Your Eminence, do you think that I would be capable of deceiving Benedict after he entrusted me with this position?"

That very evening, at the pope emeritus' request, I telephoned the Substitute at the Secretariat of State, Archbishop Edgar Peña Parra, who asked that I meet him early the next morning in his office on the second *loggia* and bring him up to date on what had happened because he had an appointment with the Holy Father at 9:15 a.m. and he had mentioned he wanted to talk about it. I waited for him as he met the pope. After the audience, Substitute Parra said to me, "Pope Francis has decided that the statement will not be released. You must communicate this to Cardinal Sarah and tell him that, for now, he shouldn't do anything."

I immediately tried to get in touch with the cardinal to tell him. Only when I got back to the monastery was I told that, after his meeting with Benedict the previous evening, Sarah had released two posts on Twitter: "Because of the endless, nauseating, false polemics that have not ceased this week since the publication of the book *From the Depths of our Hearts,* I met Pope Emeritus Benedict XVI this evening," and "I was able to ascertain with Benedict XVI that there was no misunderstanding between us. I left this beautiful meeting very happy and full of peace and encouragement."

Obviously, I felt that it was completely out of line for the cardinal to launch those tweets, just as it was for him to divulge on January 14th—without authorization—personal letters he had sent to the pope emeritus. I was even more dismayed a few hours later when a journalist, Guénois, contacted me to ask whether it were true that Benedict had read and even edited and added some things to the responses Sarah had given him for the interview published in *Le Figaro*. I explained to him that the pope emeritus had seen the interview only after it had already been published. Guénois, in turn, explained to me that it was Diat—Cardinal Sarah's agent—who had misled or lied to him about this. (Diat, in fact, was primarily responsible for organizing the publication of the book. The front matter reads: "Book published under the direction of Nicolas Diat.")

David Cantagalli, director of the publishing house that had acquired the rights to publish the Italian version of the book, also told me that he had contacted Fayard and was led to believe that the cover of the book should remain just as it was in the original edition. I explained to him what Benedict and Sarah had agreed upon. He called the French publishing house once more and received the reply: "Our contact for the cardinal is Nicolas Diat, who told us to leave the book as it is." In the end, on January 22nd, a conciliatory statement was released to the press, emphasizing that "the Introduction and the Conclusion were written by Cardinal Robert Sarah, and they were read and shared by the Pope Emeritus." This was simply to say that Benedict XVI had not expressed any objections to Sarah's text, mostly because the contents were not particularly original or innovative.

Benedict's explanation

On 12 February 2020, Benedict received a copy of the Apostolic Exhortation *Querida Amazonia* from Pope Francis and sent a thank-you letter on the following day. The pope emeritus knew that the text had not been modified since it had been approved by Pope Francis on December 27th. Therefore, Cardinal Sarah's book had no influence—directly or indirectly—on the fact that there was no mention in the exhortation of the ordination of married men. Nevertheless, Benedict felt it necessary to clarify the matter once and for all, and so he wrote to Francis, "Holy Father, I would like to briefly tell you the whole story, which I'll write as soon as I am able."

Four days later, on February 17th, Benedict's reconstruction of events was complete and he sent Pope Francis his text: "Dear Holy Father, as I had promised you in my letter of 13 February 2020, I would like to tell you the story of how my text on the Catholic priesthood got published in Cardinal Sarah's book. Around 20 July 2019, I had communicated to Cardinal Sarah that I was working on a text on the Catholic priesthood without any intention of publishing it. I was only doing it out of personal interest. The impetus for the text was that, in its excellent decree on the

Catholic priesthood, the Second Vatican Council had not touched upon a central point in the Lutheran controversy: that is, that the Catholic Church, in the late-second and early-third centuries, had begun to consider the ministry of presbyters and bishops as a priesthood and not merely as a pastoral ministry in consequence of the fact that the Holy Eucharist was considered not only a meal, but as the presence of and participation in the sacrifice of the cross. This development in Catholic doctrine was rejected by Luther as a recidivistic return to the Law; as an extremely grave error incompatible with the purpose of the Law. The Second Vatican Council had not spoken about this central point in the controversy between the Reformation and the Catholic Church. A few ecumenists claimed that the liturgical reform of the Second Vatican Council withdrew the doctrine of the Mass as a sacrifice and restored the interpretation of the Mass as a meal without a sacrificial character. Consequently, the ministers of the Church should not be considered to be exercising a priesthood, but only a pastoral service. Even if this was not a widespread position among Catholic theologians, the question was nevertheless not defined with sufficient clarity at the Second Vatican Council. This problem has occupied my mind for a long time. I never intended to publish a text on this topic; I only wanted more historical and theological clarity for myself."

On the heels of this premise, Benedict went into the details of the debacle with Cardinal Sarah: "While still working out these thoughts on paper, I received a letter from Cardinal Sarah on 5 September 2019 asking me for a reflection on the priesthood, particularly on the topic of priestly celibacy, obedience, and poverty. Surprised by the request, I responded on September 20th that I was already writing some reflections on the priesthood, but I noticed that my strength was not sufficient to render it a theologically robust text. Nevertheless, I went back to the work and sent it to the cardinal, saying, 'I leave it up to you to decide whether these notes, which I honestly think are insufficient, can be of any use to you.'"

Essentially, what happened was that, after some quick revisions, Benedict sent the text to Cardinal Sarah, who sent an acknowledgement on October 31st: "I thank you from my heart for sending your wonderful and deeply appreciated reflections on the priesthood. I am sure that they will be a great contribution to the Church, and especially an expression of your paternal support for priests throughout the world. I am truly grateful and deeply moved by your interest and your fatherly care. I am studying and working to see how I can best present them to priests and to the entire Church. As soon as I have finished the project, I will send a draft to Your Holiness for your feedback and approval."

Benedict continued his explanation to Francis: "Sarah, grateful for the text, then sent me a few lines in which he simplified the particular intention behind my own text as a kind of interpretive help for readers engaging what I had written. When the cardinal learned that I had written seven pages—strictly for private use—to help interpret my text, he asked if he could see those notes. I responded that his clear, half-page interpretation was more useful that my long document of seven pages, and that only these words of his should be considered as written by me.[15] In a letter dated November 20th, Cardinal Sarah added a few other brief explanatory notes. I had added three interpretations of fundamental texts to my reflections on the priesthood as expressions of my personal experience. So, I thought I managed to touch upon the question of celibacy without entering into current debates on the topic."

The letter to which Benedict was referring, dated November 20th, makes it clear to whom the individual texts are attributed: "I would like to publish the book on the Epiphany of the Lord, January 6th, if that is agreeable to your Holiness.[16] As you can see, the full text is divided into four parts: an introduction, your reflection, my text, and a conclusion.[17] I took the liberty of making a few additions to your text, which you will see marked in red. First of all, I added an introductory text with the intention of giving the reader some background for the reflections that follow. Furthermore, on page 5, I inserted a quote from Saint Clement of Rome to emphasize the historical continuity. Finally, on pages 9 and 10,

15 Author's note: Benedict wanted to emphasize that, apart from that "half page," he didn't want any other text attributed to him.

16 Author's note: From this, it is clear that the cardinal was intending to release the book after the publication of Pope Francis' Apostolic Exhortation.

17 Author's note: Here, there is absolutely no doubt that the only text of Benedict was "his reflection."

I added a quote from you to underscore the reflection on celibacy. As I have said, these are only suggestions and Your Holiness can make any changes you see fit."

On November 25th, the pope emeritus replied: "Your Eminence, I cordially thank you for the text you sent including my contribution, and for all the work you've done. I was deeply touched by the way you understood my latest intentions. I had written seven pages to explain the methodology I used in my text, and I am happy to say that you have boiled it down to the essentials in half a page. In my opinion, the text can be published in the form you've proposed."[18]

The conclusion of the letter Benedict sent to Pope Francis on February 17th sheds light on the deep regret the pope emeritus felt for what had happened: "I have decided to publish nothing else in whatever life I have left on this earth. Holy Father, I hope I have cleared up the story of my text in Cardinal Sarah's book, and I can only express sadness on how my contribution was abused in public debates." There was no need for Francis to respond, since it was nothing more than Benedict's acknowledgment for having received the pontiff's apostolic exhortation. But, as far as I know, he completely understood the good faith of his predecessor and appreciated his honesty and openness.

In any case, if further confirmation is needed that things transpired in the way that I have described, it can be found *ad abundantiam* in this: On 31 May 2005, Benedict XIV/Joseph Ratzinger signed over the publishing rights of his material to the Libreria Editrice Vaticana (i.e., Vatican Publishing House). Thus, Benedict never signed any contract with regard to Sarah's book, and he never had any contact with the Libreria Editrice Vaticana about it. Hence, the pope was entirely justified in acting on his own regarding Sarah's book because, in his mind, the only thing at stake was his very limited contribution—that is, this book was anything but a co-authored work.

Moreover, Vatican reporter Sandro Magister posted a blog on February 12th in which he offers his own detailed reconstruction of events. The title of the blog was "Francis's silence, Ratzinger's tears, and a

18 Author's note: Benedict continues to refer only to his initial text with the addition of the cardinal's half-page explanation.

declaration never published." Commenting on the Apostolic Exhortation *Querida Amazonia,* which had been released on the same day, Magister drew attention to the absence of any reference in the exhortation to clerical celibacy and the ordination of married men. He draws a hasty and incorrect conclusion: "The question immediately rises as to what extent the fiasco surrounding Sarah's book on the defense of clerical celibacy, published in mid-January, had any influence on the exhortation."

Magister also offers a dramatic reconstruction of an alleged telephone call taking place between Benedict and Sarah on the morning of January 15th: "While Pope Francis was having his weekly General Audience in Paul VI Hall with Gänswein, as usual, seated next to him—and thus far from the Mater Ecclesiae Monastery where he lived with the pope emeritus—Benedict XVI picked up the phone himself and called Cardinal Sarah at his residence. When he got no answer, he called him in his office, where the cardinal was taking a nap. Benedict XVI expressed his heartfelt solidarity with the cardinal. He confided in him that he didn't understand the reasons for such a violent and unjust attack. And he cried. Cardinal Sarah cried, too. The phone call ended with both of them in tears." As soon as I had read these words, I obviously went to Benedict to ask him what happened. He told me that he simply wanted to give some encouragement to Sarah on a personal level, telling him that he simply didn't understand the fury against the book, but he made it clear that the telephone call was not nearly as pathetic as Magister had described it.

There is one final thing I want to share about this story. I had a meeting with Cardinal Sarah on February 27th at his apartment on *Piazza della Città Leonina* in the presence of a priest both of us knew and trusted. When I asked him why Benedict's requests to have the cover changed, the acknowledgment of him as co-author removed, and the spread of private correspondence between him and the pope emeritus to cease were not heeded, the cardinal told me that he had placed everything in the hands of Nicolas Diat and that it was entirely his responsibility. When I expressed my disappointment for what he had done and the damage he had caused both Benedict and me, he mumbled that he could only say he was sorry for those things he had in no way intended to happen.

The prefect split in two

My simultaneous roles as private secretary for the pope emeritus and Prefect of the Pontifical Household for Pope Francis made me feel like both a servant of two masters and a vase made of ceramic and iron.

Benedict's hope that I could serve as a link between myself and his successor was a little misguided, in that, after a few months, I had the impression that there wasn't really an opportunity to create a strong bond of trust between me and the new pontiff, which would have been necessary if I were to be an effective bridge between them.

My appointment was customarily renewed for another five years probably out of respect for the original appointment made by Benedict XVI. But I could see from the beginning that my role was often circumvented, as Pope Francis preferred to work directly with my assistant, Father Leonardo Sapienza.

I remember, for example, the pope's visit to the Community of Sant'Egidio in Trastevere on 15 June 2014. The day prior, as we greeted one another after audiences at the Casa Santa Marta, Pope Francis, in the presence of the commanders of the Gendarmeria, the Swiss Guard, and the chauffeurs, said that my presence was not needed and that I could take the day off. He continued to insist even as I expressed surprise. On the following day, I received a phone call from the founder of the movement, Andrea Riccardi, who asked me if Benedict or I had some problem with Sant'Egidio because this was the rumor flying around after my unexplained absence from the event.

As soon as the opportunity arose, I told Pope Francis about the phone call from Riccardi, explaining that it made it difficult to manage the prefecture because my authority was seemingly undermined, and that, on a personal level, I was a little humiliated both because he didn't clarify the reason for his decision, and because he had spoken in the presence of others, thus initiating rumors that immediately made their way through the Vatican. Pope Francis responded that I was right and that he hadn't thought of that. He apologized but added that humiliation often does a lot of good. Unfortunately, similar situations happened repeatedly, especially when it came to visits to the parishes of Rome.

There were other signs—seemingly small but relatively important within curial circles—that Pope Francis did not consider the work of the Prefecture of the Pontifical Household to be that important or necessary. One example of this was the way he handled the apartment that normally serves as the residence for the Prefect of the Papal Household. It is located in one of the oldest sections of the apostolic palace dating from the time of Pope Julius II, and the Niccoline Chapel—which is sometimes visible during private tours of the Vatican—serves as its private oratory.

When my predecessor, Archbishop Harvey, was made Cardinal Archpriest of Saint Paul's Outside the Walls, he decided to move to the residence attached to the basilica, but the apartment needed some work, so he asked if he could stay in the prefect's apartment in the apostolic palace for another couple of months. I told him that was no problem at all for me. The work at Saint Paul's, however, was taking much longer than expected, and three years went by before Harvey turned in the keys to the Governatorato. Toward the middle of 2016, after some minor work on the prefect's apartment, the general secretary, Fernando Vérgez Alzaga, told me that I could take possession of it. So, I started to organize my belongings for the move, which until that time I had left in the office of the prefect at Castel Gandolfo on the ground floor of Villa Barberini.

On the morning of 22 July 2016, I was waiting, as was my custom, for Pope Francis at the *nobile* elevator in the San Damaso courtyard. As soon as he got out of the car, he said to me, "I heard that you have an apartment in the apostolic palace." I clarified for him that it was the apartment of the Prefect of the Papal Household, assigned to me by virtue of my office. "Please, don't take possession of it yet," he added. I informed him that it was normal for the prefect to reside there so that he could carry out his duties. And even if I were living at the monastery with the pope emeritus, this was only a temporary arrangement. He replied: "Wait. I have to talk to my inner circle first. Don't do anything until you hear from me again." I was disappointed to hear this because I could tell that someone in the curia was jockeying to take over the apartment.

On the following September 2nd—again, just as he got of the car taking him from Casa Santa Marta to the courtyard in San Damaso—Pope Francis said: "You've been waiting for my response, so now I am telling you to give it up. When you need an apartment, I'll see that you get one." When he saw how surprised I was, he explained that, as he had learned, the Secretary of State (Cardinal Pietro Parolin) and the Substitute for the First Section for General Affairs (at that time, Giovanni Angelo Becciu) were living in the apostolic palace, but not the Secretary for the Second Section for Relations with States. Then he simply said, "I've decided." And I noticed within a short time that, in fact, Archbishop Paul Richard Gallagher, the Secretary for Relations with States, had moved into the apartment.

In 2018, I thought it opportune to remind Pope Francis of his promise, so he asked Monsignor Vérgez to arrange something for me, and in the end, I was assigned an apartment in the old Santa Marta next to Paul VI Hall. The physical separation from the apostolic palace was only a foretaste of things to come.

At the end of January 2020, I discovered that, in fact, I was a *prefetto dimezzato* (a "split-prefect"), borrowing an image from Italo Calvino's opera, *Il Visconte Dimezzato.* On Monday the 20th of January, after the storm surrounding Cardinal Sarah's book, I asked if I could meet with the pope, and he set an appointment later that morning after audiences. I gave him the details about what had happened and I asked him for advice on how to act in the future because it was not always easy for me to prevent problems, as was clear from the Sarah case. He looked at me with a serious expression and said to me, completely unexpectedly: "From now on, you stay at home. Stay close to Benedict. He needs you. Be his shield."

I was completely shocked and remained speechless. When I tried to reply by telling him that I had been doing that already for seven years and that I could continue to do it, he cut the conversation short: "You'll remain prefect, but starting tomorrow, don't go back to work." Dismayed, I replied, "I don't understand. I can't accept this humanly, but I'll do it out of obedience." He replied, "That is a great word. I know so because from my personal experience 'to accept in obedience' is a good thing." My real concern was how this was going to be communicated externally because there was no doubt that my absence would raise serious questions. But Pope Francis assured me that it wasn't necessary to do anything, and he left.

I went back to the monastery. Over lunch, I told Benedict and the Memores what had happened. Pope Benedict, half-seriously and half-jokingly, said with a hint of irony: "It seems to me that Pope Francis doesn't trust me anymore and that he wants you to guard me!" I responded with a smile, "Yes, I think so ... but should I be a guardsman or a prison warden?" I then added that presumably it had something to do with the Sarah debacle because nothing else had changed in the meantime.

Unsurprisingly, as I had predicted, a torrent of mail and messages poured in asking what had happened to me. Obviously, I had nothing to say. On Saturday the 25th, I wrote a note to Pope Francis, telling him I was receiving requests for information on what had happened to me and suggested that perhaps I could return to work after a few days of suspension. I received a written reply from him on February 1st: "My dear brother, thank you for your letter. For now, I think it's best to maintain the status quo. I am grateful for all you are doing for Pope Benedict to make sure his needs are met. I am praying for you, and I ask for your prayers. May the Lord bless you and Our Lady watch over you. Fraternally, Francis."

On February 5th, the silence was finally broken when an article came out in the *Tagespost,* written by Guido Horst, which in turn ignited other posts, comments, and a host of opinions on what had happened to the relationship between Pope Francis, me and, eventually, Benedict. Matteo Bruni, director of the Vatican Press Office, contacted me to let me know that journalists were eager for some clarification and that my superiors were formulating a response. So, in the afternoon of February 6th, journalists received a press statement—which I had not seen until it was released—stating that "the absence of Monsignor Gänswein from some audiences over the last months is due to an ordinary redistribution of various tasks and responsibilities assigned to the Prefect of the Papal Household, who is also performing the role of personal secretary to the pope emeritus."

Benedict, disappointed by this turn of events, added a final paragraph to a letter he had written to Pope Francis on February 13th: "Please allow me now to ask a question. Monsignor Gänswein is suffering greatly—more so every day—under the weight of being marginalized without any solution in sight. Therefore, I would like to beg Your Holiness to clarify the situation by offering him the opportunity of a fatherly conversation. From my part, I can only say that Monsignor Gänswein had nothing to do with the preparation of my contribution to the book of Cardinal Sarah. Having seen the cardinal's book that seemed to make me the co-author, and recognizing right away that this could insinuate a stance I was taking against your pontifical teaching, Gänswein immediately understood the gravity of the situation and he strongly insisted that the book was entirely unacceptable in this form. He now feels attacked from both sides and he is in need of paternal encouragement." A couple of days later, Pope Francis made an appointment for me to see him at Casa Santa Marta, at which he told me that nothing would change. The pope emeritus made one final appeal in a letter dated February 17th—"I humbly ask you again to have a word with Monsignor Gänswein"—but received no response.

At the beginning of September in 2020, at the Biomedical Campus, I was diagnosed with a kidney problem, which the head of internal medicine attributed to a psychosomatic disturbance. When I returned to the monastery after a couple of weeks, Pope Francis called to ask about my health, and I took the opportunity to ask him for an appointment, which we fixed for September 23rd at 4:00 p.m. I told him that I understood my suspension to be a punishment, but he responded that it was not. I furthermore told him that everyone—including the media—was interpreting it in that way. His reply was that I didn't need to worry because (and these were his exact words), "there are a lot of people writing things against you and against me, but they deserve no consideration."

In any case, when I tried to reason with him about restarting work (since, according to His Holiness, it wasn't a punishment), he replied by suggesting that I make no plans for the future and to consider some pastoral work, something which was obviously out of the question, precisely due to his own wishes that I stay close to Benedict XVI at the monastery. Then, once again, Pope Francis told me about some of his difficult assignments in Argentina, saying that whenever he felt stuck in them they eventually contributed to his growth.

In the end, we talked about the possibility of appointing a pro-prefect for the benefit of creating an appropriate atmosphere when the Holy

Father had formal audiences. But he concluded that things could continue the same way they had been. Only with the publication of the Apostolic Constitution *Praedicate Evangelium* on the Roman Curia did I understand the reason, for the role of the Prefect of the Pontifical Household had been radically reconfigured. In *Pastor Bonus* of 1988, the prefect was "at the service of the Supreme Pontiff, both in the Apostolic Palace and when he travels in Rome or in Italy." Now, however, according to *Praedicate Evangelium,* "the Prefect assists the Pope only on the occasion of meetings and visits that take place within Vatican territory."

In any event, in regard to my future, I can only repeat what I said in 2016 (indeed, at a time free of suspicion): "Having been a collaborator at the Congregation for the Doctrine of the Faith, a secretary for Cardinal Ratzinger and subsequently for Pope Benedict, I evidently wear the 'mark of Cain.' Externally, I am easily 'recognizable.' That is just the way it is: I have never hidden my convictions. In some ways, the public has managed to make me out as someone with heavily right-leanings or a 'hawk' but have no evidence for that characterization. So, I can say it firmly, both now and in the future: I have not made—and am not making—any career plans."

9

The Productive Silence of the Monastery

A rhythm of prayer

It's useless to beat around the bush. However awkward it may be to admit, this is the utter truth: When we moved to Castel Gandolfo on 28 February 2013, Benedict was absolutely convinced he didn't have much longer to live. Doctor Polisca and I also thought this was the case because we had witnessed Benedict's accelerated decline from up close. Even the pope emeritus' brother Georg was convinced he would outlive his younger brother.

The only time we made any reference to the resignation was when I showed him the photograph of lightning striking the dome of Saint Peter's Basilica, taken by Alessandro Di Meo of Ansa news agency on the evening of February 11th. We obviously heard the violent storm raging outside the apostolic palace, but we didn't see the flash of light. Benedict was struck by the image and asked me if it were fabricated. I told him, "No," adding teasingly, "it seems nature had something to say!" He added nothing in return.

In the first weeks following his resignation, the pope emeritus was completely exhausted. He continually stooped when he walked and spoke very little. The doctor didn't detect any serious psychological depression, but he did attribute the symptoms to severe physical and mental exhaustion from which he expected the pope emeritus to recover gradually. The peace of the papal residence at Castel Gandolfo helped Benedict immensely. It gave him plenty of time to read (Gregory the Great, Augustine, as well as more recent authors including Romano Guardini and Eric Peterson), to listen to sacred or symphonic music *via* a compact-disk player he kept in his bedroom (Bach, Mozart, Beethoven, Liszt, Bruckner, Schubert, Brahms, and others), and he gradually starting playing the piano again.

The fact is that Ratzinger had had a series of health problems over the years, including a stroke in 1991, which had weakened the vision in his left eye. A couple of falls in 1992 and 2012 led to stitches on his head, and he underwent surgery to repair a fracture in his right wrist in 2009. He needed to have a pacemaker installed in 2003 to regulate an irregular heart rhythm, which was replaced twice (in 2012 and 2022).

Thankfully, however, Benedict never suffered from any serious degenerative illnesses, and his death was ultimately the result of the slow but steady natural process of aging. In fact, he had been registered as an organ donor for a long time, though that was obviously cancelled after his election to the papacy. The greatest difficulty he had in his final years was with speaking due to his weak lungs. Yet he accepted even this with his typical sense of humor, saying on several occasions, "God has taken words from me so that I can appreciate silence more."

Just as he intended, life in the monastery was heavily marked by prayer, as expressed in one of his favorite maxims: "I begin every day with the Lord and finish it with the Lord, and we'll see how long that lasts." This was basically in line with something Ratzinger had already said in an interview with Peter Seewald in 1996, published as *Salt of the Earth:* "The older I get, the more I notice how my strength is not enough to do what needs to be done; that I am either too weak, incapable, or simply not up to the task. That's when it's time to turn to God and say, 'Now you must help me; I can't do it on my own anymore.'"

I always tell people that the Mater Ecclesiae Monastery was not a house of rest, but of work, especially spiritual work. This is all I meant by a terribly misunderstood phrase I used when I referred to "a wider papal ministry: one with an 'active' element and a 'contemplative' element." Benedict chose to live within the Vatican precisely because he had a clear vision of what his future mission would be. In fact, I had proposed alternatives, such as some space that could be blocked off within the papal summer residence at Castel Gandolfo. We discussed the possibility during one of our afternoon walks, but he had already made his decision and never doubted it for a moment.

Sometimes, both as cardinal and as pope, Benedict had gone to celebrate Mass at the monastery. As he was pondering his resignation, he recognized it as the perfect environment for his personal disposition and his desire to live a simple life, of which he had a foretaste on several occasions. For example, in October of 2011, during a visit to the Carthusians at the Church of the Charterhouse of Serra San Bruno, Benedict said, "Every monastery—male or female—is an oasis where we find a deep well to draw 'living water' to quench our deepest thirst." During a visit to the Basilica of San Gregorio al Celio in March of 2012, he said, according to Camaldolese Prior Enzo Gargano, "I feel like a monk just like all of you. Among monks, I feel at home."

As we were deciding how to reorganize the monastery, Benedict told me he was undecided whether it was best for the four Memores sisters to stay with us because he didn't want to "take advantage" of their kindness. After consulting with me and them directly, he agreed that the original intention was to create a true family, so it would be best to keep it that way until his death. Hence, the second floor was dedicated to their use, including four bedrooms and a common living room. On the first floor was the pope emeritus' bedroom, living room, and library, in addition to my room and a study for Sister Birgit. On the ground floor was the apartment occasionally used by Benedict's brother Monsignor Georg on one side, and on the other, the kitchen, dining room, and reception parlor.

While in lockdown during the COVID pandemic, we used to joke about how we passed the time according to an aphorism Cicero wrote to his friend Varro: "[I]f there is a garden next to the library, you lack nothing." In reality, however, Benedict never wished to live in complete isolation. This was clear from his initial private conversations with Pope Francis about the living arrangements, when they both agreed that "it would be better to see people, to go out, and to participate in the life of the Church." It made us grin when Francis acknowledged him during a meeting with the elderly in Saint Peter's Square on 28 September 2014: "I have said many times that I am glad to have him live here in the Vatican because it is like having a wise grandfather in the house," to which Benedict jokingly replied, "Well, truth be told, there are only nine years between us, so perhaps it would be more accurate to call me a 'big brother!'"

In any case, contrary to what many have said, Benedict never ceased to keep up with world events. Unfortunately, during a previously mentioned speech at the Rosetum in Milan, Vittorio Messori got it wrong when he said, "Benedict receives no news. He doesn't watch television and he doesn't listen to the radio. He just gets the *Corriere della Sera.*" The truth is that, besides reading the *Corriere della Sera,* which is the most widely distributed newspaper in Italy, Benedict always watched the news on television, and he was always up to date with the latest press releases from the Secretariat of State. He also pored over the daily Vatican newspaper *L'Osservatore Romano,* as well as the German *Frankfurter Allgemeine Zeitung,* and the Catholic weekly *Die Tagespost.*

Moreover, we always kept him abreast of things that might be of interest to him or involved him in some way. For example, I told him about the television series, *The Young Pope* and *The New Pope,* as well as the film, *The Two Popes,* even though he didn't show much interest in any of them. While scenes of the latter were being filmed in Rome, actor Anthony Hopkins—who was playing the part of Benedict XVI—requested a private audience, but it was deemed inappropriate since such a meeting would certainly have become public and perhaps suggest that Benedict somehow approved of the film, which in fact presented a series of fictitious events. In fact, Anthony McCarten's book, upon which the film is based, contains "facts" that not only have no historical basis, but are even a bit offensive, such as when Pope Ratzinger "commissioned a perfume manufacturer to create a fragrance just for him, which he never failed to wear."

A series of unfounded claims

Benedict, for one—and I for another—had never imagined that his words and gestures would be dissected so meticulously and distortedly as to lead to illusionary attempts to reconstruct his life along the lines of a Dan Brown novel rather than along a path of logic and reason. At times, the first thing to come into my head was the famous phrase of American policemen: "Anything you say can and will be used against you."

One of the first major challenges to his resignation was the battle ram constructed by journalist Andrea Cionci, who questioned the use of two Latin words in the pope's declaration—*munus* and *ministerium*—both of which are usually translated as "ministry." It was even suggested that, in the preparations of the new Code of Canon Law published in

1983, John Paul II and Cardinal Ratzinger agreed to make a juridical distinction between two aspects of the pope's responsibility: *munus* indicating the Petrine title, and *ministerium* indicating the relative exercise of power. (The reality is that such a distinction simply doesn't exist in the Code.)

The hypothesis is nothing but absurd, and is based on a certainty of three successive future events: First of all, the election of Cardinal Ratzinger to the papacy (in 1983, he was barely 56 years old and Wojtyła was only 63, so they were concerned with anything but succession at the time); secondly, the development of personal and ecclesial matters that would have successively led Benedict to resign; thirdly, a truly exceptional future situation, which Cionci identifies as an "impeded see," defined by the Code of Canon Law in this way (can. 412): "An episcopal see is understood to be impeded if by reason of captivity, banishment, exile, or incapacity a diocesan bishop is clearly prevented from fulfilling his pastoral function in the diocese, so that he is not able to communicate with those in his diocese even by letter." It goes without saying that this is a far cry from the way Benedict XVI lived at the monastery, where he would meet face-to-face with anyone he wished, could write to whomever he wished, and publish anything he thought opportune.

The simply reality is that, for the sake of stylistic elegance, Benedict decided to use two Latin synonyms to indicate what had been entrusted to him at the conclave and what he had accepted. Perhaps a canonist pope would have just stuck with *munus.* But, being a theologian, Benedict drew upon his own expertise. According to him, the Second Vatican Council applied the term with the objective of explaining more precisely the concept of *tria munera* (the "triple function" or "duties")—that is, the participation of all the faithful in Christ's triple mission of priest, prophet, and king.

However, from a theological point of view, Ratzinger was not in agreement that the concept of a *tria munera* is grounded in the Church Fathers or the Catechism of the Council of Trent. In his opinion, the concept was foreign to classical theology and was substantially formulated precisely as an invention of the Second Vatican Council. Hence, he preferred the term *ministerium,* which he thought to be the correct word and one with a stronger theological footing.

Many tried to contrive conflicting and dubious translations of Benedict XVI's Latin text announcing his intention to resign. But none of us, including the canonist Bertone, had ever imagined such equivocations were possible. Nevertheless, perceiving that some were leaning toward such an interpretation, Benedict XVI, during the General Audience of February 27th, made it abundantly clear what he had meant by using the word *officio* ("office" in English), which is precisely the Italian word used to translate the Latin term *munus:* "I no longer bear the power of office for the governance of the Church, but in the service of prayer I remain, so to speak, in the enclosure of Saint Peter."

Another phrase Benedict used in the Latin text needs to be placed more carefully within the context of his intention—namely, his specification of the convocation of a conclave "by those whose competence it is." This is, in fact, a precise translation corresponding to all the vernacular languages in light of article 38 of the Apostolic Constitution *Universi Dominici Gregis:* the convocation of the cardinal electors is done "by the Cardinal Dean, or by another Cardinal in his name," and this is precisely to what "those whose competence it is" refers to. As has been said many times, the expression was chosen as a synonym for "the cardinals." One might critique the style, but not the meaning of the phrase.

The coat of arms and the white cassock the pope continued to wear after his resignation were also criticized as "inelegant," to use a euphemism. I repeat that the pope emeritus did not think that he was going to live as long as he did. So, even if he wasn't able to say it out loud, he thought it was useless to modify symbols that would, in fact, "disappear" as soon as he passed away.

Obviously, the response Benedict gave to Vatican journalist Andrea Tornielli on 18 February 2014 also gave rise to curiosity: "Maintaining the white cassock and the name of Benedict was simply a practical matter. When I resigned, there was nothing else to wear." With his typical dry humor, he was simply trying to make a joke because he knew that he was wearing the white cassock in a way that was clearly different from the way Francis wears it. But if in retrospect it wasn't a very felicitous response, I must point out that once the interview was printed I could not suggest any changes.

The real problem was identified by Benedict in correspondence he had with Cardinal Walter Brandmüller, who expressed perplexity both with respect to the pope's resignation, and with his selection of title "pope emeritus" (and he was perceived as a close friend of Benedict, even though he "happened" to show a journalist his personal correspondence with the pope emeritus, which was then divulged): "If you know of a better choice and therefore hold the right to criticize what I've chosen, I beg you to let me know what it is." In short, the question of what to wear and how to act as a pope emeritus was unprecedented, but certain decisions had to be made, even with the knowledge they would never be perfect. One thing was sure: Whatever choice we made, it would certainly be criticized by someone.

Unfortunately, I was not spared from being pulled into the polemics. Sometimes in good faith, but in most cases not, some of my more emphatic statements were exploited to support fantastic theories with no basis in reality. This is essentially what happened when I introduced Fr. Roberto Regoli's book on Benedict XVI's pontificate entitled *Oltre la crisi della Chiesa* (2016).[19] I had anticipated some misinterpretations, but I dared to use the phrase "a wider Petrine mission," not thinking it was so out of place that the intended meaning could be turned entirely upside down. I thought it would be a useful image to describe the novelty of the ecclesial situation in which we were living, and I have to say that I didn't notice any strong reactions when I used it at the conference. Over time, however, others seized on the opportunity to stretch my words in other directions. In any case, I can say now that I always shared my public speeches with the pope emeritus only after I had given them because I didn't want him to feel obligated to assumed a professorial role, but also to affirm unambiguously that I was expressing my own thoughts and was not in any way acting surreptitiously as his spokesperson, as many hypothesized.

Eventually, things got even more ridiculous, as when some asked why the old episcopal coat-of-arms was still on the letterhead of my stationery—that is, the coat-of-arms in which Pope Benedict's coat-of-arms

19 Roberto Regoli, *Beyond the Crises in the Church: The Pontificate of Benedict XVI* (St. Augustine's Press, 2023).

was quartered—and why I waited until 2017 to replace it with a new version in which Francis's coat-of-arms was quartered instead. The explanation is simple. I did indeed officially change my coat-of-arms right after Bergoglio was elected, replacing the part that showed Benedict's heraldic symbols with those of Francis. But just a few weeks before the election, the Vatican printing press sent me letterhead stationery and envelopes with the old coat-of-arms. Obviously, I wasn't able to tell them *not* to print a new batch before Benedict announced his resignation, for that would have raised suspicion. So, I continued to use the old stationery for correspondence in my capacity as Benedict's private secretary, whereas for official correspondence as Prefect of the Papal Household I used the new stationery with the modified coat-of-arms. I would have considered it a total waste to throw all that expensive stationery in the trash, but I never imagined it would have provoked such outlandish speculation.

The family caught in the fray

In the initial days of Francis's pontificate, Benedict XVI eagerly read the *L'Osservatore Romano* to keep abreast of everything his successor was saying and doing. I remember that Benedict was immediately struck by Francis's words at the first Sunday Angelus on 17 March 2013, when he cited a book about mercy written by Cardinal Walter Kasper, especially since he himself (for example, at the Regina Caeli on 30 March 2008) had affirmed with conviction that "mercy is the central nucleus of the Gospel message; it is the very name of God" (as Francis himself later admitted when he explained that Benedict was his inspiration for the title of the book-length interview published by Andrea Tornielli, *The Name of God Is Mercy*).

The pope emeritus also followed with keen interest the two phases of the synod on the family, and, with a certain clairvoyance, noticed that—well before the opening of the synod on the theme "Pastoral Challenges of the Family in the Context of Evangelization" (5–19 October 2014), followed by the ordinary synod on "The Vocation and Mission of the Family in the Church in the Contemporary World" (4–25 October 2015)—the theological-pastoral outlines of the synod were already highly developed in a presentation Cardinal Walter Kasper gave at the extraordinary consistory of cardinals in February of 2014.

Benedict had known the German cardinal for decades and had at times entered into theological debates with him, and he was somewhat concerned with what Kasper had said at the consistory. In fact, the text was presented as a beacon for the ensuing assembly discussions, and Benedict was equally surprised when Francis decided to deliver a similar speech, which clearly may have had a significant impact on the synodal fathers, indicating that the purpose of the synod was "to deepen the theology of the family and discern the pastoral practices which our present situation requires. May we do so thoughtfully and without falling into 'casuistry,' because this would inevitably diminish the quality of our work."

Another reason Kasper's speech caught the attention of the pope emeritus was that he had referred to Ratzinger both as Prefect of the Congregation for the Doctrine of the Faith and as Roman Pontiff: "The Congregation for the Doctrine of the Faith already issued a statement in 1994, declaring that the divorced and remarried were not able to receive sacramental communion, but they could make a spiritual communion. Ratzinger reaffirmed this as Pope at the International Meeting of Families in Milan in 2012. This, of course, does not pertain to all divorced persons, but only to those who are not properly disposed spiritually. Nonetheless, many people will be grateful for this response, which is a true opening. But it also raises several questions. In fact, whoever receives spiritual communion becomes one with Jesus Christ; so how can it be in contradiction with Christ's commandment? Why can't that person also receive sacramental communion?"

These are certainly delicate and serious questions, but Ratzinger never shied away from wrestling with them and responding to them. Even as pope, he remained firmly planted in the congregation's 1994 concise expression: "A series of critical objections against the doctrine and praxis of the Church pertain to questions of a pastoral nature. Some say, for example, that the language used in the ecclesial documents is too legalistic, that the rigidity of law prevails over an understanding of dramatic human situations. They claim that the human person of today is no longer able to understand such language, that Jesus would have had an open ear for the needs of people, particularly for those on the margins of society. They say that the Church, on the other hand, presents herself like a judge who excludes wounded people from the sacraments and from certain public responsibilities. One can readily admit that the Magisterium's manner of expression does not seem very easy to understand at times. It needs to be translated by preachers and catechists into a language which relates to people and to their respective cultural environments. The essential content of the Church's teaching, however, must be upheld in this process. It must not be watered down on allegedly pastoral grounds, because it communicates the revealed truth. Certainly, it is difficult to make the demands of the Gospel understandable to secularized people. But this pastoral difficulty must not lead to compromises with the truth."

Benedict was even more perplexed after the publication of the Post-Synodal Apostolic Exhortation *Amoris Laetitia.* Even though there were many passages he admired, he was confused by some of the footnotes, which usually are there simply to cite sources. But in this case, they contained highly significant content. As he continued to follow debates in the wake of the publication of the exhortation, he was increasingly unsure why it would leave such important matters so highly ambiguous, because this ushered in equivocal interpretations.

The pope emeritus, of course, did not publish anything in this regard, nor did he respond to numerous requests for comment, because he did not want to intervene unnecessarily and undermine the pope's authority. However, listening to some of his cursory remarks, I understood that he was not in agreement with the strategy of leaving the issue open to so many contrasting interpretations, and then choosing to favor one as evidenced in something printed in the official *Acta Apostolicae Sedis* (the compilation of the official acts of the Holy See)—namely, a letter sent to Pope Francis by the bishops of Argentina, with the former commenting that "their explanation of chapter 8 of *Amoris Laetitia* is commendable and complete. Other interpretations are not possible."

Benedict XVI guarded his silence even more when a letter of *dubia* was published by Cardinals Walter Brandmüller, Raymond L. Burke, Carlo Caffarra, and Joachim Meisner. These four cardinals sent the letter to Pope Francis in September of 2016 and only made it public a couple of months later when they had received no response. None of them had ever spoken to the pope emeritus, neither during that period nor after, when in the spring of 2017 the four of them once again asked Pope Francis for an audience to receive some clarification. From a human point of view, Benedict found it quite surprising that these cardinals did not even receive a response, even though Francis normally had shown himself available to anyone desiring an audience.

In any case, Benedict's desire to send a message of condolence on the death of Cardinal Joachim Meisner in July of 2017 was in no way intended in association to this affair. He sent it simply at the invitation of Cardinal Rainer Maria Woelki, Archbishop of Cologne, who invited the pope emeritus to do so based on an enduring friendship with Meisner, which was evident in the fact that Benedict had spoken with him just days prior to his death: "What particularly impressed me from my last conversations with the now deceased cardinal was the relaxed cheerfulness, the inner joy, and the confidence which he had come to. We know that this passionate shepherd and pastor found it difficult to leave his post, especially at a time in which the Church stands in particularly pressing need of convincing shepherds who can resist the dictatorship of the spirit of the age and who live and think the faith with determination."

Benedict added one more observation about Cardinal Meisner, implicitly suggesting he wished to imitate the holy priest in this respect (even though it ruffled some feathers when he referred to a boat "on the verge of capsizing"): "However, what moved me all the more was that, in this last period of his life, he learned to let go and to live out of a deep conviction that the Lord does not abandon His Church, even if the boat has taken on so much water as to be on the verge of capsizing." The final reference was really to the Church in Germany, where Cardinal Meisner had to face a host of problems. Moreover, Benedict was well aware of the great esteem that Pope Francis had for the deceased cardinal, whom he called "sincere, clear, and Catholic" in a conversation I had with him.

A letter covered with whiteout

Toward the end of 2017, Monsignor Dario Edoardo Viganò, at that time Prefect of the Secretariat for Communications of the Holy See, informed me that the Libreria Editrice Vaticana was about to publish some volumes written by various theologians on the magisterium of Pope Francis, and he asked if it would be possible for Benedict XVI to write a preface. I suggested that he send me the texts and a written request indicating precisely what he was looking for. The material reached the monastery on 12 January 2018, and I passed it on to the pope emeritus.

A few days later, Benedict said that he had looked over the material and was surprised to find that Peter Hünermann had prepared a contribution. Both before and during Benedict's pontificate, Hünermann created serious problems and had been a staunch adversary of Ratzinger (after Hans Küng's faculties to teach Catholic theology were revoked in 1979, Hünermann succeeded him at the University of Tübingen). "Out of love for Pope Francis, I would like to agree to Monsignor Viganò's request, but there are simply too many volumes for me to read. Besides, I can't remain silent about Hünermann," he told me.

Since the Prefect Viganò had asked me directly, I told the pope emeritus that I would be willing to respond myself, but would obviously show him a draft of the response before sending it. But Benedict replied that he would see to it himself, so he set himself to writing a letter that he then mailed to Viganò on February 7th in an envelope labeled "personal and confidential."

The official presentation of the book series took place on March 12th. That evening, we saw Benedict's letter appear on the evening news broadcast on *Tg1,* partially hidden under a pile of eleven books. Attention was given to only two passages in Benedict's letter: "I applaud this initiative as a needed reaction against the foolish prejudice according to which Pope Francis is only a practical man with no special theological or philosophical formation, while I was only a theoretical theologian who knew little about the concrete lives of Christians today. These brief volumes rightly show that Pope Francis is a man of deep philosophical and theological formation, and they will therefore help to show the interior continuity between the two pontificates despite differences in style and temperament."

The following day, Vatican journalist Sandro Magister regrettably posted another passage from the letter, more sensitive than those divulged the previous day: "However, I don't feel as if I should write a 'brief but dense theological commentary' on the texts. Throughout my entire life, I have made it a principle to only write about and express opinions on books I have carefully read myself. Unfortunately, even from a physical point of view, I am unable to read all eleven volumes in the near future, especially given the other commitments I have already taken on."

After a few more days, the entire letter was made known, the final paragraph of which read: "As a final—but more marginal—comment, I would like to express my surprise that Professor Hünermann was chosen to contribute to the series, who was placed in the spotlight throughout my pontificate for spearheading anti-papal initiatives. He had a large role to play in the publication of the so-called *Kölnder Erklärung* (the "Cologne Declaration"), which presented a vicious attack against the magisterial authority of the pope, especially in questions of moral theology as expressed in the Encyclical *Veritatis Splendor.* He also founded the *Europäische Theologengesellschaft,* which was established precisely as an organization opposed to the papal magisterium. In the following years, the ecclesial sentiments of many theologians have blurred the original intent of this organization, turning it into a normal forum for theologians to meet and discuss theology."

I have no idea how Magister came to know of this letter, and, normally, I wouldn't even take the trouble to deny that I was the one who divulged it, but an unequivocal clarification is obviously necessary: Anyone who claimed that it was I, spread a defamatory lie—a lie, sadly, that even the head of the German section of Vatican Radio had fallen for. A story even reached Casa Santa Marta that it was I who had divulged the letter, not only because I wanted to damage Viganò's reputation, but because I also wanted to attack the reform of the Curia undertaken by Pope Francis, a large part of which was the restructuring of Vatican communications. The absurd claim was that I had been looking for an opportunity for revenge ever since the reorganization had taken place.

Anyone who knew Benedict knew that he would never agree to keep silent over something he felt strongly about just to please his successor or some collaborator or other. No matter the dynamics of his relationship with someone, Ratzinger—as a theologian—would never look someone in the face and simply tell him what he wanted to hear. When commenting on books, articles, or other texts, he would never hesitate to make any observation he deemed appropriate or necessary, and always offered his own honest thoughts. In any case, Benedict was aware of this controversy, but he wasn't much interested in it, even though he expressed disappointment and perplexity over the manipulative act of partially displaying his letter in a television broadcast.

I remember that Monsignor Viganò called me on my cellphone on 17 March 2018 while Pope Francis was on pilgrimage to San Giovanni Rotondo, and asked if we could meet. At the appointment, he tried to justify the partial showing of the letter by saying that we had given authorization for him to do that, but I told him in reply that he had accomplished nothing but create "fake news." We never had any contact after that. Pope Francis never brought up the matter with me, but I heard from various sources—and I myself had foreseen it—that Viganò was asked to submit his resignation, which he did on March 19th. It was accepted on March 21st, and he was assigned to a new role as *assessore* in the same secretariat.

An interruption in the work of reconciliation

Flipping through *L'Osservatore Romano* on 16 July 2021, Benedict XVI discovered that Pope Francis had released a *motu proprio* entitled *Traditionis Custodes* on the use of the Roman liturgy predating the reform of 1970. He understood immediately that this was directly connected with his own *motu proprio* entitled *Summorum Pontificum,* promulgated on 7 July 2007. He also noticed that the method of releasing the document was similar, in that Francis's *motu proprio,* like his, was accompanied by a letter explaining the contents of the new magisterial document. So, the pope emeritus carefully read both in an attempt to understand what the changes were and the reasons for them.

When I asked him what he thought, he replied that the reigning pontiff has the responsibility of deciding what is best for the Church and of acting accordingly. Personally, however, he thought that it was a change in direction and a mistake since it placed in jeopardy steps toward reconciliation that had taken place fourteen years earlier. In particular, he thought it was a mistake to prohibit the celebration of the old rite in parish churches, since it was always dangerous to shove a group of faithful into a corner, making them feel persecuted and instilling in them a sense that they need to safeguard their own identity at all costs from someone they perceive as an "enemy."

A couple of months later, Benedict happened to read the transcript of Pope Francis's meeting with Jesuits in Bratislava during his apostolic journey to Slovakia. One of Francis's answers to a series of questions puzzled him: "Now I hope that with the decision to stop the automatism of the ancient rite we can return to the true intentions of Benedict XVI and John Paul II. My decision is the result of a consultation with all the bishops of the world made last year."

Francis then shared the following anecdote that troubled Ratzinger even more: "A cardinal told me that two newly ordained priests came to him asking him for permission to study Latin so as to celebrate well. With a sense of humor he replied: 'But there are many Hispanics in the diocese! Study Spanish to be able to preach. Then, when you have studied Spanish, come back to me and I'll tell you how many Vietnamese there are in the diocese, and I'll ask you to study Vietnamese. Then, when you have learned Vietnamese, I will give you permission to study Latin.' In this way he made them 'land,' he made them return to earth."

As a *peritus* at the Second Vatican Council, Benedict remembered well how the Council insisted that "the use of the Latin language is to be preserved in the Latin rites" (*Sacrosanctum Concilium,* 36), and that all seminarians were to acquire "a knowledge of Latin which will enable them to understand and make use of the sources of so many sciences and of the documents of the Church" (*Optatam Totius,* 13). He himself, with good reason, noted in his *motu proprio* entitled *Lingua Latina* that "in addition, precisely in order to highlight the Church's universal character, the liturgical books of the Roman Rite, the most important documents of the Papal Magisterium and the most solemn official Acts of the Roman Pontiffs are written in this language in their authentic form."

As is evident in his books *The Feast of Faith* (1984) and *The Spirit of the Liturgy* (2000), Ratzinger the theologian was initially favorable to the liturgical reform. It was a topic always dear to his heart because he thought it was fundamental to the Catholic faith. So, it was no accident that he wanted the first volume of his *opera omnia* to be dedicated to the liturgy, even if the original project planned it to be the eleventh.

However, witnessing successive developments in the post-conciliar liturgical reform, Ratzinger recognized that there was a major difference between what the Second Vatican Council envisioned and what the commission established for implementing *Sacrosanctum Concilium* was actually carrying out, such that the liturgy became a battleground for opposing camps, and Latin in particular became either a bullwork of defense or the target for a full, frontal attack.

Benedict always worked assiduously so that the liturgy might be celebrated in its full beauty given that it is nothing less than the celebration of the presence and work of the Living God, and he considered the Eucharist to be the Church's most fundamental and divine act of adoration and prayer. In his view, every attempt to reform the Church must start with the liturgy, insofar as the liturgy alone can incarnate a renewal of the faith, which always begins from the inside out. As a theologian, he affirmed, "Just as I learned to understand the New Testament as the soul of theology, so I also have accepted the liturgy as the reason for theology's life, without which theology simply dries up."

On the basis of this conviction, Benedict XVI, with the promulgation of *Summorum Pontificum,* wanted to facilitate the possibility of priests celebrating the liturgy according to the ancient rite, reducing the need to refer everything to the diocesan bishop and widening the field of competency to the *Ecclesia Dei* Commission. In any case, it was always clear in Ratzinger's mind that there was only one rite, subsisting in the coexistence of an ordinary and extraordinary form. The one intention of his *motu proprio* was to repair the gaping wound that had formed over time, be it voluntarily or involuntarily.

This was anything but a clandestine operation, as some have thought. In fact, the dicastery primarily responsible for *Summorum Pontificum* was the Congregation for the Doctrine of the Faith with the involvement of members of the *feria quarta* and the plenary sessions. Pope Benedict closely followed progress on the document through edits made by the Prefect of the Congregation for the Doctrine of the Faith, Cardinal Levada, which were brought to his attention during *tabella* meetings. After its publication, Pope Benedict regularly consulted with bishops during their *ad limina* visits about how the norms were being implemented in their respective dioceses, and he always received positive feedback.

This is precisely why it is completely misleading to construe Pope Ratzinger's "true intentions" to be anything other than what he had already said. For example, in *Light of the World,* he asserted that "my main reason for making the previous form more available was to preserve the internal continuity of Church history. We cannot say: Before, everything was wrong, but now everything is right; for in a community in which prayer and the Eucharist are the most important things, what was earlier supremely sacred cannot be entirely wrong. The issue was internal reconciliation with our own past, the intrinsic continuity of faith and prayer in the Church."

It remained a mystery to Benedict why the results of the consultation with bishops made by the Congregation for the Doctrine of the Faith were never made public. That certainly would have helped the faithful understand more precisely why Pope Francis decided to turn in the other direction. Similarly, Benedict was surprised at the decision to transfer competency on these matters from the Congregation for the Doctrine of the Faith and split it up among the Congregation for Divine Worship and the Discipline of the Sacraments, and the Congregation for Institutes of Consecrated Life and Societies of Apostolic Life, especially since the Congregation for the Doctrine of the Faith had done such extensive preliminary work and research on the issue.

Always taking a stand against abuse

The horrible issue of clerical sexual abuse reached its highest critical point during the years Ratzinger was prefect and pope. In both roles, he fought this plague with all his might. As Prefect of the Congregation for the Doctrine of the Faith (and even before as Archbishop of Munich), he was part of the team that put together the new Code of Canon Law promulgated in 1983. Canon 1395 states that "a cleric who in another way has committed an offense against the sixth commandment of the Decalogue … with a minor below the age of sixteen years, is to be punished with just penalties, not excluding dismissal from the clerical state if the case so warrants."

The underlying reason for the rage of abuse occurring in the Church was clear to Ratzinger then. As he recounts in *Light of the World,* "After the mid-sixties … it [i.e., canonical penal law] was simply not applied any more. The prevailing mentality was that the Church must not be a Church of laws but, rather, a Church of love; she must not punish. Thus, the awareness that punishment can be an act of love ceased to exist." At the same time, he witnessed a deteriorating social fabric in which sexual norms were completely thrown out the window, having dire consequences on the formation and lives of priests.

He explains this analysis further in a famous unpublished essay he began to write simply as a personal reflection on a serious pastoral concern that weighed heavily upon him as pontiff—that is, his concern for the life and ministry of priests. In fact, the tragedy of clerical abuse represented a crisis of priestly credibility, as well as a crisis of priestly identity with regard to their mission and their ability to proclaim the Gospel.

When Benedict heard that there would be a meeting at the Vatican of presidents of episcopal conferences from across the globe on 21–24 February 2019 to reflect on the crisis of faith and the crisis in the Church in the wake of the abuse scandal, Benedict decided to send a text to Pope Francis *via* the Cardinal Secretary of State Pietro Parolin, asking for his consent to make it public. A few days later, Cardinal Parolin telephoned me on behalf of Pope Francis, asking me to tell the pope emeritus that Francis agreed that the text should be published.

Giving a detailed reconstruction of events, Benedict does not shy away from denouncing the freedoms sought in the Revolution of 1968, which included an "all-out sexual freedom, one which no longer conceded any norms," asserting that "part of the physiognomy of the Revolution of 1968 was that pedophilia was then also diagnosed as permissable and appropriate." (There are still memoirs and manifestos from the period penned by members of the cultural elite.) At the same time, "Catholic moral theology suffered a collapse that rendered the Church defenseless against these changes in society" based on the presumption that "morality was to be exclusively determined by the purposes of human action that prevailed.… There no longer was an (absolute) good, but only the relatively better, contingent on the moment and on circumstances."

Subsequently, in the late-1980s and 1990s, "the crisis of the justification and presentation of Catholic morality reached dramatic proportions.… On 5 January 1989, the Cologne Declaration, signed by fifteen

Catholic professors of theology, was published. It focused on various crisis points in the relationship between the episcopal magisterium and the task of theology.... Pope John Paul II, who knew very well the situation of moral theology and followed it closely, commissioned work on an encyclical that would set these things right again. It was published under the title *Veritatis Splendor* on 6 August 1993, and, in effect, it included the affirmation that there are actions that can never be rendered good ... [and] values which must never be abandoned for a greater value and even surpass the preservation of physical life."

Jumping back in time to 5 March 2014, I remember when Benedict read an interview between Ferruccio De Bortoli and Pope Francis in the *Corriere della Sera.* The pope emeritus wondered what Pope Francis had missed when he was asked about "non-negotiable values, especially in bioethics and sexual morality." The answer Francis gave was: "Values are values, and that's it. I can't say that among the fingers on my hand one is less useful than another. Therefore, I don't understand in what sense there can be negotiable values." Without uttering a public judgement, Benedict, on a personal level, understood Francis's affirmation to be a change of direction and a veiled criticism of John Paul II, as if the pope were saying that everything is negotiable.

On a practical level, toward the end of the 1980s, Cardinal Ratzinger began receiving appeals from bishops from various countries (but especially the United States), asking for help in confronting the problem, given that canon law did not seem sufficient in giving guidelines on how to equally guarantee the juridical protection of the accused, the victim, and the good in question.

Benedict explains in the unpublished essay: "In principle, the Congregation of the Clergy is responsible for dealing with crimes committed by priests. But since *garantismo* dominated the situation to a large extent at the time, I agreed with Pope John Paul II that it was appropriate to assign the competence for these offences to the Congregation for the Doctrine of the Faith, under the title *Delicta maiora contra fidem.* This arrangement also made it possible to impose the maximum penalty, i.e., expulsion from the clerical state, which could not have been imposed under other legal provisions.... But both the dioceses and the Holy See were overwhelmed by such a requirement. We therefore formulated a minimum level of criminal proceedings and left open the possibility that the Holy See itself would take over the trial where the diocese or the metropolitan administration is unable to do so."

This explanation is confirmed by letters sent decades earlier by Cardinal Ratzinger to brother Cardinal José Rosalío Castillo Lara, President of the Pontifical Council for the Interpretation of Legislative Texts. The letters were subsequently published in the *L'Osservatore Romano* in December of 2010. In a letter written on 19 February 1988, Cardinal Ratzinger complained that, judging from petitions for dispensation from clerical obligations coming from priests guilty of scandalous behavior, a reduction to the lay state was considered a "grace" rather than a "punishment," thus compromising the good of the faithful in the face of such serious crimes.

But the Code of Canon Law couldn't be forced to do something it wasn't designed to do. Therefore, Ratzinger tried to invoke article 52 of *Pastor Bonus,* which granted the congregation the duty to examine "offences against the faith and more serious ones both in behavior or in the celebration of the sacraments." But the absence of any further description of what constitutes these "more serious" crimes impeded a precise and consistent application of the norm. This concern led John Paul II to fill in the gap in April of 2001 with the *motu proprio* entitled *Sacramentorum sanctitatis tutela,* which was followed in May by the letter *De delictis gravioribus* to facilitate the implementation of new procedures in regard to cases of clerical pedophilia. So, in 2003, the congregation adopted new internal guidelines for treating cases of sexual abuse of minors by clerics. These norms were made public in 2010, extending the term of prescription of a criminal action from ten to twenty years (one of the longest in the world and, in the case of minors, with a time limit that only begins to calculated when a person is no longer a minor), and adding as delicts the acquisition, possession, or distribution of pornographic images of persons under the age of fourteen.

One of the most striking ways in which Pope Benedict XVI manifested an unwavering commitment to uncovering crimes, even when the person in question had been protected at high levels, was the investigation into Fr. Marcial Maciel, the founder of the Legionnaires of Christ, who was ultimately spared a canonical process due to his advanced age and delicate health. But the collected documentation clearly pointed to his guilt, such that, in May of 2006, he was ordered to a life of prayer and penitence and removed from all public ministry until his death (occurring on 30 January 2008). Ratzinger had clearly shown what he thought of the figure of Fr. Maciel, having avoided participating in the celebration of his 60th anniversary of priestly ordination in Rome in the Fall of 2004, even though several highly-ranking cardinals of the Roman Curia participated.

Even Pope Francis, during the press conference on the return flight from his apostolic voyage to Mexico on 18 February 2016, publicly acknowledged Ratzinger's work when replying to a question about the "Maciel case": "Here allow me to honor a man who fought even when he did not have the power to step in, yet he did: Ratzinger. Cardinal Ratzinger deserves applause. Yes, a round of applause for him. He had all the documentation. When he was Prefect of the Congregation for the Doctrine of the Faith, he took everything in his hands, he conducted investigations and he pushed forward, forward, forward ... but he couldn't go any further in the execution.... [H]e was a brave man who helped so many open this door. Thus, I want to remind you of him because sometimes we forget all this hidden work that laid the foundation for 'taking the lid off the pot.'"

During his pontificate, Pope Benedict took drastic measures to make sure that priests found guilty of the abuse of minors were reduced to the lay state. There were more than 550 of them between 2008 and 2012, including some bishops (there were other bishops who resigned ahead of time when it was clear they had covered up abuse committed by priests in their respective dioceses). And let's not forget that Benedict was the first pope to meet victims of clerical sexual abuse during his apostolic voyages. He did so in the United States (April 2008), Australia (July 2008), Malta (April 2010), the United Kingdom (September 2010), and Germany (September 2011). In his usual style, he maintained the utmost discretion and confidentiality in these circumstances.

Unfounded accusations from Munich

Considering all this, it was entirely understandable why Benedict was so terribly saddened when accusations were aimed at his brother Georg in 2010, dating back to his time as director of the choir in Regensburg. The investigations confirmed that abuses had occurred in the school attended by many members of the choir, but that Monsignor Georg had nothing to do with them. But obviously his was the only name that circulated in the press during the investigations.

It was even more shocking when, in January of 2022, the finger was pointed directly at Ratzinger as allegations arose dating to the time when he was Archbishop of Munich in Bavaria between 1977 and 1982. The item in question was a dossier commissioned by the diocese to shed light on the period between 1945 and 2019: a period of seventy-four years in which 497 cases of abuses had been committed by 235 individuals (173 priests, 9 deacons, 48 school employees, and 5 pastoral workers).

There were only four cases alleged to be the result of negligence on the part of Ratzinger. Yet, of course, these were the only ones that the media had any interest in, and it was impossible to react to the avalanche of news unleashed within hours of the diocesan press conference. The reality is that Benedict had already prepared a response to twenty or so pages of questions that had been sent to him by attorneys working on the case. He sent eighty-two pages in response on 15 December 2021. Some legal experts helped him prepare the responses, one of whom made a mistake in his timeline, writing that the cardinal was absent from a meeting of the Council of the Ordinariate that took place on 15 January 1980. One of the abuse cases was on the agenda for that meeting.

It was nothing more than a typo, and the pope emeritus apologized for it as soon as it came to his attention. It was anything but an act of deception. The minutes from that meeting, kept in the archives, indicated that he was indeed there in person. This is further affirmed in his biography published by Peter Seewald in 2020, in which we read: "When he was bishop, in 1980, he had agreed at a session of the diocesan council to allow the priest concerned to come to Munich for psychotherapy."[20] And yet this was enough to accuse him of lying. He couldn't help but reply to this false accusation in a letter dated 6 February 2022: "To me

20 Peter Seewald, *Benedict XVI: A Life, vol. II* (Bloomsbury Continuum, 2021), p. 422.

it proved deeply hurtful that this oversight was used to cast doubt on my truthfulness, and even to label me a liar."

In an emotional defense, Benedict bares his soul: "In all my meetings, especially during my many Apostolic Journeys, with victims of sexual abuse by priests, I have seen first hand the effects of a most grievous fault. And I have come to understand that we ourselves are drawn into this grievous fault whenever we neglect it or fail to confront it with the necessary decisiveness and responsibility, as too often happened and continues to happen. As in those meetings, once again I can only express to all the victims of sexual abuse my profound shame, my deep sorrow and my heartfelt request for forgiveness. I have had great responsibilities in the Catholic Church. All the greater is my pain for the abuses and the errors that occurred in those different places during the time of my mandate. Each individual case of sexual abuse is appalling and irreparable. The victims of sexual abuse have my deepest sympathy and I feel great sorrow for each individual case."

Benedict obviously sent the letter to Pope Francis on February 3rd to keep him informed. Two days later, the pontiff—who had already called him personally on January 26th to express his support, confidence, and a promise of prayers—expressed his gratitude for the letter and reaffirmed his material and spiritual support, adding that he too was saddened for comments made by some priests and bishops.

The most widely publicized of the four cases involved a priest from the Diocese of Essen who, in 1980, was sent to Munich for medical therapy. His bishop, without giving any explanation of the priest's illness or the medical treatment in question, asked if he could stay at the residence of the canons in the diocese, which was under Ratzinger's leadership at the time. At the above-cited meeting taking place on January 15th of that year, the request was granted. The minutes from the meeting, however, are not clear as to whether there was any discussion about the priest's pastoral activity, or any mention of a suspension from duties due to accusations of sexual abuse against children.

The three remaining cases also involved no direct accusations of sexual abuse that took place during the period when Ratzinger was Archbishop of Munich. One involved authorization given by the vicar general to an elderly priest to return to retirement within the diocese after he had finished a prison sentence for sexual misconduct, as an act of grace so that he could die in peace in his native land. The other involved a priest who had photographed nude children while they were putting on costumes for a theatrical performance. He was immediately sent by Cardinal Ratzinger to a retirement home with a prohibition against any further contact with minors.

The last involved a young priest—a nephew of a certain bishop—who wished to study at the University of Munich. After having been seen swimming nude in the local Isar river, he was sent home. With regard to this case, the dossier asserts that Benedict XVI showed himself defensive since he downplayed the events, writing that the priest "was known to be an exhibitionist, but not an abuser in the proper sense of the word." In reality, the issue is that Benedict's phrase was abused, since the pope emeritus defined abuses—including exhibitionism—as "terrible," "sinful," "morally reprehensible," and "irreparable." The simple fact is that the legal experts assisting Benedict XVI in the preparation of his responses wanted to make the historical clarification that the Code of Canon Law in force at the time—published in 1917—did not specify exhibitionism as a delict, since the norm in force did not make any distinctions regarding behaviors that would fall under this crime.

For the sake of historical accuracy, it is worth pointing out an affirmation in the dossier asserting that there is no proof that the archbishop had any knowledge of the cases in question. Indeed, during the press conference at which the dossier was presented, a journalist asked if the legal counsel could demonstrate whether Cardinal Ratzinger was aware at that time of the fact that the priest was an abuser, and what the annotation "highly probable" meant in that context. The legal expert replied: "Highly probable means we are presuming with higher probability!"

"Prophecies" for our time

In November of 2004, a few months before being elected pope, Joseph Ratzinger gave a firm response to Vatican journalist Marco Politi who asked him about his attitude toward the future. Benedict responded that "optimism and pessimism are emotional categories: I think I am a realist."

This, in fact, is the attitude that always guided him, both as a theologian and professor, as a cardinal and as pope, in his attempt to arrive at clear judgments and to develop reasonable, persuasive arguments.

During that same period, a book entitled *Without Roots* was published, which was essentially an exchange of ideas with then-President of the Italian Senate, Marcello Pera. In the book, Ratzinger offers an incisive analysis of the times with words that crystalize the reasons for which the Christian faith and its majestic message struggles to reach the people of Europe today.

In his opinion, the primary reason is that Christianity does not appear to be an attractive form of life because it "seems to place limits on everything. It seems to sap the joy out of life. It seems to restrict man's precious freedom and to lead him not to open pastures—as the Psalms say—but to a narrow, restricted path." As a response to this, Ratzinger suggests the urgency "to show a Christian model of life that offers a livable alternative to entertainments that are increasingly more shallow in society that worships leisure, a society forced to make increasing recourse to drugs because it is sated by the usual shabby pleasures. Living on the great values of the Christian tradition is naturally much harder than a life rendered dull by the increasingly costly habits of our time. The Christian model of life must be manifested as a life in all its fullness and freedom, a life that does not experience the bonds of love as dependence and limitation but rather as an opening to the grandeur of life."

The second reason is that Christianity seems to have been displaced by science and a disordered elevation of rationality in the modern era. One of the reasons for this are theological currents that "have wasted too much time in minor defensive squabbles and in debating minute details. Theology has not tried hard enough to confront the big, fundamental questions: What is Revelation? In what ways do God's revelation and the development of human history intersect? How does the long course of history, with all its trials and tribulations, reveal that there is some 'Other' guiding it, who acts within this history and creates something new that cannot have arisen from man's own action?" It was therefore Ratzinger's wish that theology, "in its encounter with science and in dialogue with the philosophies of today must cling once more to the fundamental question of what holds this world together. A true civil religion will not conceive of God as a mythical entity, but as Reason itself that precedes and makes it possible for our reason to seek It out and recognize It."

In various conversations with Benedict over meals and while strolling in the Vatican gardens, I listened closely to his thoughts after meetings with bishops from all over the world who came to Rome for their quinquennial *ad limina* visits. He was left with a deep impression of how difficult the pastoral challenges truly are, especially with regard to the sacraments that have become nothing more than habits: baptisms of infants whose parents had no relationship with the faith and with the ecclesial community; first holy communions of children who had no idea of Whom they were receiving in the consecrated host; confirmations of adolescents for whom the sacrament does not represent full adhesion to the Catholic Church, but rather their graduation from it; marriages that did nothing more than serve as opportunities for big family get-togethers.

His conclusion was that we need to respond to today's crisis of faith by placing the question of God once more at the center of ecclesial life and of the Church's proclamation, rather than trying to manage structural reorganizations that end up being nothing more than cold institutions themselves, always at risk of conforming themselves to the mainstream of the world and of our times. This "detachment from the world," however, in no way means a "retreat from the world." On the contrary, it is the Church's responsibility to ensure that her missionary witness—even by critically revisiting privileges she had enjoyed over time—is not only presented more clearly, but formulated in a way that makes it more credible.

This diagnosis had actually been developing in Ratzinger's mind a long time ago with breathtaking clairvoyance. Already in 1958, in a lengthy article entitled "The New Pagans and the Church," he expressed the conviction that "whether the Church wants it or not, after an internal, structural transformation, sooner or later there will be an exterior transformation that will lead to a 'little flock,'" and that in the long run the Church "will not be able to avoid dismantling piece by piece its congruence with the world, in order to return to being that which she is: a community of believers. In effect, her missionary efforts will not be able to grow except through these external losses. Only when she quits being a cheap, cheesy banality, only when she begins to present herself once again as that which she really is, will her message be able to reach the ears of the new pagans, who until now have been happy to live under the illusion that they really are not pagans at all."

In 1969, Ratzinger participated in some German radio programs in which he offered an analysis according to which "the future of the Church will come about through new saints; and hence through men and women whose perception goes beyond words, and who precisely for this reason are 'modern.' It will come about through men and women who know how to see further than others because their lives look out onto a wider horizon."

As a result, according to Ratzinger's vision, "a greater power will arise from this interiorized, simplified, smaller Church. A day will come when people, in fact, will feel totally isolated from one another in a world that will be entirely banal. When God will have completely disappeared from their interests, people will experience a complete and terrifying poverty. And they will then discover this little community of believers as something completely new. They will experience it as a hope that concerns them too, as a response to questions they have always asked themselves in secret. It seems certain to me that very difficult times are in store for the Church. Her true crisis is just beginning. She must anxiously take stock of this. But I am also certain about what will remain in the end: not the Church of a political cult, but a Church of faith. Certainly, she will no longer be the dominate force in society in the same way she was until relatively recently. But the Church will experience a new flourishing and will open up to men and women as a homeland that gives them life and hope beyond death."

The lucidity of his observations made it possible for him to anticipate many issues that now are at the center of debates in the Church. This is nowhere clearer than in the book-length interview he gave in 1996, printed under the title *Salt of the Earth.* Regarding gender, for instance, he said, "the bold revolutions against historical forms of sexuality are culminating in a revolution against biological presuppositions. No one wants to admit that 'nature' has anything to do with it.

The human person must be molded on its own desires. Man must be free from any presuppositions about his being. He makes whatever he wants of himself." And with regard to environmentalism, "[O]ne can engage in ecology from a Christian point of view, beginning with faith in creation, which places limits on man's will, which gives some criteria for freedom. One can also go about it in an anti-Christian way, such as on a New Age model, beginning with the divinization of the cosmos." With regard to the cults of Gaia and Pachamama: "The idea of 'inculturation,' particularly in Latin America, wants to restore a pre-Columbian culture and religion, freeing itself in some way from the excessive penetration of European elements imposed from the outside. They have emphasized the cult of Mother Earth and, in general, of the feminine side of God. The cosmic elements of this restoration of ancient religion are encountered in New Age movements, which strive toward a fusion of all religions and a new unity of man and the cosmos."

These views toward the future gradually led Benedict XVI to devote more attention to Marian apparitions, which in reality had never intrigued him that much in his youth. Indeed, whenever there were claims of private revelations, Cardinal Ratzinger was very cautious. If events of this nature continued in some part of the world, the congregation would be sure to collect documentation carefully, and then report developments to the Holy Father. Even with regard to events surrounding the alleged apparitions in Medjugorje, he put together an international commission of experts to investigate the case (who then subsequently delivered their report to Pope Francis), and he entrusted a careful analysis and assessment of the alleged tears of the *Madonnina a Civitavecchia* to qualified theologians and canonists without taking any preliminary stance on its authenticity.

His involvement with the apparitions of Fatima were more intimate. He became more deeply involved at the request of John Paul II, who asked him personally to explain the text of the third secret at a press conference on 26 June 2000 during which the handwritten note of Sister Lucia dating from 2 January 1944 was made known (in which she reports the words that she heard the Virgin say on 13 July 1917).

Both at the time he was prefect and while pope, Ratzinger has never given his own detailed interpretation of the enigmatic description: "And we saw in an immense light that is God: 'something similar to how people appear in a mirror when they pass in front of it' a bishop dressed in white 'we had the impression that it was the Holy Father.'" After the resignation of Benedict and the election of Francis, some interpreted this image as a prophecy of the two popes, especially since Francis had said that he perceived himself, above all, as the Bishop of Rome ("You all know that the task of the conclave was to give a new bishop to Rome," he said during his first greeting after the election).

With the passing of time, Benedict rather cultivated his understanding that the prophecies uttered by Our Lady had to be considered more carefully, with particular attention to her precise words. For example, in the final part of the secret, there is a reference to persecution in the Church culminating in the martyrdom of many people, including the pope, who "passed through a big city half in ruins and half trembling with halting step, afflicted with pain and sorrow, he prayed for the souls of the corpses he met on his way; having reached the top of the mountain, on his knees at the foot of the big cross he was killed by a group of soldiers who fired bullets and arrows at him."

Even John Paul II had associated these words in some way with the assassination attempt against him on 13 May 1981, inspiring him to give the bullet fired by Ali Agca in Saint Peter's Square that day to Our Lady of Fatima. But it is also true that the pontiff was not killed that day. (Perhaps a more accurate prophetic allusion to the event can be found in the prophecy given by the Virgin to Mélanie Calvat and Maximin Giraud, the visionaries at La Salette in France: "The Pope will be persecuted from every side: someone will shoot at him, someone will want to kill him, but he won't be able to do it.")

It was in the context of these considerations, grounded on the hypothesis that the prophecy had not yet been realized and therefore was open to be fulfilled in a more or less distant future, that led Benedict to say the following in his homily in Fatima on 13 May 2012: "We would be mistaken to think that Fatima's prophetic mission is complete." At the same time, in order to avoid any equivocation, I should add that Joseph Ratzinger never had any extraordinary supernatural revelations about this or any other matter.

Catechesis within the family

The disciplined rhythm of life at the monastery gave Benedict the peace he needed for ongoing meditation supported mainly by the daily celebration of the liturgy. More particularly, it afforded him the time to prepare homilies for the Sunday cycle of readings, which the Memores kindly recorded and transcribed. He did this mostly as a service to our own little family (there were periods when his brother Georg was present and, more rarely, other guests), which was evident in the way he customarily opened his homily with *cari amici* ("dear friends"). These were the fruit of spiritual conversations throughout the day, over meals, and during walks.

He began to prayerfully reflect on the upcoming Sunday reflections the Monday before, using the Greek text as his basis. For the Old Testament, this meant the Septuagint, and for the New Testament, he used the version edited by Erwin Nestle and Kurt Aland. He also had at his disposal several vernacular translations, such as the Jerusalem Bible in German and the Missal approved by the Italian episcopal conference in 2008. He would continue to meditate on the readings throughout the week, and on Saturday morning he would dedicate a couple of hours to writing an outline of his homily in a special notebook, which he didn't have in front of him while delivering the homily on the following day.

Sometimes, on feast days commemorating important saints, he would give a brief overview of their lives at the beginning of Mass, since, as he said, "the best interpreters of the Gospel are not the exegetes with their critical studies, but the saints with the witness of their lives."

After his resignation, he gave his first 'private' homilies in the chapel at the apostolic palace at Castel Gandolfo. They were generally short, and Benedict focused on the most essential aspects of the faith: "Learn to live a joyous faith; learn to live with the Father, to live according to the Word of God: this is true happiness and fullness of life" (10 March 2013); "Conversion is not just the autonomous act of a subject, but the fruit of an encounter, and in this sense it is a gift, but a gift that then naturally involves one's own activity: We are conquered in order to conquer" (17 March 2013); "God finds men in every part of the world and at every moment in history. This is how the reality of the

Church shines through: it seems poor and simple in the world, but, if we look at the world in its totality, we see a family that surpasses all boundaries" (21 April 2013); "[P]rayer implies two gifts: the Savior and the Holy Spirit. But we have to add that these two principal gifts are preceded by a more fundamental gift—namely, creation. God's first gift is life, and we must put this gift into action" (28 April 2013).

When we returned to the Vatican after our stay at Castel Gandolfo, the chapel of the Mater Ecclesiae Monastery became a stable home in which he could develop these reflections. They opened up to a more catechetical horizon, embracing contemporary world events and offering keen analyses of them. For example, in his first homily at the monastery, the pope denounced "more subtle persecutions of Christianity—that is, its marginalization from intellectual life, creating an overtly anti-Christian culture" (12 May 2013). He developed this point later, identifying "two main threats to the Church: the wind of ideologies that want to destroy our cosmos, and waves of political and militaristic power that persecute and strive to destroy the faith" (10 August 2014). He was most unambiguous in his stigmatization of laws permitting abortion, assisted suicide, and homosexual marriage: "All three of these say that I have complete power over my own life. I can destroy it if I want to. It is my own property, my sovereignty, my autonomy. But if we look deeper, we see that this triad implies a 'no' to the future: for abortion, it means we don't want any children. Suicide, homosexual marriage: these make a similar statement, since they necessarily exclude children" (22 September 2013).

As we face this complex situation, we find help in the words of the Gospel: "Jesus does not ask whether or not we have salt within ourselves. He decisively says, 'You are the salt of the earth!' (Matthew 5:13). In essence, we Christians must be salt for our history. We must show that the strength of the Cross of Christ is within us by defending life against the forces that seek its destruction. Otherwise, as the Lord stresses, our Christianity will end up conforming to the world and we will lose the courage and passion for the truth. A Christianity that seems modern, that seems up-to-date, will actually be flavorless and devoid of any real newness" (9 February 2014).

Looking more closely into the reasons underlying the surprising victory of Christianity over ancient religions, Benedict concluded that the most important factor was "the witness of a distinctive life. In a world where corruption, violence, immorality, and the lack of common commitment to the good prevailed, the early Christians lived with uprightness, integrity, goodness, and suffering, but doing no harm to anyone. This kind of life was such a radical and clear sign that it convinced others, precisely because it could not have been achieved by human effort alone, but could only demonstrate that God is the one who gives this life. Thus, the witness of the Christian life will be equally decisive for the victory of Christianity tomorrow" (25 May 2014). He persistently stated that "faith is not of our own invention; it is a gift of God to safeguard and to live. Hence, it is not something at our disposal. We cannot change it however we want. It is a gift of God and only in this way will it grow and deepen. Even the pope is not an absolute monarch. He cannot do whatever he wants. He is rather the guarantor of obedience to the gift of God, which is a true treasure for the world" (29 June 2014).

Benedict closely examined the Gospel image of the shepherd who leads his sheep, countering the modern tendency to place human autonomy as the highest good and rejecting the Christian attempt to place it under a yoke: "Yes, it is true that we are free persons endowed with reason, free will, and love, but it is equally true that our freedom is in need of enlightenment because we do not know the way, and we need a compass to find it. The Lord's parable speaks of mercenaries and wolves, and we have seen such wolves in our own time. Think of infamous dictators—Hitler, Stalin, Pol Pot, Mao Zedong —who all said: we are bringing humanity to its true happiness. They were wolves who destroyed the world in an incredible way, and underlying them are philosophers who created these erroneous ideals. Think of Nietzsche, who mocked Christians as weaklings, countering them with the Superman who destroys. Think of Marx with his promise of a paradise without God, which turned out to be nothing but an enormous concentration camp. Think of Freud, who proposed that it was best to do entirely away with the soul. The world will always fall into the hands of wolves, and at this moment we can only cry out to the Lord, 'Do not let your creation fall into the mouths of wolves! Don't let them destroy truth with their lies, love with their hate, and unity with their division!'" (26 April 2015).

In fact, the relationship between freedom and obedience was always one of the most important topics for Benedict's reflection: "There are two contrasting ideas at play. To follow Christ means to walk behind him, to follow his way, to leave aside one's own will and conform oneself to his will, while freedom means following one's own will, aiming to fulfill one's life-plan. In reality, to follow Christ is to enter the fire of love and thus to enter into the freedom that frees us from all our attempts to justify ourselves exteriorly. Saint Augustine used a bold expression to capture this, but it's true: 'Love, and do what you want.' If we have the true love of Christ crucified, by doing whatever this love tells us, we will always be on the right path, in communion with the One who is Love. And in this way, we will understand that to follow Christ is to realize our very selves because in that way we become the image of God and we fully realize our personal vocation" (30 June 2013).

Benedict often liked to unpack the meaning of ancient, biblical phrases and images. One at the center of many of his last homilies was "climbing the mountain." "To believe is to leave the plain of everyday life, the place of daily anxieties, the place that obscures our hearts, and to climb the mountain as Christ did, to go there to pray, to be with the Father, leaving behind all the thoughts that destroy our soul" (6 October 2013). He also went on to describe the descent from the mountain: "To go down from the mountain is also part of the Christian vocation. We must ascend, but we must also have humility once again, the willingness to go down into the valley of everyday life, into our daily tasks and responsibilities. It is precisely in this descent that we are on Christ's path, who, before opening up the path that leads upward, came down from divine glory, descended even to the point of dying on the cross" (16 march 2014).

One of his most developed homilies was delivered on 17 November 2013, centering on the "eschatological discourse" of Chapter 21 in Luke's Gospel, where Jesus "is not painting a picture of the last period in history, but pointing to some elements of this last phase of history. If we consider more attentively what he is telling us, we are surprised because it doesn't include a fundamental element in modern philosophies of history—that is, the basic concept of 'progress.' According to the philosophy of progress, history is always an upward trajectory. There are always aberrations and setbacks, but all in all, in the end we arrive at a more just and fraternal society, a better world, a kind of earthly paradise. Jesus, however, speaks of natural disasters, increasing violence, wars, and anarchy; of persecutions and a waning of faith, essentially showing us that human history remains the same until the end. Therefore, we need to take seriously the way he commands us to respond to these phenomena."

Basically, we need three things: "First of all, we need sobriety. To not put credence in fantasies and in false messianic lies, but to work with patience and humility. Work is man's task: not only after sin, as some think, since from the very beginning the Lord commanded man to subdue the earth—not in the sense of abusing creation, but to impart to creation the perfection desired by the Creator. Work therefore entails faith in God's will and trust in our capacity to transform the world for the better. Secondly, we need courage. When faced with hatred for the faith, we must remember that the light of God is stronger than human darkness. God the Creator is also the Savior, and he doesn't let history slip from his hands, since, even if power seems to be in the hands of liars, God's power is stronger. Finally, we need perseverance. Even after we have converted, the effort of the journey remains, which we must pursue tirelessly by continuing to follow the path of goodness."

Perhaps it was no accident that the last homily he gave on 2 April 2017—when he was already having trouble speaking—centered on the topic of eternal life: "Man seems to have been made to live forever, he wants to live forever, and at the same time he lives in a world structure where death is essential. What are we to say to this? In his dialogue with Martha (John 11:21–27), the Lord responds to this fundamental issue by raising it to a new level, and only in this way is he able to overcome the contradiction. Jesus says to Martha, 'Your brother will rise again.' She responds, 'I know that he will rise again in the resurrection of the last day.' But the Lord replies, 'I am the resurrection and the life. Whoever believes in me, even though he will die, he shall live.' He is telling us that we are not dealing with a life that will begin again at some unknown moment in the future because we do not know when we will reach this 'last day.' No. It is a life that begins now and it is indestructible because we are held in his hands, and therefore we cannot fall back into death."

A faithful farewell

Throughout all these years, Benedict XVI's days were spent in a remarkably structured way, beginning around 6:30 a.m. In his last days, since he had mobility problems, a religious brother from the Fatebenefratelli community who worked at the Vatican pharmacy helped him to bathe and dress, and in the evening he was likewise assisted by another member of the same community who came to help him prepare for bed.

He celebrated Mass at 7:30 a.m. (in the last years, I performed the role of main celebrant while he concelebrated from a seated position), followed by morning prayer and breakfast. The pope liked to read in the morning, take care of his correspondence, write, and dictate notes to Sister Birgit. Around 12:45 p.m., we would recite the office of readings or midday prayer together. After lunch at 1:15 p.m., we would take brief stroll on the terrace and then take a nap.

Later in the afternoon, we would take a longer walk in the Vatican gardens and recite the rosary near the Lourdes grotto (the schedule would vary depending on the season). On some Fridays, we would pray the *Via Crucis* in front of the beautiful stations in the chapel. When he wasn't able to walk well anymore, he would go outside in his wheelchair, and in his last years, he would use an electric one that his brother Georg had given him.

After returning to the monastery, he would recite vespers and take the opportunity to read, write, or meet with guests. Toward the end of his life, he preferred that someone read articles to him from the newspaper or from passages in books. For the latter, he liked to alternate between biographies and theology (among the books he appreciated the most were Cardinal George Pell's memoirs about his trial and incarceration in Australia).

Once a week, he would receive a special massage to improve his posture, and twice a week he would perform a set of breathing exercises, while on the other days of the week he used a special machine to help clear mucus from his bronchial tubes. His health condition and medical needs were always carefully monitored by Doctor Patrizio Polisca, his personal physician, who had become a personal friend over the years. He was assisted by other specialists and some extremely well qualified nurses.

Dinner was served at 7:30 p.m., followed by the news on television. Then we recited compline, always adding a special prayer for the priests of the Diocese of Munich in Bavaria who had died in the last fifty years (he remembered so many of them and described them to me in striking detail with an impeccable memory up until the time of this death). Then he would turn in for the night at around 9:00 p.m.

The routine was a bit different on Sundays and feast days, with Mass celebrated at 8:30 a.m. and the recitation of the Angelus at noon with Pope Francis, which we watched together on television. The afternoons we dedicated to cultural recreation. In the early days, we would listen to lyric operas and concerts on CDs, and in the latter years we would watch them on DVDs. At the end of the day, one of the Memores would read a book out loud to us. One of Benedict's favorites was the series of stories about Don Camillo and Peppone written by Giovannino Guareschi.

Benedict's diet throughout the week was classically Mediterranean: breakfast, taken with lemon tea, consisted of bread and jam or yogurt; lunch and dinner began with a first course of pasta or rice, followed by fish or fowl (rarely a steak fillet), a vegetable or potato side dish cooked in a variety of ways; and then dessert, which was either fruit or, occasionally, a sweet. Only the dinners on Sunday were served in Bavarian style, and they were a little more rustic, including rye bread, sausage and salami, and occasionally a meatloaf known as *leberkäse,* and, obviously, a beer (though Benedict himself would drink a lemonade spiked with squirt of beer). I must add that Benedict never had problems with digestion!

He began to seriously prepare for death a long time before it happened, as he confessed in one of his last conversations with Peter Seewald in 2016: "Even with all the trust I have in the fact that the Good Lord cannot abandon me, the closer the time comes to seeing his face, the more aware one is of all the mistakes made along the way. So, one feels the weight of this guilt, though naturally, a deep sense of trust is never lacking."

More recently, in 2022, he said publicly: "Quite soon, I shall find myself before the final judge of my life. Even though, as I look back on my long life, I may have reason for fear and trembling, I am nonetheless of good cheer, for I trust firmly that the Lord is not only the just judge, but also the friend and brother who himself has already suffered for my shortcomings, and is thus also my advocate, my 'Paraclete.' In light of the hour of judgement, the grace of being a Christian becomes all the more clear to me. It grants me knowledge, and indeed friendship, with the judge of my life, and thus allows me to pass confidently through the dark door of death."

It's not that he was anxious in the face of death; to the contrary, he lived in expectation of that final moment by having a foretaste of what faith permits us to hope for, as he wrote in a letter to old friends: "Next time, we'll meet in that place where we'll be able to tell one another everything we're unable to tell each other face-to-face today."

On 24 December 2022, I presided at Mass as usual in the Mater Ecclesiae chapel while the pope concelebrated from his wheelchair. At 6:30 p.m. on Christmas Eve and 9:00 a.m. on Sunday, December 25th, we celebrated Christmas Mass with the four Memores and Sister Birgit in attendance. Then we watched Pope Francis' *Urbi et Orbi* blessing on the television and enjoyed a simple and relatively quiet Christmas meal.

Benedict's health seemed relatively good that day, so I felt comfortable going through with plans to visit my family in Germany a couple of days later. I took a flight in the afternoon of Tuesday, December 27th, but the next evening I received a phone call from the monastery informing me that there had been a sudden worsening in his condition due to severe respiratory problems. I immediately spoke with Doctor Polisca, who, in the meantime, had assembled a small medical team to stabilize his situation. I returned to Rome the following morning.

Pope Francis had been informed of the situation, so at the end of the general audience on Wednesday, he added, "I would like to ask you all for a special prayer for Pope Emeritus Benedict, who is supporting the Church in silence. Remember him—he is very ill—asking the Lord to console him and to sustain him in this witness of love for the Church, until the end." After the audience, he immediately went to visit the pope emeritus, prayed over him, and imparted his blessing. In the meantime, news of his condition quickly spread throughout the world.

That afternoon, Benedict went into respiratory distress, but he was very lucid. I proposed administering the sacrament of anointing, and he immediately agreed. He had just seen his confessor, a priest from the Penitentiary at Saint Peter's Basilica, a few days earlier.

From that moment on, all of us took turns sitting by his side in the bedroom on the first floor of the monastery, together with other doctors and nurses who had gradually gathered around him between Thursday the 29th and Friday the 30th. They had noted that there was a slight improvement in his condition, even though he was at an age where a natural decline was to be expected.

We never considered admitting him to the hospital since we already had all the medical care possible right there at the monastery: a resuscitator, an IV machine, a respirator, a supply of oxygen, and an assiduous medical staff. Moreover, I was absolutely convinced that he had no desire to go the hospital, so there was no need to even ask.

Around 3:00 a.m. on Saturday, 31 December 2022—the memorial of Pope Saint Sylvester—the nurse keeping watch over Benedict saw him turn his gaze to the crucifix on the wall and say in a soft but clearly distinguishable voice, *"Signore, ti amo!"* ("Lord, I love you!"). These were his last comprehensible words because he was unable to express himself orally after that. When I would ask him questions, he would understand and would try to respond with gestures. I prayed morning prayer aloud by his bed, and then, around 9:00 a.m., he began a precipitous decline.

We began to recite litanies and prayers to accompany him on the journey, and imparted to him a plenary indulgence when he was at the point of death. His heart stopped at 9:34 a.m. The entire pontifical family was present at that moment, together with Doctor Polisca and the rest of the medical staff. After his last breath, I said a final prayer in German and give him a blessing.

I immediately called Pope Francis on his cellphone, and within ten minutes he was at the monastery. He sat next to the bed, made the sign of the cross over the pope emeritus, and prayed in silence for a while. We then discussed how to announce the death through the Vatican press office and plans for the public viewing, funeral, and burial in Saint Peter's Basilica.

That same evening, at first vespers of the Solemnity of Mary, Mother of God, Francis said, "[M]y thought naturally goes to the dear Pope Emeritus, Benedict XVI, who left us this morning. We are moved as we recall him as such a noble person, so kind. And we feel such gratitude in our hearts: gratitude to God for having given him to the Church and to the world; gratitude to him for all the good he accomplished, and above all, for his witness of faith and prayer, especially in these last years of his recollected life. Only God knows the value and the power of his intercession, of the sacrifices he offered for the good of the Church."

We arranged a chapel of repose in Mater Ecclesiae, and then I celebrated a memorial Mass at 8:00 p.m. on 31 December 2022. We then took turns throughout the night praying in the chapel so that someone from the pontifical family was always present. I offered Mass again on the morning of 1 January 2023, after which various people from the Vatican came to the chapel to bid a final farewell.

I celebrated Mass again on the morning of 2 January 2022, after which members of the pontifical family, in deep sadness, accompanied the hearse on foot as the bier was transferred from the monastery to the Basilica of Saint Peter, where Benedict XVI's remains were available for public viewing by the faithful until 4:00 p.m. Our hearts and eyes were filled with such grief, but our minds were filled with immense gratitude for the example of ardent faith, profound teaching, and abiding joy that he had given us for so many years.

On 5 January 2023, Pope Francis presided over the funeral Mass for the Supreme Pontiff Emeritus Benedict XVI, after which Benedict's remains were buried in the Vatican Grotto in the place that had previously been occupied by Saint Pope John XXIII (from 1963 to 2000) and John Paul II (from 2005 to 2011) before their remains were transferred to the upper basilica. Benedict was buried in the red vestments he had worn for World Youth Day celebrations in Australia in 2008 and for Palm Sunday in 2009, along with the episcopal cross he had worn as pope emeritus, the ring bearing the Benedictine symbols, a rosary, and a crucifix that I had given as a gift for the burial.

Someone asked me what I was going to do with Benedict XVI's papers after his death. The truth is that there was no question about what would happen to them since he left me precise instructions that I was strictly bound to obey in good conscience. He also made known his wishes about what to do with his books, manuscripts of books, documentation relative to the Council, and personal correspondence. For the rest, he simply said: "Private documents of any nature are to be destroyed. This is to be done without exception, and no loopholes."

I have also been asked about my opinion regarding his eventual beatification and canonization. Personally, I have no doubt about his sanctity. However, Benedict XVI did express to me privately his feelings regarding such an occurrence, so I will not permit myself to take any steps to accelerate the canonical process. My personal suggestion is to let all questions about his long life settle first, particularly surrounding his pontificate and years as emeritus pontiff, so that the heroic virtues of Joseph Ratzinger—which, I repeat, are unquestionable—may appear with utter transparency and may be demonstrated and shared by all.

His last wishes were contained in two notes enclosed in an envelope and kept in his desk drawer. The notes, regarding the destiny of his personal belongings, were updated every year until 2021, and I was appointed executor of the will.

He wrote a brief spiritual testimony in his mother tongue during the first months of his pontificate, which was completed and signed at Castel Gandolfo on 29 August 2006. The text has not been modified since. The following is an English translation of the text in its entirety:

> If in this late hour of my life I look back at the decades I have been through, first I see how many reasons I have to give thanks. First and foremost, I thank God himself, the giver of every good gift, who gave me life and guided me through various confusing times; always picking me up whenever I began to slip and always granting me once more the light of his face. In retrospect, I see and understand that even the dark and tiring stretches of this journey were for my salvation and that it was in them that He guided me well.
>
> I thank my parents, who gave me life in a difficult time and who, at the cost of great sacrifice, with their love prepared for me a magnificent abode that, like clear light, illuminates all my days to the present moment. My father's lucid faith taught us children to believe, and my faith has always been a trustworthy beacon the midst of all my scientific inquiry. The profound devotion and abundant goodness of my mother represent a legacy for which I can never give enough thanks. My sister assisted me for decades selflessly and with

affectionate care. My brother, with the lucidity of his judgments, his vigorous resolve, and serenity of heart, has always paved the way for me; without his constant guidance and companionship, I could not have found the right path.

I thank God from the bottom of my heart for the many friends, men and women, whom He has always placed at my side; for my collaborators at every stage of my journey; for the teachers and students He has given me. I gratefully entrust all of them to His goodness. And I want to thank the Lord for my beautiful homeland in the foothills of the Bavarian Alps, in which I have always seen the splendor of the Creator shining through. I thank the people of my homeland because in them I have been able again and again to experience the beauty of faith. I pray that our land remains a land of faith, and I beg you, dear countrymen: Do not let yourselves be turned away from the faith. Finally, I thank God for all the beauty I have been able to experience at all the phases of my journey, especially, however, in Rome and in Italy, which has become my second homeland.

To all those whom I have wronged in any way, I heartily ask for forgiveness.

What I said before to my countrymen, I now say to all those in the Church who have been entrusted to my service: Stand firm in the faith! Do not let yourselves be confused! It often seems that science—the natural sciences on the one hand and historical research (especially exegesis of Sacred Scripture) on the other—are able to offer irrefutable results at odds with the Catholic faith. I have experienced the transformations of the natural sciences for a long time, and I have been able to see how, on the contrary, apparent certainties against the faith have vanished, proving to be anything but science, but rather philosophical interpretations only apparently pertaining to science. On the other hand, it is through dialogue with the natural sciences that faith, too, has learned to understand better the limit and the scope of its claims, and thus its specificity. It is now sixty years that I have been accompanying the journey of theology, particularly through the Biblical Sciences, and with the succession of different generations, I have seen seemingly unshakable theses collapse, proving to be mere hypotheses: the liberal generation (Harnack, Jülicher etc.), the existentialist generation (Bultmann etc.), the Marxist generation. I saw and still see how the reasonableness of faith emerged and continues to emerge from a quagmire of shaky assumptions. Jesus Christ is truly the way, the truth, and the life—and the Church, with all its insufficiencies, is truly His body.

Finally, I humbly ask: Pray for me, so that the Lord, despite all my sins and shortcomings, welcomes me into the eternal dwellings. To all those entrusted to me, my heartfelt prayer goes out day after day.

Postscript

No one knew and supported Benedict XVI throughout the years of his pontificate and retirement more than Archbishop Georg Gänswein. Having shared in the late Pontiff's daily life, first in the apostolic palace and then at the Mater Ecclesiae Monastery, Monsignor Gänswein was able to delve into the thoughts and actions of one of the most culturally refined and theologically adept pontiffs in the Church's history.

Joseph Ratzinger, both the man and the pope, was not fully understood during his lifetime precisely due to his extraordinary intellectual and spiritual gifts. These were qualities that shook up the instability of an unbalanced society feeding itself on hedonism and the ephemeral, bent only on "finding meaning in history, even if history has no meaning" (to use an expression of singer Vasco Rossi), happy with being postmodern and fluid, since "change is the only permanent thing and uncertainty is the only certainty" (according to an aphorism that sums up the teaching of sociologist Zygmunt Bauman).

Staying in daily touch with the papal magisterium for many years as a Vatican reporter since the time of John Paul II, I have been able to recognize how Ratzinger's entire existence was marked by extreme consistency.

In fact, the singular, driving concern of every phase of his ministry was to give full witness to the Truth. This, in fact, is the common denominator between Pope Ratzinger and Monsignor Gänswein, as evident in the similarity of their episcopal mottos: *Cooperatores veritatis* ("Coworkers of the truth") and *Testimonium perhibere veritati* ("To give witness to the truth").

"Truth" understood with an uppercase "T," since Joseph Ratzinger/Benedict XVI's main mission was always to revitalize a timeless faith. But "truth" also with a lowercase "t," in that these pages give us a fresh look at the ordinary life of a figure who was characterized so unfairly and so inaccurately, perhaps because he displayed so many gifts that prevented him from being summed up in a single definition.

Author Roberto Rusconi has suggested that Ratzinger lived several lives: "The first consisted of his life as an academic theologian; the second, in which he showed himself to be an inflexible Cardinal Prefect of the Congregation for the Doctrine of the Faith; in the third, he was catapulted to the highest position in the universal Church as pope, taking the name Benedict XVI. There was even a fourth, in which he suddenly became 'pope emeritus' after his resignation and continued wearing white vestments." Archbishop Gänswein shows that Ratzinger, in fact, did not live four lives, but rather a single existence in four different phases, even if the present book focuses on those periods in which Gänswein knew him most personally, which began during his service in the Vatican.

Relying on the generous availability and total trust of Don Georg, I only asked him to assure me of one thing in the process of writing this book—that is, to be completely honest and to not "sugarcoat" the truth. The risk I encountered in writing several other books of this type—something between a biography and autobiography—is that heartfelt feelings cloud the memory, something that ends up being a great disservice both to the subject of the book and the author. The unforgettable Prefect of the Congregation for the Doctrine of the Faith, and pontiff eternally marked by his free resignation from the Petrine ministry, has no need of that.

This narrative is written in the first person rather than as an extended interview, and there is good reason for that. Having written many books of the latter genre, I know well how a journalist can lead—and sometimes determinedly by force—the tone and content of the dialogue. By writing a first-person narrative, however, the writer assumes the unique role of accompanying the author to a deeper level of what he really wants to communicate, bringing to the surface viewpoints that over the course of several years have been more clearly crystallized in his head and that have made Monsignor Gänswein the most authoritative witness to help interpret this man of faith, a priest according to the heart of Jesus, and a protagonist in some of the most difficult and exciting times in the history of the Church and of the world. This is the essence of the pages of this book, the success of which will be determined by the individual reader.

One final note. When, with the help of postulator Monsignor Sławomir Oder, I was writing a biography of John Paul II entitled *Perché è santo* (*Why He's a Saint*) in 2010, I had the opportunity to consult the confidential testimonies offered by several high-ranking ecclesiastical authorities in the process of John Paul's canonization. One of the most beloved spiritual sons of Padre Pio da Pietrelcina recounted a prophecy that he had heard from the saint in the 1960s regarding the future of the Church. Recalling vaguely an encounter he had had with Karol Wojtyła at San Giovanni Rotondo, the stigmatic saint explained to this friar that there would be a Polish pope who would become "a great fisher of men," followed by another pope who "would greatly strengthen his brothers in the faith." Then, with a smile, he added that one day, both would be proclaimed saints.

Saverio Gaeta